PIT BULL NATION

by CINDY MARABITO

This book is dedicated
to T-Rex, to Junior, to Little Piggles,
and all the ones I couldn't save.

Table of Contents

Chapter One
Rebel

Cut Across Shorty
by Marijohn Wilkin and Wayne P. Walker

It all started with a dog. It has been a long, incredible journey from there to here, but one I would repeat even with all the sad times. I am going to tell the story of my experiences with dangerous dogs. I am not a doctor nor am I a trainer. I am just a person who happened to find a dog. I have never bought a dog or a cat in my entire life, but the ones who've crossed my path have brought me as much joy as the rarest of bred dogs must have brought to their ancient emperors. Speaking of emperors, it seems appropriate to begin my story with the tale of Fu Manchu, a magnificent black Chow Chow. We did not find him while contemplating the Great Wall of China, but on the down low corner of Homer and Henderson in Dallas, Texas.

We were preparing to move to Port Harbor, California in 1995. I had always wanted to move back to California. I knew there was something going on I needed to be a part of. My animal stuff kept creeping up back in Texas and I would do a little bit here and there while pursuing my real goal, filmmaking. I had studied film and pursued a career in film, but all the while, some sickly pigeon or stray dog or cat would show up in my path. I would need to find them a home or nurse them back to health. I didn't have a clue that caring for animals would turn out to be my chosen path. At the time, I would have laughed out loud had someone told me I would spend all my waking hours trying to find good homes for pit bulls on death row.

Right as we were ready to load up, our dog, Fu, tragically died. Fu Manchu was a majestic dog. He wandered up to our doorstep as a young dog, about a year old. Fu Manchu had been living in the streets most of that past year. He was the neighborhood stray dog, known to everyone who lived within spitting distance. As a small puppy, the crack-dealing owner had given him the boot. Fu had been wandering those same streets until the day he wound up on our front porch.

The neighborhood locals were happy we adopted Fu.

It wasn't much of a decision on our part, because Fu really adopted us. It seemed he'd already made up his mind to move in with Scott and me and the cats. He just began sleeping on our porch until we got used to the idea and made it official. Fu was so proud the first day we took him on a walk with his new purple leash and matching collar. He was regal and he was owned. I learned something that day from Fu as he pranced down the sidewalk with his nose pointed up high into the air. Dogs love to be owned.

Fu came to us with a severe heartworm infection. He also needed a kidney operation, had cherry eye and of course, he was still intact. The heartworm treatment was the worst. The cure for heartworm infestation used to be a shot of arsenic into the main artery of the heart. You then waited to see if your pet would join the 50 percent who survived while keeping them on a short lead and lots of bed rest for the two-month procedure. Fu pulled through. The recovery period was harsh. When we were finally allowed to go for walks, Fu would just lay down and refuse to move. This was before cell phones and I'd have to prevail upon the kindness of a neighbor to call Scott for a ride home.

Fu was quite a legend. There was something about him that made him everybody's dog, but yet a dog who belonged to no one person. Fu had a natural proud and regal bearing that set him apart as if he were being carried on another level from the rest of us. Chows have a colorful and interesting history going back thousands of years. Bred to guard the palace, most chow lovers will agree that the chow has retained this quality.

I hadn't had much experience with chows, but had noticed them in our little neighborhood. There was one sassy red male who literally manned the streets. I imagine he was responsible in part for some of the chows that populated our part of town. Fu was Scott's dog, all the way. He was totally devoted to Scott and followed him everywhere. He became Scott's best friend and companion. I loved Fu, but dogs have

favorites just like we do. Scott was Fu's favorite person in
the whole world. When I'd get home from my job printing
photographs all day, Fu and I would turn up Soundgarden and
listen to our song, "Black Days". We'd hug each other hard. All
the troubles of the world would melt away. It was just me and
Fu and the radio.

We needed extra money for the move, so I got a part
time job at a local vet hospital. This wasn't the nice vet who'd
cared for Fu throughout his four surgeries. This veterinarian
was a very strange man who ran a very strange hospital. He
was a real piece of work who refused to hire anyone of color.
One of the vet techs pointed this out to me on the first day.
Looking back, I realize I should have listened to my own gut
instincts about that place. This wouldn't be the first time I'd be
sorry I didn't listen to my inner voice. I let the cheap medical
care for employee pets take priority over my feelings. I made
arrangements to have our cats' and Fu's teeth cleaned at the
rock bottom price of just $10 per pet. What a bargain!

The day before Fu's appointment, I took him down to
the hospital for a groom and three hour spa treatment. He had
come to us with horrible skin problems and oozing hot spots.
My home cure at the time was to keep him shaved down and
shampoo with medicated oatmeal shampoo. Amazingly, Fu was
completely healed by now and his luscious black coat was shiny
and full after we finished. He gleamed like a show dog.

Fu had the first appointment the next morning. Being
very anal about medical records, I had given the receptionist
the folder containing Fu's history and treatments. This would
update the vet in regards to Fu's condition as well as providing
a clear picture of exactly what procedures Fu had endured to
date. I was in the middle of learning how to process a stool
sample when I heard the emergency call from the operating
room upstairs. I knew instantly something was wrong and that
something involved Fu. My shock system set in and I continued
to fidget with the sample I was working with. I remember

trying to block out the voices on the PA system. I didn't want to know what they were saying. I tried to concentrate on the fecal matter I was holding between the glass slides in my hand. Time stood still and so did I. I just stood there.

A technician came and told me they needed me upstairs in surgery. I arrived to find Fu lying on the operating table completely still. I knew he was dead without even touching him. The vet was distraught and upset. They had given Fu a big shot of Sodium Pentothal, a drug no longer even being used for surgical procedures in modern hospitals. To compensate for his weight, they'd given him an extra large dose, killing him instantly. No one had bothered to look at his file, still downstairs on the receptionist's desk.

The staff began to ask questions about what to do with his body. I was amazed at the callousness. This was my beloved Fu Manchu and they were talking about him like some sort of high class garbage which needed disposing of. I took his body outside to wait for Scott. When Scott got there, he pulled up and left the car running in the road with the door open. "Give me my dog!" he yelled and tried to grab Fu in his arms. I had never seen Scott so upset. He dropped Fu in the street and scrambled to pick up Fu's lifeless body. The hospital sheet flew off and blew down the street.

We took Fu home and buried him in the yard. I was still wearing the raspberry colored scrubs I'd been issued at the vet hospital. People began dropping by to pay their last respects to Fu. Lulie came from the store across the street, Emeralds to Coconuts. Lulie and Joan, the manager, had tried to save many dogs and cats happening to wander into our neighborhood. At the time, chows were as numerous where we lived as pit bulls are today. Joan had three chows, each with beginnings similar to Fu's story.

As the day wore on, so many people came to say goodbye to Fu. It was amazing to me the number of lives this dog had touched in his own quiet way. Sometime after

7 o'clock, it was dark and already getting cold when the last person left. I was still in those scrubs and noticed the chill in the air. To some people, the loss of a pet is much like losing a child. To those of us lucky enough to share our lives with animals, to those of us who hear too often that we don't know real love, because we don't have children, to those of us who must keep our grief a secret from other people who do not understand, this kind of loss is devastating and sad.

I didn't go back to work at the vet hospital or even try to sue for losing Fu so tragically. What amount of money could square off the life of that incredible dog who had brought so much to so many people? The hospital did ask me to return the scrubs. They also sent out the standard sorry for the loss of your beloved pet card that veterinary hospitals send out after the loss of a client. I felt empty and helpless. Scott was even worse. He had suffered the loss of his best friend and soul mate.

We had managed the first day without Fu and made the attempt to get on with our lives. I was dressing the next morning when I heard banging and yelling at the front door. Scott was calling my name over and over. He was standing there when I threw open the door with the scroungiest and funniest looking orange ragamuffin dog I'd ever seen. Red like a little fox, he was grinning ear to ear. Scott had driven over to the barrio to pick up some workers and this puppy had run up to him.

"Look what I found," he said. I told Scott there was absolutely no way I could take on a puppy right now. No way. Scott said, "well, I can probably take him back where I found him."

"No," I said. "Let me give him a bath and we'll put his photograph up at Lulie's. We can find him a home."

I started running water in the bathtub and put the little dog in. He was so smiley. He was so silly looking. He had short legs and a squatty stout body. His face was Chow Chow with perky housetop ears. A filthy kite string was tied around his neck. As I lathered him up, he looked up at me like I was the best person he'd ever seen. Right then, I knew I had myself a new dog. He wasn't going to have his picture in Lulie's window. He wasn't going anywhere. I knew Fu had sent this little one to take care of us and for us to love. Rebel.

Chapter Two
Mookie

Master's Song
by Leonard Cohen

Mookie

We said our goodbyes and headed out for California.
We must have looked something like the Animal Planet Beverly
Hillbillies driving down the road in our U-Haul and towing a
Caddy full of cats. Rebel sat up front with us. Set for adventure,
he parked his little elbow on the armrest and wide-eyed, he and
I took in every tree and mountain the country had to offer us.
Candy, Roy, Ray and Buddy were tucked comfortably into two
Vari-kennels facing one another with the doors removed so
they could have a litter box. Candy sat on the litter side all the
way to California, guarding it from the boys just like she does at
home, the litter queen.

The trip was wonderful. We stayed at pet friendly
motels along the way. At night, we would drag in all of the
animals and pile up in queen size beds to watch movies.
Although, we'd gotten some tranquilizers for the cats, they
never needed sedating and were perfect traveling companions.
Rebel was the one who needed a pill! He was barely four
months old and wanted to play all night. A word to the wise, no
pork ears for a puppy traveling in close quarters. Pee-yew!

We reached Port Harbor in the middle of rainy season.
I'm from a town called Beaumont, Texas, 17 inches under sea
level and very humid, however, I'd never in my life seen so
much rain. Scott was fighting off the flu and had a hard time
getting well in all of the moisture. The trailer needed to be
unhooked from the U-Haul and re-attached so we could search
for a place to live. My dad was keeping the birds with him in
Texas until we got settled. We tried to lease a flat while still in
Dallas, but it was near impossible. The Symbionese Liberation
Army used to pick up and move into gorgeous Victorians in the
middle of the night, but we couldn't find housing because we
had cats!

We boarded the cats and tried to keep Rebel with
us while we continued to look for a rental. We were having
trouble even finding a motel room that would allow Rebel. No
motor inns would allow pets in Port Harbor. We finally found a

11

place with greasy sheets and shag carpeting. Half the letters in the neon sign were burned out with 'otel-daho' flashing on and off in the darkness when we'd come dragging back worn out and dejected after looking for a place to live all day. The lady who ran the motel told us Rebel could not even sleep in the car. I broke down when we finally had to board him with the cats. All the sadness and grief from Fu's death and the stress of the move came tumbling down on my at once. I cried like a baby when they took Rebel from my arms at the boarding facility.

After that, we hit the deck running and got real serious about finding a place to live with our animals. We had some checks with us, but couldn't deposit them due to the holding period. We were getting low on cash and beginning to worry. We had looked at so many places to live and not one had been appropriate. Some of these dumps were wetter inside than it was outside in the rain.

Then, like magic, we found George. George was the landlord of an old Victorian in the smack dab center of the hood. It might have not been the best part of town, but we would have the entire top floor and the entire property was fenced. Rebel would have a yard to run around and play in.

By that afternoon, we had retrieved our cats and Rebel and were all moved into our new home. There was some work to be done, but most of it cosmetic. We figured we could paint once we were moved in. There was a big yellow kitchen with windows all around. It was my favorite room in the house. I had always wanted a kitchen big enough to fit a table and chairs and yellow was my favorite color. The kitchen would set the tone for every house I would live in after that, yellow.

There was a place for everyone in our new home. The cats had two big bedrooms to hang out in. The birds would entertained by the goings on in the backyard trees in view of the kitchen windows. Rebel was easy. He was comfortable anywhere and soon to begin exploring every corner of Port Harbor.

Just as we got the last of the boxes unloaded and hauled upstairs, I heard a very strange noise. It was definitely the sound of an animal, but not one I'd heard before. Kind of a yowl howl growl is the best I can describe. I set off downstairs to investigate. Walking around the side of the house, I spied the culprit. There was this big German Shepherd tied to the back of the house. Literally. He had a rope noose around his neck, anchored directly to the house. He would be strangled by the noosed rope were he to attempt to escape.

Our downstairs neighbors were white Rastas and Mookie was their dog. They agreed to allow Mookie to play with Rebel. He was about a year older than Rebel and the two of them became instant best friends. Their special game was to run around and around the house. Suddenly, Rebel would hide behind the same bush and wait for Mookie to circle again. Rebel would then spring from the bush at Mookie, barking and growling ferociously. Over and over and over, they would perform the same theatrics never growing tired of the game. Mookie must have known Rebel was behind that bush, but never once did he let on. He would stand there erect like a cardboard cutout of a German Shepherd while Rebel barked and barked, melodramatically. It was like watching a Chuck Jones sheepdog and wolf cartoon when the same shrub and rock would pass over the screen again and again.

One night I woke up to the sound of Mookie crying. He was always tied up outside unless he was playing with Rebel. He was lonely and cold. I heard, "shut-up, shut-up, Mookie!" Mookie cried louder. Back in those days, I was better at minding my own business, so I just went back to sleep. There were many mornings when I would wake up to the sound of Mookie crying and barking.

I have come to learn a little about Shepherds. These incredibly sensitive, intensely social dogs are dedicated to their person. My first and only previous German Shepherd experience had been with Missy, the family dog of my childhood friends, the Powell family. Our moms were best friends as were the kids. The Powell's next-door neighbors were also part of our pack. The three family's daughters, Dixie, Bernadette and myself were best friends. It was 1966 and we were twelve. We had the world by the tail.

Missy was everybody's buddy, the neighborhood dog. She went everywhere with us kids and we were all over the place. Our stomping grounds were as green as the back roads of Fiji and brimming with opportunities for mischief. Missy always had our backs. If we'd wrestle, though, Missy would instantly come to the defense of the Powell kids. Protecting them was her job and she was darn serious about it. We learned right quick not to play too rough with the Powell kids.

Mookie was the only other Shepherd I'd known up close and personal. He reminded me so much of Missy. This must be one of the pitfalls of attributing qualities to a dog in regards to breed. We tend to rob the individual dog of his unique personality, the very essence of what connects us to them. Mookie was a German Shepherd in the classic sense, but he had such an abundance of emotion, it was hard for him to contain himself at times. Mookie was soft and beautiful like a rainbow of the colors brown. He was a special and precious dog.

That first day when I met Mookie tied up to the side of the house, I broke all the rules of meeting a strange dog. Often, I will encounter someone while walking a dog. They will approach my dog gingerly while holding out the back of their hand for the dog to sniff. I know the reasoning behind this, but still have to wonder what would happen if that dog decided to bite. Would he snap at the hand coming at him? Would it matter if the palm or other side of the hand were offered first? Wouldn't one prefer to have the palm bitten instead of the more tender outside of the hand? My own palms are much tougher than the backs of my hands. And all those veins!

I went right up to Mookie and committed a dog savvy faux-paus. I put my face right up in his face, something you're never supposed to do. I wasn't attempting to gain entry to Mookie's personal territory, but just wanted to make friends. I knew I would be OK, because I felt it. I had a connection with Mookie from that first day. I knew it and so did he. When I bent down and stuck my face into his, he started this low weird growl, a habit peculiar to his nature and a trait that I grew to love. That day, it did surprise me. He then opened up his big old German Shepherd mouth, must like one of those 'beware of dog' signs you buy at the hardware store with drops falling off the cartoon fangs. He let out the loudest succession of barks I'd ever witnessed. I jumped backward, shocked. Later, I learned this was Mookie's signature greeting. He was a vocal dog and had a lot to say, very loud and proud.

After many years of playing face Kong with Mookie, which I repeatedly lost, I learned to get my face out of the equation pretty quick. Mookie taught me if you wanted to learn dog behavior, you learned from a dog. Playing with Mookie, I saw how a game like face Kong could result in an injury. Mookie and I had a dynamic. We knew it was a game and we knew the rules of the game. I wondered how many dog bites involving kids had begun with an innocent game. Maybe our game was not safe, but we knew how to play. We knew our boundaries, just as Mookie and Rebel had evolved a system in their daily game of hide and chase. Running, charging, barking, growling, attacking and retreating were all part of their game. I never once saw either one break the rules they established all those years ago in our yard chasing and never catching the other one.

As our own family grew close to Mookie, Scott and I became concerned about Mookie's wellbeing. We met someone who offered to help us. Ewen was an Animal Control Officer in Port Harbor. He rode a motorcycle and wore black leather chaps and a biker jacket. The Rasta guy who owned Mookie was running a small time pot operation. One day, Ewen dropped in to see us and left his card with Mookie's dad. An impression had been made. Mookie's owners started treating Mookie a little better. I tried to mind my own business and tried to hope for the best.

One day, I heard Mookie squealing and crying. I was on the phone and ran downstairs to see what was happening. I saw Mookie's owner punch Mookie with one hand while holding onto the rope around Mookie's neck with his other hand. I lost it. "What the hell do you think you're doing?" I asked. The guy dropped the rope, his voice raising an octave. "He was barking too loud." I remember swinging the phone over my head, using it to emphasize my point. I told him the days of punishing Mookie for barking were over. He just squeaked and nodded in agreement, his voice gone. The more I talked, the more worked up I got. I let him know if I heard so much as a peep coming from Mookie, I would drop a dime on him and his pot operation would be history.

One other thing German Shepherds are known for is loyalty to their masters. Most Shepherds are one man dogs which has contributed toward their reputation as guard dogs. In fact, where I come from, it's not unusual to hear someone refer to a German Shepherd as a guard dog as a breed rather than a job. Mookie broke the mold on that one. The whole time I'm screaming at the Rasta, waving the phone like a handgun, Mookie is calmly sitting by my side, very ho-hum. He was like, 'buddy, you're on your own with her."

Like Fu Manchu before him, Mookie began sleeping at the top of the stairs by our front door. Even though he legally belonged to the folks downstairs, he was telling us that he was our dog now. The Rastas even bought him a beautiful teal collar after that incident. Today, when I see that shade of greenish-blue, I think of Mookie. That became his color. The wife strangely enough worked for a large holistic grocery chain and began bringing home avocados she would mix in with his dog food.

One day, the couple knocked at our front door and asked

if they could speak with Scott and me. They were moving to San Clemente and wanted to give Mookie to us. We asked if we could think about it. Now that I look back on it, I find it hard to imagine what we possibly needed to think about. We considered the Mookie adoption in depth and discussed at length adding another dog to our family. We talked about it for a month. I don't recall ever taking that long before or after to make a decision during our married life. We weighed all of the pros and cons, hard, long, back and forth. It was as though we were considering having a baby. We finally told the couple we would take Mookie, although Mookie already knew he was ours. He'd made that decision long before we had. Weirdly, they asked us to keep him intact and I immediately had him altered.

We had inherited a dog who'd never been to a dog park, was chronically abused, both beaten and screamed at, had never slept inside a house and had a load of maladies to show for it. The first thing we did was take Mookie to the dog park. Before we adopted Mookie, Rebel and I would take off on all day long treks. Everywhere we went looked like a movie backdrop, a scenic nirvana. To hike and climb all day and find yourself and your red chow chow in the public rose garden, fully abloom, or blazing the fire trails through John Steinbeck's 'tawny backs of lions' was pure heaven on earth. I felt guilty leaving Mookie tied to the side of the house. He would cry as Rebel and I left. It was not the first time I felt sorry for a dog and wished I could do something to help.

Now I had the opportunity to make up to Mookie for all of the times Rebel and I closed the fence gate on his crying. As we opened the gate, we were met by the neighborhood mailman, Maurice. Before anyone knew what was happening, Maurice put his pepper gas can right in my face. I was shocked. "Are you pointing that at me?" I asked him.

He was just as startled and answered that he was trying to protect himself from the dogs. Mookie and Rebel were on leash and trying to get themselves into the car. Neither dog was even aware of the mailman. I tried to explain this to Maurice, but he wasn't having any of it. The situation escalated into a disagreement and ended with my telling him I was going to report him to the post office.

I was a little apprehensive about taking Mookie to the dog park for the first time. I didn't know how he would behave. So far as I knew, he'd only been around Rebel. Mookie surprised us all by behaving like a perfect gentleman. He was respectful of all other dogs he met. He liked people, kids, big dogs and small ones. He met a large intact Rottweiler, a feisty female Jack Russell terrier and loved everyone. Mookie was having the adventure of his life. He was enjoying himself as he so deserved to.

Mookie became best friends with the Jack Russell whose name was Lois. She was a ball hog. When we'd visit the seaside dog park, her dad, Kevin, would throw the tennis ball far out into the water. Mookie would jump in beside Lois and swim all the way out with her to retrieve the ball and escort her back to shore. They would go on like this for hours. A few years later, when Kevin moved to Los Angeles, Mookie and Lois would talk to one another by speaker phone.

We stopped by the post office after the dog park to complain about Maurice and the pepper gas. Redirected through the building in search of the complaint department, we were finally able to speak to someone. Way in the back of the warehouse by the loading dock, a lady came to the desk we'd been instructed to wait by. I started to introduce myself and she said, "oh, I know who you are. You the one with the bad dog."

"Bad dog?" I was totally surprised.

At this point, Scott tried to explain what had happened outside our gate that morning. We were beginning to learn a first hand lesson that not everyone likes dogs and not all of the citizens of this town were old flower sniffing leftovers from the summer of love.

18

The incident was less about dogs and more about these redneck sounding people from Texas with their big old dogs. It seemed Maurice had run right back to the post office and filed a vicious dog report against Mookie. In the report, Maurice claimed that Mookie had attacked him. We were floored. Mookie is one of those dogs who lives up to the saying, 'all bark and no bite'.

Our mail delivery was cut off as of that day. From then on, we had to retrieve our mail directly from the post office. For months, I had to drive down to the post office every day to get our mail. In addition, the mail was mysteriously lost each day. I would wait in line and the clerk would return saying he could not find the mail. Maurice also filed a report with the local animal care and control stating that Mookie had attacked him. This was brazen behavior considering Scott and I were both involved and could testify that no such attack took place. Postmen, as public servants, are sworn by oath to tell the truth.

Here was this wonderful dog who'd been abused his entire life. I was not going to allow a false accusation to create a black mark on Mookie's record. It was not fair. Suppose another incident should occur in the future? I couldn't take the chance of having an unfounded complaint compromise Mookie's second chance at a happy life. I decided to file a complaint myself. I was getting my first little taste of animal rights. Animals depend upon us to protect them. I had not agreed to adopt Mookie with just the intention of slapping a bowl of kibble in front of him. There was more to the arrangement than that. To me, adoption was a complete commitment, like a marriage.

We embarked on an adventure together that would take up the better part of a year and would begin to change the course of my life. I started by making phone calls. I telephoned the local postmaster and tried to explain what had really happened the day of the complaint. The postmaster replied he would need to investigate the matter and would get back to me.

Fair enough. He then sent me a letter stating that other carriers had experienced 'threatening encounters with' my dogs. He went on to say their own 'safety had been jeopardized'. I found out then that Maurice had pepper-gassed Mookie through a fence knothole while Mookie was still owned by the Rastas.

Before Mookie moved in with us, he was a backyard dog. The neighborhood kids would bang on the fence and taunt him. I understand that workers and mail carriers must come into contact with dogs and respect the work they do. However, we had a study and high privacy fence surrounding the property. The dogs were certainly no threat to Maurice or any other person.

Until the matter was resolved, we were instructed to continue picking up our mail at the downtown post office. This was not only inconvenient, but complicated by inconsistency on the part of mail clerks to locate our mail each day. It had become such an issue, that I began to collect stamped receipts stating the mail could not be found. Upon occasion, a bundle of our misplaced mail would turn up in strange places throughout the building. Scott was becoming increasingly irritated with the whole mess and demanded that it be resolved. He told me to settle it once and for all, but I wasn't about to concede to a false charge involving my dog. I was not going to jeopardize Mookie's wellbeing simply to have my mail delivered.

I wrote up a description of what really happened the day Maurice claimed Mookie attacked him. I had everyone who witnessed the event sign the document. Even the neighborhood children who were playing in the street signed the account. I still have photos of the children who would run to me when I came home from work every day. They would pose for pictures and beg to play with Mookie and Rebel. Mookie was a special character in that neighborhood. These kids had sad, grown up eyes that had already seen life's rotten side. In a place where days of innocence are few, these kids were defenseless against the poverty and drugs and destruction. They were happy to see

Mookie saved from an abusive situation that reflected their own lives. They were our friends and truly loved Mookie and Rebel.

Flowers peeked through the dirt and cracks and birds and bees went about their business. Life went on and Mookie and Rebel chased each other around the house endlessly. I'd sit on the steps by the tomato and pepper plants and watch them play. The kids loved both the dogs, but Mookie had been one of them, locked behind that fence, baited and tormented by everyone who walked by. They had heard him cry when the Rasta would punch him for barking. They were sad when he was punished. They had grown up with Mookie and were happy when the Rastas moved away and Mookie moved in with us. They were happy when Mookie got to go on adventures with Rebel.

Mookie was an absolutely joyful dog. Destination didn't matter to him. He was so happy to get to go anywhere, to the ocean or the mountains; on long trail walks with Rebel or to the dog park. It didn't matter to Mookie. Anywhere was a party. He wore a big grin on his face most of the time. So when the postman lied and said Mookie attacked him, the kids did not approve and signed the petition. Once this was reported to the local postmaster, we received a typewritten apology for any rudeness we might have felt we had experienced. It was a back handed statement and went on to explain the carrier's apprehension due to the many dog attacks occurring each year. The postmaster asked for a letter advising my intensions within 10 days.

George padlocked the gate so the carrier could leave the mail without apprehension. I then received an additional letter from the postmaster regarding yet another attack on a postman at our address. This latest supposed attack involved three dogs according to this latest claim. Since only two dogs lived at our address, Rebel and Mookie, this was strange indeed. The postman had filed a written complaint with animal care and control and I received a copy of that report. Not one of the descriptions of the three dogs resembled Mookie or Rebel. This new accusation was suspicious, especially in light of the newly padlocked gate.

I wrote to the postmaster general in Washington and asked for help. I had tried to follow the chain of command, but realized we were getting nowhere. Scott was irritated at the entire situation. His position was to basically end it and get our mail delivered. I was not quite ready to throw in the towel. My instinct was to stand my ground. An inspector was dispatched from Washington to set up shop at our local post office and investigate the matter. He began by interviewing me and then spoke with Maurice. He finished up with the second carrier who issued the three-dog attack claim. This whole thing had turned into a big mess.

All the unpleasantness did not stop us from having fun, though. Mookie added such a spark of life and made our day trips a blast. We enjoyed watching him thrive and become the dog he was meant to be. Looking back on the way Mookie has been treated, I did not feel as bad about the beatings as I did about his being anchored to the house. For a dog like Mookie who loved to run and feel the wind, it must have been torture to be chained up 24/7 and to watch us leave with Rebel.

Now we had the opportunity to make it up to him. We would go to Bolinas for the day. Bolinas is right next to Dog Town and quite hard to find, because the townspeople keep hiding the sign. Every July 4th, Bolinas has a tug of war with Stinson Beach. The losers get pulled into the lagoon. We always rooted for Bolinas. Bolinas is more dog friendly as Stinson Beach has strict dog restrictions. If you have your dog on a leash, Bolinas natives holler, 'no dogs on leash!' What a great custom.

I had made a super 8mm movie about Rebel going AWOL from the army called "Mi Nombre is Rebel". Rebel is a Tex-Mex dog and the 'is' remains true to Tex Mex lingo. His travels take him through the Berkeley Hills to Oakland's Jack

London Square and then on to San Francisco's Fisherman's Wharf. He rides a fire truck and a city bus, gets chased by a policeman out of the BART station until he finds his way back home to Scott. Scott wouldn't quit eating his lunch while I was trying to film the movie, so we just foleyed in his lines post production. Rebel was the star and the only actor who followed direction. We even got permission to use "Rebel Yell" from Billy Idol's people.

I spent many hours in my big yellow kitchen writing and calling people for help with the Mookie post office situation. I loved being in this room of the house. It reminded me of the kitchen in "Member of the Wedding", the kind of room you shelled peas and drank coffee in. It was a family room and the heart of our home. Mookie's being there with us made our lives full and complete.

The man from Washington stayed occupied while investigating Mookie-gate. Right away, the second dog attack report fell apart. That had a great deal to do with animal control becoming involved. Even though a government official had documented under oath he'd been attacked, the story lost credibility when it was discovered there were not three dogs on that property. The post office began to lose some points.

I got my hopes up for nothing, though. The Washington guy finally closed the case with a request that our dogs be secured inside the gate when the mail was being delivered. The mailbox was to be attached to the outside of the fence in front of the gate so that the postman would have no opportunity to come into contact with the dogs. Even with all of the new stipulations, the fence, gate and mailbox remained the same as before Maurice and the pepper gas incident. The only difference was the padlock being added to the gate so only residents could enter the actual property.

We continued about our lives with only one fly in the ointment. Scott was watering the lawn one afternoon when Maurice delivered the mail. He claimed Scott sprayed him

23

with the water hose! This time, he was claiming Scott attacked
him! We received yet another letter from the postmaster
regarding the water hose incident. This was the last written
communication we received from the post office in what
had turned into a real life mini-series. So far as the city was
concerned, meaning animal control, Mookie's record was
expunged. In a tiresome and ridiculous battle that had lasted
over a year, Mookie was able to resume his life and just be a
dog.

We moved down south to a small tract house in a
suburb. I still can't remember why we moved other than to be
closer to Scott's job. The day we moved in, a yellow notice was
taped to our door, courtesy of the post office. It was a vicious
dog notice. I assumed they just wanted to have the last word
after all. Our new postman, Ricardo, was a wonderful guy. I
made it a point to introduce myself along with Mookie and
Rebel. He was a dog lover and thought is was funny when
Mookie and Rebel barked. He carried cookies in his pocket
and would reward Mookie for barking. I don't think Mookie
knew how to handle getting a treat when he was so accustomed
to being beaten. It was funny to see Mookie's lip catch on his
canine tooth, giving him a silly, quizzical expression. Ricardo
let Mookie and Rebel know that all mailmen weren't dog haters
and in return, they let him know how much they loved their
new postman. They looked forward to the mail delivery every
day from their place at the window. Or a cookie.

Despite the great new arrangement with our postal
service, I was not a fan of the town or the house we lived in.
I loved the backyard, though. We sat right on about 30 acres
of property owned by the airport. Everybody in the hood
trespassed. It was don't ask, don't tell and some of the locals
claimed to have walked their dogs on the land for 32 years.
There was rarely anyone walking when Mookie, Rebel and
I took off for our hike every day. We had our own personal
dog park with tons of room to romp and run. There was a

eucalyptus grove along the western side shading a deep creek that ran the length of the property. Mookie would swim the creek and clear the long tree branches floating in the water. Some of the branches were fifteen to twenty feet long and Mookie would systematically dive in and grab onto a branch with his teeth. He'd then run clear out to the middle of the field where he'd place the limb. Mookie took to his new job like a Navy Seal. Keeping that creek free of tree limbs was Mookie's new purpose in life.

We tramped that land whether it was cold and rainy or hot and muggy. We didn't care what the weather decided to do. I remember the three of us saturated by the storms. We just had that much more fun. Mookie and Rebel were so happy. They reveled as the wind would howl and eucalyptus trees blew down horizontal with the land that tried to hold them. The town didn't seem so dull and the house so cramped. We had a fantastic wilderness to ourselves right in our own backyard.

One day, Ricardo was laughing when he brought our mail. "Boy, do I have some news for you. You know the postman who gave you and the dogs all that trouble?"

I nodded. Who could forget?

Ricardo shook his head. "Well, he's gone."

"What do you mean by gone?"

Ricardo shrugged his shoulders. He answered that Maurice had been fired, but it was speculation. Either way, Maurice was no longer at the post office and the postmaster was gone, too. Ricardo didn't know the details and said no one was talking. The one sure thing was both Maurice and the postmaster were no longer employed at the post office. I had to believe it had something to do with Mookie. Somebody smiled on Mookie from heaven. I still have the file I compiled about our long ordeal with the United States Postal Service. Talk about postal! I gave Mookie an extra big helping of dinner that night. It was cause for a celebration.

Chapter Three
Angel Divine

Learning to Fly
By Tom Petty

Angel Divine and Marty

We moved again. This time, it was into our own
very precious cottage in Port Harbor. The minute our rent
house had been sold, the airport property was boarded up to
trespassers. This move had been a stressful one. While the
house was on the market, we had to crate all the cats and load
the dogs up and leave while they showed the house. Ray was
especially distressed. He had always been a sprayer, but stepped
up his game during this period. Before the move, his spraying
was so bad we had to use extreme measures to protect the house
from damage. We lined the rooms with the kind of plastic
runners old grandmas use to protect the staircase. On top of
those, we laid down boards and bricks with towels. All this
was changed out once a day. This was long before pheromone
sprays hit the market.

Right as the house sold, we were able to move into our
dream house. When the day arrived, we had been loading the
last of the boxes when I had a surprise visitor. I had installed
a kitchen window bird feeder outside which played host to a
myriad of birds. One day, I had a sense I was being watched. I
looked out to see a teenage red-shouldered hawk at the feeder
staring right at me. From time to time, he would fly overhead
and I'd feel his shadow cross me just like the words in Neil
Young's 'Helpless'. On this day, he circled deep three times
and then flew away. I never saw him again, but I knew he was
telling me goodbye in his way. It was one of those moments you
know in your knower. Whenever I see one of these magnificent
raptors, I think of my avian friend down south and know that I
had, for a moment, one small moment, a connection with the
wild, with nature and the very spirit of life.

Our new house was almost perfect. Our neighbors on
each side were animal friendly. There were little parks tucked
away in our neighborhood which Mookie, Rebel and I made
good use of. We were near a lovely city lake surrounded by a
five mile hiking trail. There was an old army fort turned into
a huge dog Mecca within walking distance and the playground

hosted tons of dogs from all over the county. I swear there were dogs of every breed from every part of the world in that park. We had landed in a dog groover's paradise.

The front gate opened to a precious flower garden. I planted hibiscus and Scott added lush rose bushes that were mindful of the rose garden where Rebel and I had whiled away so many happy hours. Our backyard was sizable compared to most in the community. Our cottage was one of seven built in the 30's on a hill, something like the blue-collar version of the famed painted ladies in San Francisco. Our yard was covered in ivy and vine and slanted down to the fence line of the adjoining property. My first order of business was to get rid of that ivy and create an area for the dogs to play chase. I also had another card up my sleeve, a little surprise for the cats.

I would come home from work each day and grab my pick-axe before heading out back. I do believe that ivy vine was prehistoric. My neighbor would catch me going at it and ask what I was doing. I'd answer, "20 to life" without missing a beat. We tried to use organic methods to extinguish all of the weeds and foxtail, but the vines were left to my trusty pickaxe and me. I had come by my dislike of English Ivy honestly. My grandfather once cut back all of the ivy in his yard with hand clippers. He'd spent days and weeks on the project. Instantly, the stuff grew back and bigger! He hated English Ivy and taught me to feel the same way. I didn't like foxtail either. Mookie had sniffed one up his nostril the previous summer and had to be taken to the vet. I've since found that homeopathic remedies can expel foxtail, but at the time I didn't know any better and hit the panic button. The vet hospital performed surgery on Mookie, but no foxtail was recovered from his nasal passage.

We put in grass seed and waiting patiently for the little blades to peek through the earth. Mookie and Rebel continued to visit surrounding parks so they wouldn't trample the new lawn. It was almost time to realize our dream of letting the cats enjoy the great outdoors as well. They had always been indoor cats, but we had discovered a way to safely convert them to be able to use the outdoors as well. It was called the Radio Fence.

We had begun to research the Radio Fence when the package featured a photo of both a dog and a cat on the box. When we were finally ready to try it, there was only a dog on the box. The cat had been photo-shopped over. I called the company and was told that cats were no longer considered domestic animals. The company was only allowed to market their product to be used on dogs. We decided to go ahead and use the Radio Fence with our cats.

We love our cats and wouldn't hurt them for anything. The Radio Fence, however, delivers a small monitored warning signal. We set our signal extremely low. Scott even tested it on himself. The receiver is attached to a collar worn about the neck. We put the cats through an intensive two-week training period that involved little white flags. It was kind of like that EDS commercial about herding cats. It's funny when someone else tries to train a cat, but not as humorous when trying it on your own. Our cats are very smart and caught on quickly. The main offender was Buddy, who would not leave the deck and refused to participate in the training. I would pay dearly for slacking with Buddy's training.

The day finally arrived when we were ready to spring our plan into action. It was very exciting. We put the little collars around their necks with the receivers. The radio wire ran around the perimeter of the property. With Roy, Candy and Ray, we only had to employ the correction once. Buddy just sat on the deck and refused to move. Buddy had 'escaped' a couple of times back in Dallas. He had figured a way out of the bathroom leading down to an alleyway behind our house. We would find him every time in a neighbor's shed just sitting by himself on a stool in the middle of the room. When he was indoors, Buddy was a needy little creature, but outside, he considered himself wild. He would hiss at me as though I was some sort of monster.

Our little dream cottage became just that, a home filled with love and animals. There were a few flaws with our new system. Candy began to house hop from rooftop to rooftop. I could relate to the mothers whose teenage daughters sneak out at night. Buddy would withstand the radio signal to escape. He had found another neighbor's shed similar to the one in Dallas. I would find him holed up in there, fangs bared and hissing when I'd try to pick him up. Aside from these small snafu's, though, we got along pretty well.

Something happened that completely altered my life. Scott would take Mookie and Rebel to the top of the hill at the end of our street to play. From that point, there was a panoramic view of the city. One evening, they met a stray female pit bull at the top of the hill. When Scott told me she'd been playing with Mookie and Rebel, I about hit the roof. I'd heard about these dogs. The evening news was full of stories about pit bulls. They were known to be fierce fighting beasts with no respect for life. I could not believe Scott had allowed one to play with our pets.

The next day, I saw this dog trotting in front of our house. She stopped at our gate and looked inside the courtyard. I went about my business and pushed any concern out of my head. She was probably just lost. Her owners would find her. The next day, I heard whimpering and went to see what was the matter. She was limping and had blood running down her legs. Even though I didn't like pit bulls, I approached her and she let me pet her. I took her inside the gate and got her some water. I went to call for help.

I found out really quick there was no resource for pit bulls. First, I called Coastal County SPCA. While I was holding the telephone, I had been thinking how wonderful it was we'd moved to a place that cared for animals and wanted to help them. Back in Texas when we'd find an injured bird, there was no one to call at that time. Often, the most humane thing would be to put the animal out of his misery rather than let him suffer. I felt grateful to be surrounded by organizations devoted to helping animals. Finally, I got a live person who directed me to call Coastal County Animal Care and Control, CCACC. I was told that the CCSPCA did not take in stray pit bulls. The woman did go on to tell me that should the dog pass all temperament tests at CCACC, the CCSPCA would accept her into their program.

I then called CCACC and was asked to bring in the dog myself. Since I could not, they told me an officer would be dispatched to pick her up, but there would be a wait as they were very busy. Because she was a pit bull, CCACC was the only avenue for this dog. They assured me her medical needs would be met. Later, I would find that usually meant an x-ray and a bandage. I was offered the option to place a call interested party in her computer record. This would insure that I would receive a call before she was put to sleep.

At that time, CCACC allowed six adoptable pit bulls to be adopted at any time. These dogs were kept in a room containing six kennels. Unclaimed and otherwise relinquished dogs earned their places in the pit bull room after completing the stray period and passing a series of temperament and medical evaluations. The behavior assessment at that time consisted of taking the dog into a hallway and facing off with another dog of the same sex and size, both leashed. If the dog showed any aggressive or fearful tendencies as interpreted by the person conducting the test, that dog was destroyed.

The lucky dogs, ones who'd passed the test, were transferred to the available side. Any time a new dog needed to be temperament tested, one of these dogs were pulled from his or her kennel and tested again, sometimes over and over again. These dogs were often tested when they had not had opportunity for a walk or to relieve themselves. One can only imagine the stress these animals feel in a strange cold place surrounded by terror, noise and barking.

The dog we had turned in was cleaned up after being x-rayed. She was bruised, but luckily, nothing was broken. She passed her temperament test with flying colors and was moved to the adoptable side after her stray period was over. The downside of this system was the dog was euthanized to make room for a new dog. The dog in availables longest without being adopted was the one put down. To be pulled at random and pass temp test after temp test only to lose your life by an unlucky throw of the dice is sad. I called every day to see if our girl was still alive.

I met someone who was to become very special in my life. Layla Williams was rescuing dogs and fostering them in her home for a local dog and cat rescue. I had met Layla on a street corner with her hair dyed bright blue and her arms loaded with dogs on leashes. She looked like an advertisement for something, but what? We had talked and exchanged cards. I called her for advice about the stray girl. Layla's house was full of foster dogs at the time. I believe she had something like 25 dogs living with her at that time. Over the years, 25 was a lowball number for dogs sharing Layla's quarters. She just can't say no to a needy pooch. She told me to keep monitoring at CCACC and just not let them euthanize the dog.

After six long weeks, the dog was adopted! I was beside myself. I tried to find out who had saved her, but was told this would be in violation of some code or law or some sort of thing. I was referred to the assistant deputy director at CCACC, Jill Burns. She, in turn, offered to refer my name to the adopter. After a couple of weeks, I received a call from Marty, the wonderful person who had saved her. Marty had renamed her Angel Divine. We began an enduring friendship lasting over the years. I got to see Angel evolve from the poor hurt dog walking down our street to the girl nicknamed the Princess of Beach Boulevard. She made her daily rounds with Marty to all of the local shops where proprietors would give Angel treats. I've seen her ride the kiddy airplane ride at a carnival and wearing her yearly Halloween costumes. Sometimes, Angel and Marty don't even wait for Halloween to dress up. No matter what day it is, in costume or not, Angel cannot disguise her smile. She always wears the biggest ear-to-ear happy grin and is truly an ambassador to the breed.

I wanted to give something back, so I began volunteering at CCACC. I became the photographer for the website. My job was to take photographs of the dogs and cats and upload the pictures to the CCACC website along with a short bio for each animal. I would spend one or two afternoons a week taking the photos and uploading them to the city's website I still had misgivings about the pit bulls and rarely visited the pit bull room I noticed the public avoided the room also. They would view the other dogs and when most people reached the pit bull area, somebody would usually say, "oh, this is where they keep the pit bulls," and shut the door to the kennels. They were fearful and I must admit, I was scared, too.

I dedicated my picture taking to the cats and other dog breeds, because I was afraid of pit bulls. I had seen the stories on the news and heard the tales about triple locking jaws. I had heard how pit bulls would snap for absolutely no reason and turn on their owners, often mauling them to death. CCACC had a rule in place that only more experienced 'green' volunteers were allowed to handle and walk the pit bulls. I was a novice 'blue' volunteer. We were color-coded by the shade of our aprons we wore while volunteering.

I began to feel pangs of guilt for excluding the pit bulls after a couple of months into my volunteering. I would walk past their kennels and feel surprised when they didn't lunge out and attack the cage as I had expected them to. Deep down, I began to suspect that these dogs just wanted someone to love them. I began to feel a connection when I would look into their eyes. I was still pretty green, even though I wasn't wearing a green apron. I hadn't yet learned to trust my instincts. That would come later.

After a few months, I decided to obtain my green status as a CCACC volunteer. This way, I could take photographs of the pit bulls and at least give them a fair shot at being adopted. The supervisor at the time was Colleen Blanchette. She was a full figured girl who bolstered an immense amount of self-confidence as well as demeanor. One came away from spending time around Colleen with the idea that she knew all there was to know about pit bulls. She came off like she knew everything about all dogs. Debbie's Devil Dogs was contracted by CCACC as the group who trained the county's dogs. Debbie worked very closely with Colleen to supervise the dog program and train all of the dog volunteers.

The day I was set to achieve my green status, I had expected to work with Debbie, however, Colleen met with me in the front lobby. I would be following her around for a couple of hours while she assessed some dogs. Our first dog was an adult female Rottweiler mix. Colleen enjoyed listening to herself talk. She also liked the position of power in deciding a dog's fate. She had a good deal of braggadocio and seemed sure of each comment made regarding dogs and pit bulls. I had no reason to doubt her and tried to take in as much as I could. Later, I later discovered her previous experience had been clerking in a chain pet store. Until she had landed the CCACC position, she had rabbits as pets, but no dogs. Many of the people I would come into contact with who held supervisory positions in county animal control loved holding meetings and lecturing. I would have to learn to separate the science from the bullshit.

Colleen had an opinion about the way a dog would hold her ears, her stance or the hackles raised on her back. These could be read as signs of aggression, she told me. I remember her telling me the current trend was to breed dogs small for fighting. She warned me that should I see a smaller breed of pit bull in the shelter, say a Staffordshire bull terrier, I must beware. Most likely, that dog had been bred for fighting. While on this subject, she pointed out the fire hose outside. Should I ever be concerned for my safety, I was to turn on the hose full force and point it at the dog. The hose was in the side recreational yard and used mainly to water in the poop. The water pressure was so strong that it gouged a huge hole into the ground. This fire hose packed a mean punch.

After my training session, I was nervous, but ready to take my first picture of a pit bull. I went to the kennels and asked for help. For the first few sessions, I was to have a kennel attendant accompany me. Most days, the staff was overworked and could not spare an extra person to watch me. The kennel tech on duty just told me to take one of the dogs into the get acquainted room and I'd most likely be fine.

I was nervous, but jumped in there and took out my first pit bull. His name was Rainbow and he wasn't really a pit bull. He was classified as a pit bull and therefore, faced the same fate as faced the rest of the pit bulls at CCACC. Rainbow was huge and pointy. He looked to me more like a greyhound mix with the long slender snout and whip of a tail. He was brindle with hues of gold, caramel and black with a giant white blaze carried across his chest. Perhaps the brindle coat inspired him to be categorized a pit bull. Over the years, I have met a lot of these so-called pit bulls who qualified due to their brindle coat and not much else.

Rainbow had a boatload of energy. What Rainbow had running through his veins could give Red Bull a run for their money. I was a tad apprehensive to say the least. Was he going to maul me to death once we got out of the kennel? Or could I even get out of the kennel with him at all? At this point, I did not trust my own feelings. I could usually tell if a dog was scared or nervous without the training, but all of the volunteer orientations had caused me to doubt my gut instincts.

It took me a good while to get a collar and leash on Rainbow. By the time we made it out of the kennel, down the hall and into the get acquainted room, I was drenched with sweat. The small room was just big enough fit a person and a dog. It was designed for small dogs or petting a cat, but certainly not for a big rollicking dog Maybe if I just let him jump around awhile, he would wear out, but no. The camera belonging to the volunteer department was extremely unforgiving. Digital had just hit the market and although innovative, still complicated and rife with kinks. By the time the shutter would register, Rainbow would be a brindle streak across the room. After a lot of effort and heavy panting, I finally got the money shot and took Rainbow back to his kennel. We had been going at it the better part of an hour, but I had the photo I needed and I was still in one piece. Maybe the media wasn't all that smart after all. What if all these dogs with so-called pit bull in them were not sadistic killers who turned on you in a second.

Rainbow was one of the lucky ones. He was rescued by a volunteer and fostered to a family who adopted him. I saw him at a park with his people about a year after he left the shelter. He had settled down tremendously. Sometimes, a little love can work a miracle. I believe in my heart that love is the main ingredient for training a dog, but a good obedience class doesn't hurt either.

Chapter Four
Martha

Save Me
By Aimee Mann

Martha

Sometimes, a volunteer gets the opportunity to name a dog. My practice is to change the name of the surrendered dog. I want to give that animal the chance at a new life and am a little bit superstitious in this respect. I believe with a new name, the dog has a bit of extra luck. To give up a dog or a pet you've shared your life with is something I have a hard time understanding. I hope I am never faced with having to make that decision. We live in a world with many resources for rescue animal and believe me, I would exhaust every extreme to avoid giving up my companion. I have built two whole rescues by practicing what I believe.

There is not a day that goes by in my life I don't think about Martha. My sister's name is Martha and I named this girl Martha, too. She wasn't that much to look at. In fact, she was another brindle girl mixed with just enough pit bull to wind her up in the pit bull room at CCACC, enough to become a member of the club that killed its seventh member when the room got too full.

Layla had just formed her own rescue group, Outer Space Rescue. Layla refers to these dogs as having the brindle curse. She felt that brindles had a harder time getting adopted. I don't understand why, because I've always had better luck with brindles than some of the other colors. Brindle dogs remind me of tortoiseshell cats. Martha had that rich dark brindle found in Torties, lots of inky black and deep sienna oil paint brown. If you spread the hair between your fingers, you might see cream or a funny orange like a piece of burning wood. Brindles come in many shades and hues. Lots of dog breeds share the fraternity of having a brindle coat. Greyhounds, Bull Terriers, whippets, Boxers, Bullmastiffs, Presa Canarios and little French Bulldogs can sport a brindle coat to name a few.

I was still taking photographs of the cats and dogs at CCACC and was a bit overwhelmed with the scope of work I'd taken on. We had actually seen a flurry of adoptions with my updated internet photos. I took my commitment very seriously.

I could see a difference. Even though I worked full time, I was coming in at least two days a week to try and get as many cats and dogs up and running as possible. I wrote alluring and quirky bios so the animals might have a chance at finding a special home.

Cats had a better opportunity, because the CCSPCA would come over daily to take a few under the 1994 adoption pact between the two facilities. The CCSPCA is a huge facility. It set the standard for such organizations throughout the rest of the country. Cats lolling in rooms with televisions and comfy cat furniture greet CCSPCA visitors as they walk through the front lobby. What the public doesn't see are all of the animals in small cramped kennels warehoused in the back of the building. All one has to do is step back and look at the size of the building to realize the cats up front are the few of the many. Complicating the issue is the no-kill reputation infused by the media. The adoption pact is referred to among rescuers as Coastal County's dirty little secret. Unbeknownst to the public, the city is not a no-kill city. In fact, more animals than most fall under the 'disease' or 'behavior' caveat to the agreement. Shamefully, most of the animals being euthanized are turned away systematically by CCSPCA on a daily basis. The animals are put on the daily euthanasia list, offered to CCSPCA where most fall under the 'sick' or 'behavior' clause. The animals are then routinely euthanized. Every single animal I have ever saved from CCACC was on that list and turned down by CCSPCA.

But, back to Martha. I had placed this pressure on myself to try and get some of these dogs adopted before their time ran out. Martha had no redeeming characteristics to attract the average family. She was not particularly good looking. She didn't even have that great a personality. To tell you the truth, she and I had more in common than I'd care to admit. It's funny, the ones who get under your skin. The first few times I bypassed her kennel, she looked just like another brindle pit bull mix. I had to agree with Layla, there were certainly a lot of brindle dogs and it was a kind of curse.

I started Martha's photo session by taking her outside and letting her run around a little. I thought she might get tuckered out and I could time that lazy shutter enough to get a decent shot of her. Then, perhaps, the photo would appeal to that wonderful person out there who'd been looking for a Martha all their life and would rush in and jump through all of the hoops to adopt her. Animal control made it as difficult as possible to adopt a pit bull. First and foremost, they required landlord permission to have a pit bull on the premises. This was always put to the landlord very bluntly, something to the effect of, "do you want a pit bull living at your residence?" Many of these dogs weren't even pit bulls outright, but more often than not, were cheated out of a good home. In addition, the prospective adopter had to have pit bull experience. At that time, not many people on the street had pit bull experience on their resume. Should the adopter pass all of the mandatory conditions, he then had to sign up for training. The training was given at CCSPCA, the same organization who would refuse to take the dog in their caveat. All dogs should take an obedience class, but I would rather send the dogs and their people to a trainer who works with shelter dogs.

CCSPCA makes a lot of money through dog training classes; however, they take in relatively few pit bull breeds from CCACC. They had recently begun teaching a class called Bark Class. This was geared for aggressive dogs and cost $400. I had to wonder what would happen to the dog whose owner dropped dead of a heart attack in class. That dog would be sent right around the corner to the county shelter and held in the stray side for what used to be five days. He would then receive his temperament test and medical assessment deciding whether or not he was 'adoptable'. His record already reads 'problematic' with a paragraph from the $400 dog behaviorist. Ultimately, Fido winds up in room 132 where he gets a dose of blue juice administered to other 'behavior' dogs every afternoon at 3 p.m.

No one is suggesting that dangerous animals be released to the unsuspecting public, but one can't ignore the fact that a lot of money is being made on their behavior. I would think more than twice before purchasing a book written by a famous dog behaviorist when the department headed by that person won't take a dog who looks scared, frightened, hesitant, nervous or basically any dog who doesn't already look trained and socialized. If you can't train a dog that isn't already trained, then I want to know what you are doing in the dog training business?

I became a green volunteer and allowed to handle difficult dogs. I believed I was in the company of others who loved animals as I did and wanted to help them. I thought the other volunteers like myself, were there for much more than walking the dogs. How can you walk a dog you know is probably going to die? Most of the other volunteers subscribed to the Devil Dog training program. Because she was the resident dog trainer at CCACC, Debbie's group became a nucleus for dogs and dog business. I began to notice more control issues in relation to the dog department than other animal programs at CCACC. These attitudes were not restricted to animals solely. There were definite lines between the paid staff and the volunteers who donated their time freely. Most staffers looked down upon the volunteers with an air of superiority.

But, again, back to Martha. I took Martha's photograph and posted her on the CCACC website. Sadly, very few animals were being adopted from the site. There was also a public access television spot featuring the website's cats and dogs along with their bios. The television show was slow to turnover, though, and all too often, the morbid parade of photos would be of animals already put down. It was not unusual to tune in and see euthanized dogs pictured one right after the other, over and over again.

The first day when I photographed Martha outside, I found out something quite incredible about her. I had been trying so hard to listen to those more experienced and knowledgeable about dog behavior and had forgotten to listen to my own heart....my own dog language. This was a God given resource I'd brought to the party. Dogs talk to us. No matter what the breed, each dog is an individual just as we people are. Each one has something to say. That is why the definitive dog book has not yet been written.

The kennels filled with dogs say, "hey, you! I've been bred to work and they've got me locked up in this tiny cage with an old tennis ball in the corner. Can you please get me out of here? Or could you just come inside and pet me? I need human contact. I am a social being. Do you know what one little five minute walk would do for me? Do you know the difference you could make by putting your hand on my head and petting me? I'm going crazy! What did I do wrong to be put in here? I didn't hurt anybody. I've always liked people. Please help me. Look at me. Don't just walk by."

I had been listening to the dog experts who believed public speaker and kennel owner, Sue Sternberg wrote the bible. I had forgotten to listen to me! I took Martha outside. She was what I like to call a busy girl. After running around a few minutes, she went to the potty outside. This was a dog needing to go potty outside and would hold it until she could do so no longer. This is a girl who is potty trained and waits and waits for a volunteer to show up so that she can go potty outside like a good girl. When no one comes that day, she and so many others will go potty in their kennel. This is so sad, because they are trying to be good, to do as they have been trained to do. They do not understand that they are in a new location, that somebody has changed the rules and forgotten to tell them. They are on a new schedule, somebody else's time frame and the old routine is history. Many of these dogs have come from a background in which they were punished for having an accident, having their noses rubbed in their excrement or spanked. Here they are, most at the end of the line, still trying to be good dogs.

Martha was all about the ball. She was a two-ball dog, meaning she immediately went for that ball when it was thrown and wouldn't release until you gave her the 'leave-it' command. Martha stepped up the game a notch. She would not release until you showed her the new ball. She would then gently set the ball in her mouth on the ground beside her and tear out after the new ball as far and as fast as you could throw it. Then, Martha would return like clockwork for the next round. This would go on and on. She never, I mean, never tired of the game. She was relentless. Someone who is not a trainer, like myself, will toss the ball a little and then try to get some loving and sugar from the dog. Martha wasn't wired that way. She was there to work. Her job was that ball. If you reached down to pet her, she routinely moved her head to the side and waited for you to throw the ball again. I remember that movement so clearly, as if it were yesterday or even a few seconds ago. She was a machine. That's what I remember about Martha. I remember that about her every day.

Something funny happens to you when you volunteer or work at a city animal shelter. You have to develop skills to survive or you will go nuts. Believe me, I know. The people who wear green aprons at CCACC often cop a know-it-all attitude regarding dogs. Some of them have been to a couple of seminars and return with commonplace industry terminology peppering their conversation. Some ideas are helpful, but taken out of context in a fear-based arena such as a city shelter, these concepts can do more damage than good.

Whale eye is a term that absolutely terrifies me. When I see 'whale-eye' written on a kennel card, I want to put a leash on the dog and get the hell out of Dodge! I think there is someone who's been to a high dollar dog conference. What 'whale'-eye' means is too much white of the eye is visible round the pupil. It is supposed to denote fear in a dog and again, I'm terrified to think how many dogs have been destroyed with 'whale-eye' written on their kennel card. What I'd like to see is the dog properly assessed, then re-assessed on another day and by more than one expert. My goodness, what these dogs could teach us if we'd let them. We are here to learn, right?

Martha didn't have the opportunity to teach us much of anything. Someone put the word out that she was a bad dog. It didn't take much to remove a dog from the adoptable side. She was immediately put on the euthanasia list. I was heartbroken. I knew she was not a bad dog, but I didn't have the book knowledge or street credentials myself to prove it. There were more powerful people at CCACC who supposedly knew so much more. I went to Colleen and begged for permission to spend time with Martha in the side yard during her last days. I knew there was nothing else I could do to save Martha. She was going to be killed, put to sleep, euthanized, whatever you call it and nothing could change that fact. To her benefit, Colleen did grant my request to spend Martha's last few days with her.

What one goes through when spending time with an animal about to die are hard to weather, feelings of total aloneness and of despair. At this time, I was not aware of any legislative measures that could have enabled me to help Martha. I had no money or resources. I did not even have a place to put her were I able to save her. Martha's beauty lay in her intent to focus. To her, everything was about the ball. Here she was, literally living on borrowed time, but every bit of her intensely dedicated to working with her ball. That was her purpose in life. How many of us can say we have reached that plateau in our own busy lives? When I remember Martha, I prefer to remember her retrieving her ball out there in the side yard. She was truly a magnificent dog.

Some of the green volunteers who formed Colleen's dog department clique actually suggested I accompany Martha when she was administered the euthanasia fluid. I could not do it. I do not have that in me. To take the life of a vibrant being is near impossible for me to watch. I noticed that some of these volunteers regularly sat in on the process. We did sign a paper waiving our opinion of euthanasia when we attended the volunteer orientation, but I was beginning to question whether or not I could continue to ignore my own feelings regarding the destruction of healthy and non-threatening animals.

Martha was let down by all of us. She was betrayed by the system, by the people paid to protect her, by the volunteers who thought they knew dog behavior. Most of all, she was let down by me. Had I tried harder, I could have found a way to save Martha. I know that now.

Later on, I would speak to a woman who travels all over the United States recruiting canines to participate in the U.S. Customs Drug Detection Program. There is an extremely strict criteria applied to the squad. The program lasts a year and is structured to escalate the dog's prey drive. When I inquired regarding pit bulls, she was very clear on the matter. In fact, she had personally bought a house should her all time favorite dog in the program fail. She would be prepared to adopt the dog and offer her a home. Pit bulls are not considered adoptable due to the heightened drive it takes to complete the program. A Golden Retriever or Labrador type dog that drops out can be adopted, but pit bulls are considered too intense to transition to civilian life.

What she looks for in a dog is basically a dumb-dora, a dog all about the lure, but not too bright. She lets the dog sniff a rolled towel when scouting for qualified contenders. Without making too big a deal, she tosses the towel and watches the dog go to work. The dogs must be people friendly for obvious reasons, but ultimately all about the lure. Martha would have been a superstar. She was the best I've ever seen, hands down. If Martha had entered the course, she would have become as famous as Popsicle, the drug dealer's dog who'd been found by DEA agents in a freezer. Not only was Popsicle brought back to life, but also after training, he went on to bust tons and tons of drug dealers. Martha could have been in his league.

Harry Whittington, a famous pulp fiction writer, commented on writing westerns. He said you don't have to ride every horse to write about them, but you have to have loved that one. That's how I feel when I remember Martha. I have met my share of pit bulls and I have loved pretty much every one of them. I have loved some of these dogs more than I have loved others. It's impossible to define who and what you will love in your life. Martha was not even that lovable a dog. She was certainly not a huggy dog. She was all about business. It was a crime to put a dog like Martha to sleep. I think about Martha and what she taught me and I look forward to the time I might see Martha again.

Chapter Five
Girl

Still is Still Moving to me
by Willie Nelson

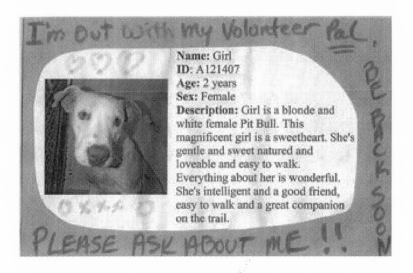

I'm out with my Volunteer Pal,

BE BACK SOON

Name: Girl
ID: A121407
Age: 2 years
Sex: Female
Description: Girl is a blonde and white female Pit Bull. This magnificent girl is a sweetheart. She's gentle and sweet natured and loveable and easy to walk. Everything about her is wonderful. She's intelligent and a good friend, easy to walk and a great companion on the trail.

PLEASE ASK ABOUT ME!!

After Martha died, I began walking the pit bulls as my primary volunteer work at CCACC. When things get bad for me, I know to walk the dogs. I still took photos of the other animals for the website, but the pit bulls had touched something inside me. I began to see more and more of the available pit bulls being exterminated just because they weren't lucky enough to be adopted. More and more, I devoted my waking moments to the dilemma facing these pit bulls. I thought surely there must be a solution for this incredibly overwhelming problem. At the time, pit bulls were never seen being walked around Port Harbor. You'd see pit bulls around town all right, but most of them wore a tow chain around their necks. How could we change that picture? What could I do?

Most of the dogs brought into the shelter were puppies and under a year old. A good many were under two, but seldom much older. I don't know if the reason most shelter pit bulls were so young had to do with the temperament test and an older dog's ability to pass. There were certainly no studies being conducted to explore why the majority of these dogs were brought in so young. I would hate to think that the American Pit Bull Terrier faced the same short life expectancy as North American Indians. What a sad comment about the first native American dog and the native people of our land. You would think we would strive to protect and cherish our history.

Years before, I took a great government class in college from a Eugene, Oregon professor. He'd guaranteed an 'A' if I enrolled for the evening class. The students were mainly nursing and criminal justice majors on their way to being cops or working in the judicial system. One night, our instructor asked us to raise our hands if we believed in capital punishment. A sea of hands bolted upright. He asked how many of our group were nursing students. About half the arms remained proudly erect. The next question was regarding capital punishment and lethal injection. He asked if we knew who actually delivered the shot. The answer, not surprisingly, was a registered nurse. The arms began to drop down as the class members considered the taking of a human life. The issue became real when we thought about putting our opinions into the action of taking a life.

The people who perform daily euthanasia at CCACC are regular people like you and me. Many of the employees started out as a volunteer or answered an advertisement in hopes of helping animals in a low kill shelter. Imagine taking a job to help the animals and then, upon reporting for work, finding out part of your daily duty was to kill those animals. In some cases, the job required removing the animal's head, maybe an animal the kennel tech had been feeding and caring for on a daily basis.

There is no counseling program at CCACC for the people who perform euthanasia. The question is a moral one. Shouldn't this sort of procedure be conducted by a professionally trained technician, meaning someone who is psychologically prepared for such work? Kennel techs are the lifeblood of any shelter. They keep the facility running smoothly. Most of these people are good human beings. I have met many animal care technicians whose own homes are overrun with other people's unwanted animals. At CCACC, technicians often work under the radar to see that the animals have blankets and toys along with an extra scoop of food.

Working in an animal care facility is debilitating work. I have seen good people break under the pressures of trying to care for the animals and more often than not, witnessing their euthanasia. One girl in particular comes to mind. Margaret was just completing her training as an animal care technician when I started my volunteer work at the shelter. She, too, had been in the volunteer program before being hired as an animal care technician. She encouraged me to obtain my green status so that I could take photos of the pit bulls. She loved the mastiffs especially and told me stories about growing up around bullmastiffs.

The day in, day out stress took its toll on Margaret. I

sensed her pull away and the light in her eyes begin to dim. I probably could have reached out to her, but I was caught up in my own whirlwind. Margaret, who had so loved the animals, was suddenly dismissed from the shelter. The people who ran the shelter did not like controversy. Issues frightened them. They were always wary of anything hinting of lawsuit. The shelter's way to handle any kind of disturbance was to quietly snuff it out.

I heard from some of the other techs that Margaret had begun to withhold food from the animals. For an animal in a shelter, or any animal for that matter, food is the high point of the day. For an animal not to be fed is the very essence of desperation. Everything about this story is hopeless to me. What I saw was this good well-meaning person being forced to kill animals every day, animals she had cared for and petted and loved. After a while, it just took a toll on her and robbed her of her soul. I have seen people respond to the pressure in many ways, but Margaret's story affected me deeply.

I increased my focus on the pit bulls. I have a lot in common with pits. When the going gets tough, I look for a loophole. Pit bulls, as their devotees will testify, are like that. They are manipulative, but in a good and funny way. Nothing is quirkier to me than watching the wheels turn in a hard-headed pit bull while she tries to figure an angle to outsmart you and get something she wants. I continued to take the photos for the website while I looked for ways to help the pit bulls. There were so many of them and more being bred every day. I knew enough not to waste time cultivating an outlet for them at the CCSPCA. They clung to their adoption pack caveat like white on rice!

Then, I met the most beautiful pit bull I have ever seen. Her name was Girl. Carol, a vet tech at CCACC named her Girl because she was such a girl! She was an American Staffordshire Terrier, grand and proud with gorgeous long shapely legs. She was definitely the poster girl supermodel for the breed. She was fawn with a lovely white face and a freckled ear. Her eyes were golden and she wore her own liner rimmed about each eye like an Egyptian princess. She had the tiniest little white lashes and her nose and mouth were framed with the dusky rose-colored shape of a heart. She stole my heart that very first day.

Girl had a huge white chest, pure muscle, which melted into her fawn torso. Her long tail looked like it had been dipped in cream. She looked like she was wearing little white socks in the back and long gloves in front. If she had a plaid skirt, she could give Britney Spears a run for the money as a Catholic schoolgirl.

Some of the pits were pretty like Girl, but for some reason, I couldn't always get a good photograph of them. They were either moving too quickly or so excited to get to go outside, they had a hard time sitting still. Girl was a natural. She took the best photos, each better than the last one. She absolutely radiated and would grin the minute I picked up the camera. She was on. It was as if she knew something was expected of her and it was her job to deliver. The first photo I took that day was perfect. That photo became a tattoo on my arm and later a logo for the most notorious pit bull rescue to hit the streets of Coastal County.

Girl was a natural athlete. She amazed me that first day when we began to play. Not all of the dogs are like Martha and hell on the ball. Some like to sniff every corner and mark it like my little shorty pants, Rebel. Some are like Mookie and survey the domain, barking at all of the birds and people and anything that moves. Some like to roll around in everything and have you rub their bellies. Girl came alive the first time she eyed a Frisbee. I had never been able to interest any of the dogs in the plastic discs lying around the side yard. For some reason, I picked up one of the Frisbees and tossed it into the air that day. Girl was off and running. She flew through the air like a very large, graceful bird. She bucked midair and snapped her jaws on that Frisbee before landing. She was a natural. Girl absolutely soared.

I couldn't believe my eyes as I watched her. It was amazing, something you wanted people to be able to share. She tirelessly went after the Frisbee. I could hardly keep up with her. She was a two-ball dog in the same respect Martha had been. She picked up very quickly what was expected of her. For dogs like Martha and Girl, this was work. Girl came alive with that Frisbee in her mouth. This was her purpose. When she'd return with it, she was hesitant to let go. She shook it a few times, as dogs do, as if to punish that naughty Frisbee. We carried on for a good while that afternoon, Girl and I. She was so happy, smiling and panting. Her big, pink tongue hung out like a cartoon version of a pit bull. Whatever they had in mind when trying to breed the AmStaff was realized in Girl. She was perfect.

I took her back to the kennel that afternoon for the first of many times over the next few weeks. As amped up as she'd been in the yard, she was equally calm when I closed the door to her kennel. In fact, rarely had I seen such a calm dog in the shelter. She smiled sweetly and sat directly in the middle of the floor as I closed the iron gate and fastened the lock into place. There was a moment between us where her eyes looked trustingly into mine as if she knew I was going to get her out of there. Animals sense things. They might not know what it is, but they know when something is up. For the first of many days, I made an out loud promise to Girl that I would save her.

I went directly upstairs to enter her data on the city's website. Everything had to be done by the book according to bureaucratic standard. The website was the only resource to find potential adopters while the clock ticked. I made posters and tried to put them in local coffee shops and pet stores around town, but so often, the dogs were destroyed before anyone had a chance to inquire about them.

I continued to work with Girl and Frisbee. I asked

everyone I met to adopt her. She was popular with both staff and the volunteers. The green volunteers were especially fond of her, because she was so calm. This group could be circumspect regarding most of the pit bulls in the shelter, but everyone liked Girl. She was even liked by Colleen, who was fostering a dog who looked a bit like Girl. They had both been apprehended in the same area and were suspected to be littermates. Colleen mentioned she didn't know pit bulls could play Frisbee. What an unusual statement coming from someone who was a pit bull expert. The pit bull rescue she was instrumental in forming, Big Top, issued a statement on their website warning against playing Frisbee with pit bulls. This was rather odd, but they eventually reversed their position and retracted their former statement regarding Frisbees and pitties.

After crossing all of the hurdles to adopt a pit bull, the last stop was Colleen. While she was CCACC Animal Control Supervisor, all pit bull adoptions had to be approved by her personally. Many dogs were put to sleep who had good homes waiting for them. Justin was a very cute young pit bull mix. Before he wound up in the CCACC kennels, his ears were deformed. His former owner had chopped them off like Mr. Spock's and sewed them up with fishing line. He wound up at the shelter with that fishing line still in his ears. That didn't stop Justin, though. He was a happy dog with no ill feelings toward anyone. He was golden colored, soft and fluffy with puppy fur. A very nice lady wanted to adopt him and had a female pittie whom she'd already introduced to Justin. They were like peas in a pod. Every criterion was met and the adoption was a go until they got to Colleen. Once Colleen found out the young lady took her social dog to a dog park, the adoption was killed. So was Justin. He was put to sleep, because Colleen and her new group, Big Top Pit Bull Group, did not believe pit bulls should go to dog parks. Justin was only one of so many dogs who lost his life due to politics and opinion.

Big Top clearly states on their website that no pit bulls

are allowed to visit dog parks. I am not overly fond of dog parks, but have seen more than a few well-trained pit bulls at the dog park in my time. It should be a case-by-case decision. In other words, some dogs are dog park dogs and some aren't. That simple. That ethic applies to all breeds of dogs. If people were more in tune with their dogs, there would be fewer mishaps at the dog parks and elsewhere, for that matter. A good 'off' and recall should be a must for all dogs. A blanket statement that all pit bulls should be prohibited from dog parks is harmful and breed specific. You're demonizing the very dog you're attempting to help.

The catch 22 at CCACC prohibited anyone from using the resources at Craigslist.org to find homes for the animals. At the time when I was volunteering, Craigslist was emerging as an online classified network. The official reason given by CCACC was fear that the public would respond en masse to save animals and overwork the staff. Even though the world 'care' preceded 'control', it was a clear case of the 'control' trumping the 'care'. Most of the CCACC staff is caring and hardworking, willing to go the distance to help an animal find a home. I had seen a smile cross even the most war torn CCACC employee's face in the rare instance of a last minute adoption. Unfortunately, these moments were infrequent.

Administration argued the public should not be encouraged to adopt animals based upon emotional reason generated by Craigslist postings. I had nine 'unplanned for' animals living in my home at that time, each one a cherished member of our family. The real reason prohibiting posts on Craigslist is known by select few in the rescue community of Coastal County. The myth perpetuated by the media, the CCSPCA and CCACC is that Coastal County is low kill. Those of us in the rescue community know the real reason animals are being unfairly euthanized for behavior and health reasons. Other local shelters and animal control agencies use Craigslist to advertise regularly with great success.

Two websites would become fundamental in helping place pit bulls and other animals in great homes. First was PBRC, Pit Bull Rescue Central. This is an online nationwide pit bull site designed to educate about the breed. Those members of the public who've found or wish to re-home a pit bull or pit bull mix have an extraordinary set of resources on this site. PBRC supports the breed with tons of materials, informative historical data, an online application process with posts of available dogs seeking new homes that can be cross-posted to other websites and lists of other organizations formed to help pit bull breeds. Petfinder.com is another national database accessible to multitudes of potential adopters. Petfinder is the most widely known of several other adoption sites which have sprung up in the past few years like Adopt -a-Pet and Pets 911. These sites have been wonderful for homeless animals, providing a network of available animals so the public will have alternative options to buying and breeding. Hope is for the day when the term 'euthanasia' will be as unacceptable as words like lobotomy or holocaust.

Girl was at CCACC for a long, long time. When her days were numbered, the annual Gay Pride Parade rolled around. We were invited to bring dogs to walk in the festivities. I volunteered to walk Girl with the ulterior motive of finding her a forever home. First, though, we had to wade through all of the red tape at CCACC. Even though Girl had been cleared to walk in the parade, some of the more seasoned volunteers approached me to express their doubts about Girl. They felt she was too shy and would be fearful in a crowd situation. Secretly, I held with my own feelings that she'd rather deal with the crowd than what was looming down the hall in room 132. At this point, though, I politely answered them with my belief that Girl could indeed handle the crowd and she would be fine so long as she was by my side. I knew we had a bond and I knew she trusted me. Anyone who has developed a relationship with a dog knows when they share a connection. There is a sense of trust involved on both parts. It's a mighty powerful thing and a gift that must be treasured. It is your duty to protect the one who places their trust in your care. When the volunteers kept it up, I replied that Colleen authorized Girl to walk in the parade. Since we were all afraid of her anyway, the objections began to fizzle. It was off to the parade for Girl and me.

The day of the big event was hotter than all creation. It was mindful of Texas weather. The CCACC van was there along with a big loudmouth Project 20 guy who wasn't even an official volunteer. Project 20 was a program allowing citizens to work off traffic fines and the like through public service. This guy elected himself our chief cook and bottle washer. He spent the whole day running around and shooting out orders at me, Girl, a fifteen year-old kid and the CCACC van driver. This went on for the entire six hours of the parade.

I lined up five potential adopters for Girl. She was such a head turner. She just shone. Although she was feeling the heat, I made sure she had plenty of water. I wasn't worried about her shyness, just her thirst and the heat index. She was just the tiniest bit of a drama queen and marched as if the event had been arranged just for her. When the parade finally got under way, it was something magnificent to behold. The original intention of Gay Pride was that, gay pride. When you are a part of that actual celebration, though, you are part of a phenomenon bigger than life itself. There is a multitude of acceptance where everyone and every being is welcomed. When I attend Gay Pride, I always feel as if this was the way life was intended to be. So when Girl and I began to walk down that main street, the cheers and smiles and happiness from the crowd absolutely took my breath away. Girl was not shy in the least. She perked up and proudly walked down that street. That day, she wasn't a pit bull on death row, but part of a greater good. As Girl and I walked, people reached out to pet her and tell us hello. It was so hopeful and joyous. We would look at each other, Girl and I, and grin. It was truly an incredible day.

During the next 48 hours, all five of the potential adoptions for Girl fell through. Her time was up at CCACC. Even the most opinionated green volunteer, Julie Chen, was distressed enough to consider adopting Girl to keep her from being euthanized. However, she'd been trying to breed her sighthound and the dog was recently impregnated. Girl's adoption was scrapped. Colleen let me know Girl was out of options. The shelter was full and more dogs needed to move to the adoptable side. The only place for Girl was Room 132. I took her outside to play. She was so pretty and calm when I put her back into her kennel that night. She looked up at me with her dog smile. How could I let her down? She trusted me.

I knew Scott would say no to the idea of fostering Girl. We had two dogs of our own along with four cats and a bird. Besides that, we lived in a tiny cottage. I had to try anyway. I begged and begged. I promised him everything I could think of. Scott's biggest fear was too may animals resulting in an accident. I told him how beautiful Girl was. I can remember seeing his eyes glaze over like, sure, right. I told him how athletic she was, how she soared through the air after her Frisbee. I think he finally consented to meet her just to shut me up so he could get some sleep. I knew if he would just meet her, he would love her as much as I did. We arranged to bring Mookie and Rebel to CCACC and meet with Colleen the next day. Colleen had to perform the temperament test with Mookie and Rebel.

The hours seemed to drag on forever until the next afternoon rolled around. I took Mookie and Scott held onto Rebel's leash as we waited for Colleen in the side yard. When Colleen arrived with Girl, we allowed the three to nose touch and it was as if Girl knew just what to do with these two confirmed bachelors. She immediately went into a play bow and wagged her tail. Mookie let out his signature 'yow, yow, yow!' Rebel usually only wanted to play with Mookie or hang by himself, but today, took an immediate liking to Girl. We let

them become completely acquainted before taking them off
leash. There was an instant air of harmony between the three
dogs. Sometimes you just know it's a fit. Even though we all felt
comfortable letting the three dogs off leash, the fire hose was
available for extreme measures. Judging from their interplay,
though, I didn't think the fire hose would be necessary for these
three dogs.

The meeting between Girl, Rebel and Mookie was
the single best introduction I have ever been party to. Their
interplay would later serve to help me gauge assessments with
other dogs. Girl and Mookie and Rebel ran around and around
the side yard at the shelter, barking and chasing each other like
long lost friends. It was almost as if they knew each other from
another time and were enjoying a happy reunion. Whenever
one would turn and play bow, the responding dog would roll
over and offer his or her tummy in submission. Each dog took
turns being the chaser and the one in pursuit, rolling over
good-naturedly when caught, legs akimbo. Not one of the
three seemed to care about being alpha or dominant. Their
agenda was fun and to have a good old time. It was as winning
a combination as I could have possibly hoped for. My heart just
about exploded. This was what I was about. I felt very blessed
and lucky to be a part of their world this day.

Mookie was something of a ladies' man. Although fixed,
the girls all seemed to melt when Mookie came around. He'd
just strut at the dog park. He knew all eyes were on him and
would make the most of it. His joy in life was to head a pack
of dogs running around without any particular destination,
yapping and yelping in his wake and most of them females.
Mookie was sort of a rock star with the gals and Girl was no
different than the rest of them. She absolutely adored Mookie
from the first minute she laid eyes on him. Watching them play
was as good as it gets.

I am terrible at dog introductions, bordering on
paranoia. I have been accused of being too careful and have

been told by trainers to lighten up. I am aware of the strength and serious nature of pit bull breeds and have let that in my way of conducting a proper dog on dog assessment. Truth be told, I'm happy to have the professionals handle this part of the job. I have been very lucky to know some of the best trainers in the business. My favorite California dog trainer, Billy Best, says not every dog likes every dog. This little statement says a mouthful about dogs and about Billy's understanding of them. That day, though, it didn't take dog training to see that Girl, Mookie and Rebel were instant best friends.

We couldn't take Girl home that day. She still had to be spayed and given all of the required shots and vaccinations. No matter how many inoculations they might have already received in their lives, by law, dogs and cats had to be vaccinated again before leaving the shelter. On the lucky side, Girl was spayed at CCACC rather than CCSPCA. I was happy about this since I'd seen my share of spay/neuters gone wrong from CCSPCA. Plus, at CCACC, the gals got a tattoo. Girl came home fixed as well as hip!

The pit bull breeds, more than other dogs I've encountered, seem to have a vulnerable almost human quality. They just love to be owned. When we finally brought Girl home, she was so happy to be a part of the family. Girl had some shyness and fearfulness about her. Her trainer felt that Girl had not been abused, but had probably come from an environment where she hadn't been handled very much. Our approach with Girl was to coax her toward me quietly by standing still and allowing her to make the move. It was hard to try and remember to handle Girl like this, but I did my very best. I am gregarious and loud from Texas which is usually quite popular with dogs and not so with Californians. Luckily, Girl already trusted me and we were bonded. She would come to me every time. To this day, when I say her name, she smiles and comes to me every time, especially when a cookie's in the picture.

I wasn't too keen on the name Girl. It sounded so from the hood. I liked Carol, the vet tech who'd named her, so I tried to think of a name that would give homage to her shelter name. I considered a lot of names. I wanted something really special, a name no other dog was named. I liked the song "Cowgirl in the Sand" and it captures her quality so. She looks like a cowgirl in the sand with her white face and fawn coloring. She is so mysterious and always seems to be sending silent messages. Cowgirl was a popular name among the bred and fighting dogs. For rotten people, they do pick out some good names. Then, it dawned on me like magic, Rowdy Cowgirl! I used to love "Rawhide" and Rowdy Yates. He was a real pretty cowboy and she was a real pretty cowgirl, such a champion. There it was. She was officially crowned Miss Rowdy Cowgirl.

We couldn't trust her to come to us when we called her every time, but she'd always come when we called Mookie. Rebel never came to anybody and still doesn't, being his own dog and all. Mookie had perfect recall and with Rowdy Cowgirl in tow. We ended up calling her Girl and never considered looking for that forever home. She was already here.

I still didn't know what it was, but I felt it necessary to do something to help these dogs. These dogs are strong and serious, but in the right home, can be a cherished member of the family. For some time, I had been entertaining the idea of forming a rescue organization myself. I was overwhelmed by advice to not rock the CCACC boat, to stick to walking the dogs. It's hard to not believe what one hears, but you can't help noticing cracks in the system. This became my quandary. I had begun to trip on the cracks and the day came when I could no longer ignore them.

One Monday afternoon, I came home to let the dogs out. We had a set routine in which the cats were collected from the backyard in order to let the dogs potty and get some exercise. I had gathered all of the cats and put them in our bedroom, but forgot to fasten the cat window. My little sweetheart pride and joy, Ray, wandered back out to the deck and Mookie began to bark at him. Girl followed right behind and snatched Ray into her mouth. What followed was a complete nightmare. I tried and tried to get Ray out of Girl's mouth. All I could think to do was twist her collar in hopes that she would choke and release her hold on Ray. I had no choice. Raw was frantic and screaming and there was blood everywhere. I can't begin to explain the panic I felt. Girl finally gagged and I was able to pull Ray from her mouth. I got him into the house where he immediately went into shock. The blood was from a gash in my finger Ray had bitten in his terrified state.

After settling the dogs, I went back into the cat room for Ray. I was able to rush him to a nearby vet who dropped everything and immediately saw to Ray. Scott came home and met us at the vet clinic. Ray was in surgery and they advised us to go back home. They promised to call as soon as they knew something. It was hard to not stay and wait for Ray, but the cut on my finger needed stitches. When we returned to the vet, the doctor let us know he was concerned about Ray. He'd suffered heavy trauma to both the liver and the pancreas. It was an especially difficult situation as one of the organs needed to eat to heal properly and the other needed to starve so that it could recover. This was how I understood what the doctor wanted to do to save Ray. He had performed a procedure to fool the organ needing starving. He allowed us to take Ray home with instructions to try and get some food into him.

It was hopeless from the get go. Ray was so sick that he had absolutely no interest in food or eating. I tried everything. I tried cooking his favorite chicken and mixing it with cooked salmon. I tried adding rice and cat food, baby food, but nothing. The next morning, I took him back to the hospital. The vet said at this point, our best chance was to insert a feeding tube and monitor him round the clock. This would require picking Ray up at the vet hospital every evening when they closed and transporting him to the emergency clinic to be observed through the night. Ray would need to be brought back to my neighborhood clinic when they opened in the morning. I would do anything I could to save Ray's life. He went back into surgery to apply the feeding tube. The operation went well, but Ray was still critical. The task at hand was to increase his strength and interest him in eating on his own.

I picked Ray up that first evening and took him to the emergency hospital. I had misgivings about this particular hospital due to a previous experience there with my bird, but it was the only option at the time. One of the vet techs from the neighborhood vet worked nights at the emergency hospital. Being familiar with Ray's case, she promised to keep close watch on him. I followed the routine for a week. He was connected to an intravenous tube and being fed with success. I began to have the tiniest bit of hope. When they brought Ray to me, I would hold him and tell him how sorry I was that I had allowed this to happen to him. I would tell him how much I loved him and how much he meant to me. He would look at me with his glassy eyed stare and I could see how very sick he was, how frail and damaged. I prayed real hard.

That Friday night, I picked him up from the vet's and headed to the emergency hospital. He would stay over the weekend. Being the weekend, the emergency hospital was very busy and everyone was running around like crazy. They took Ray to the back so they could begin to monitor him in a more stable setting. I waited in the main lobby for over an hour to sign the paperwork. Suddenly, a frantic staff member came out and yelled for the person with Ray Marabito. I jumped up. "Me! I am!"

They showed me into a waiting room and fear swept over me as had happened with Fu. This female physician came into the room. I later found out she was a high priced holistic vet who moonlit at the emergency clinic. Ray was lopped across her arms and trailing the dripping lifeless iv tube. She screamed, "Your cat is dead. He's dead! Your cat has died!"

I was in total shock. No, I had just brought him in to be monitored with the iv tube an hour ago. She held her arms out with Ray's iv tube emptying its contents onto the floor below. The doctor was in an obvious state of arousal. "Your cat's dead! He is dead!" She kept yelling that Ray was dead over and over and over while holding his body out and away from her own. I was totally freaked out. I could not think straight. I panicked. Someone came in and started asking me if I wanted to make arrangements. They were quick to finalize at this place as if death was commonplace. I was trying to talk to three people at once, ready to write up the documents. Where were all of these people when Ray needed them to check his iv tube? He had died alone with no one to hold him. That is what I remember when I think of this horrible night. There had been no time to check Ray in, but suddenly all the time in the world to make final arrangements.

All I knew is that I wanted the hell out of that place. I wanted me and Ray out of that hospital. I took his poor body and left walking down the street screaming and crying. My cat was gone. He had died alone and all by himself. We could have sat out there in the car if he was going to die. He could have died with dignity and in the arms of someone who loved him rather than that sterile, cold hospital full of workers too busy to even look over and see if the patient was alive or dead. I left that place with a newfound understanding of what hospitals mean by the word monitor.

I cried for the next month. I didn't care who heard me or saw me. I felt the sorrow of those poor women in Iran who beat their chests and self-mutilate. I was feeling sadness, loss, guilt, helplessness, but mostly, just felt empty. What helped me during this time were Bella and Lola, the beautiful Akitas I walked twice a day. They were quiet and stoic and seemed to understand the pain I was feeling. I will never forget the silent strength they provided me as we walked each day. We were a part of the rest of the world, but distant from others as we drifted by. I don't know if I realized at the time how they helped me to heal. They didn't seem to mind my tears or think I was strange to burst out crying. I was just their Cindy and for them, that was enough.

I thought volunteering more would help ease the pain of losing Ray, so I took my camera down to the shelter where I hoped I could do some good. People at the shelter asked me if I was going to euthanize Girl. I started to see a distinct line between the real animal people and the rest. This sort of thinking from people who were volunteering their time among animals whose lives depended upon them terrified me. How can a person who loves animals have no sense of animals? This was a hard lesson. When I first began volunteering, I was so naïve. I thought everyone felt as I did. I thought we were all working together to find a way to save these animals who so trusted us. I was beginning to wake up.

What Girl had done was instinctual and caused by fear. I would later find out Girl was a frenzy fighter. She won't start a fight, but once a scuffle begins, her prey drive kicks in. When I had left Frenchie the cockatiel's cage door unlatched by mistake, I came home to find his remains on the floor. My cats, Roy, Ray and Buddy had killed him. This was devastating. It was my fault as Ray's death had ultimately been through my own negligence. I certainly did not hold the cats responsible for Frenchie's death. It was horrible and I grieved and hurt as I did when Ray died. I yelled at Buddy when he meowed for his dinner that night, but I understood what the cats had done was nature at it's worst. When it was suggested to put Girl to sleep, the idea was as preposterous as putting a cat to sleep for killing a bird. We do not like it when our sweet kittens behave like jungle animals. We feel betrayed when the precious dog who sleeps in our bed behaves like a predator.

I realized what a powerful animal Girl was. I had

69

recognized it before, but now I had seen her in action. She was completely made of muscle like some genetic wonder, but Girl was a very gentle soul. I had a bond with Girl that is not easily explained. We had an unwritten agreement, a commitment signed in blood. I have listened to the am radio talk show rants. People say things like, 'if my dog was ever aggressive, I'd put it down so fast you wouldn't know what hit you!" These people sounded to me as if they were measuring their own worth by willingness to kill their pet.

I read, researched and soul searched since the day Girl mauled Ray. As has been my practice in rescue work, I tried to find a solution. I considered the levels of aggressive behavior and questioned what caused that behavior. To be honest, my ad hoc study has been an ongoing one and also an intensely personal one. It has become the enigma of my life and my work. Surely, if we could find an answer to the question of what actually causes aggression, would that not be a miracle? To consider all of the animals waiting to die in shelters, most of them here due to some sort of behavior related issue.

I never had to make that decision whether or not to keep Girl. There was never the option. I knew her power and her strength. I knew her personality. I knew she was an animal. I knew not to expect her to be a rational being like the dog owners on the radio show. I also knew that the bond Girl and I shared was not something experienced by most of the population. To pick animals over people and their politics certifies a lifetime membership with the rest of the so-called animal nuts. I once heard an animal rights activist asked the question were she on a sinking boat with a chicken and a child, which one would she save...the chicken or the child. Now, who's crazy? What would anyone be doing on a rowboat with a kid and a chicken?

One CCACC small dog volunteer came into the volunteer room with a Chihuahua in her sherpa bag. She began talking baby talk to the Chihuahua. "Ooh, be careful. We don't want Girl to think we are a kitten, do we?"

I couldn't help but think how cruel and hurtful her remarks were. Again, here's someone working with dogs and has absolutely no concept about aggression levels. This was not the first or last experience I would have with people drawn toward animals, yet who lacked the ability to love all of them. This was yet another lesson that not all people who work with animals are necessarily fond of them.

Girl and I went to work. We'd already completed the mandatory obedience class at CCSPCA, but she needed to go the distance. There was a young man working at CCACC who owned a Belgian Malinois and did very sophisticated and advanced work with dogs. He was organizing a training class at the shelter. Girl and I were the first to sign up. I wasn't surprised to see some of the green volunteers with their own pets. Girl and I were there to learn everything we could learn.

When Ray died, this young man was one of the few who understood. Rather than judge, he offered his support and talked to me about ways to prevent this from ever happening again. He assured me that Girl was a good dog and a workable dog. If I was willing to put forth the effort, we could manage the problem. He encouraged me to look at the incident from a scientific point of view. I began to try and see things through Girl's eyes. When we'd go for a walk, I would observe her reaction to small animals on the trail. When we would encounter a feral cat, she would stiffen and her tail would become rigid and erect. She became as still as a statue cast of stone.

I learned that Girl will always have this prey drive. I enjoyed many training classes with Girl over the years starting with the very basic CCSPCA obedience class. In our new class, Girl and I developed a solid 'off' command. We practiced 'off' and 'leave it' commands frequently. I wanted her to have definition of these two commands with 'off' the more resolute. I would use 'leave it' should we be passing discarding garbage for instance. 'Off' was a serious command for intense situations. Perhaps I didn't pay close attention and Girl picked up the garbage in her mouth. With a proper 'off', Girl would drop the contents in her mouth immediately.

Girl loves food more than just about anything, but she turns her face to the wall when she hears a command. She is the best for recall at the house. When I yell her name, she always comes a running. Even so, I am conscious of the possibility of a feral cat or wildlife entering our property, so I work with Girl daily on her recall.

I miss Ray every day. I have a framed etching of him hanging in the cat room so that we can remember him. The artist caught his personality completely with his pointy, pouty little mouth. Scott brought home a stained glass piece he'd found hanging in a local antique store near the beach. The glass cats amazingly resembled Roy, Buddy, Candy and Alibaba. Alibaba was an old Siamese cat who'd belonged to an h.i.v. positive man since passed away. The non-profit group whose mission it is to help those patients and their pets took Alibaba to CCACC when his owner died. I happened to be at the pound that day and took Alibaba into the Animals First group I'd started. Alibaba was the first rescue of the group. It was almost as if the stained glass came to life when Alibaba came to live with us. In the center of the four cats is another yellow tabby with a white van dyke beard just like Ray.

Years later, we moved from the little cottage. I'd buried Ray in the front garden, but didn't want to leave him there. I began to dig and found him wrapped in plastic and a towel. I had him cremated. This way, I could have him with me always and carry his memory with me wherever I go.

I think of Ray and I think of Alibaba a.k.a. Bobby when I think of Animals First. I refer to this co-op of other little rescues for animal not lucky enough to be born pit bulls. One of these rescues is for senior cats and we even have our own e-group for them called Organicats. Not only do we try to re-home these elder statesmen, but have found healthy ways to help solve behavioral and health issues through diet, homeopathy and holistic supplements.

Many of the people who call me are trying to re-home their cat due to a behavioral issue. Often, I'll tell them about Ray's spraying long before we are lucky enough to know about pheromone sprays, Australian Bush Flower Essences and Chinese Traditional Medicine. Nowadays, there are so many products and supplements; one can cure his cat of any bad habit. The callers will try a couple of these easy suggestions, solve their problem and keep the cat. I can't bring back Ray, but he has helped many other cats keep from being sent to the pound.

Chapter Six
Room 132

Room At The Top
By Tom Petty

Junior's sister, Tori

The saddest part of rescue work is when the animals end up in Room 132, the end of the line. This is where euthanasia is performed It happens at CCACC every afternoon around 3:00 p.m., the same time hundreds of thousands of children are getting out of school. The techs performing euthanasia started out wanting to help animals and somehow ended up pulling duty in Room 132. As volunteers, we signed a document in orientation waiving our opinion regarding euthanasia and stating that we believed everything possible had been done to save the animal before destruction. Both groups had been swept into a tide beyond their control.

One night, I had walked all six pit bulls in Room 116, the pit bull room. I had tucked each one into a clean blankie and each dog had a toy. I began to sing a goodnight song to them. By the last note, each dog was singing along with me. I remember one dog in particular that night, Bob. Bob was a yodeling along like the best of Slim Whitman. Bob was all white, a gorgeous boy and a bit on the clown side. Who ever knew dogs could sing? And on cue? They finished all together like a glee club. I went home that night with my heart full. It was a good kind of feeling that I get only from animals. Sometimes, a bird or a dog or a cat will give me a certain look and something zings from their eyes straight to my heart. I know it's a love note from God to me. I feel blessed and I felt blessed that night. Even though all of those dogs were sitting at the city pound, we all shared something extraordinary that night. It was a moment I will never ever forget. In another time and place, it would have qualified for America's Funniest Home Videos. There is not anything funny, though, about dogs no one wants sitting in a shelter with nowhere to go.

I went back for my volunteer shift the next day. I had a skip in my step and couldn't wait to see the doggies in Room 116. I was ready for a repeat performance like a research monkey. I wanted to re-experience the happiness I'd shared with the dogs the night before. I hurried through the check-in ritual and ran over to Room 116. The six dogs in the kennels were dogs I'd never seen before. It was like a Twilight Zone segment where someone is running down familiar streets and no one recognizes him. I found out that every dog in Room 116 from the night before had been destroyed. It was absolutely devastating. They were not even euthanized at the regular 3:00 p.m. time. Someone had been ordered to put them to sleep that morning.

These were not bad dogs. I felt their loss on a deeply personal note. I remember Bob yowling and how loud and happy he'd been. I remember his big white head up in the air yelping out the notes as if he were trying to eat the air as he sang. There is something terribly wrong with a world that allows one of God's creatures to be killed for no reason. This is a very wealthy town with a very endowed shelter. This shelter was sitting right next door to another affluent organization and in the position to make a huge difference. They were turning their backs on these animals. It seemed like everyone was turning their backs on these dogs. Something had to be done. It was time to do something. It was time for me to do something. What was it Lily Tomlin said? "I always wondered why somebody doesn't do something about that. Then I realized I was somebody."

I had a dream about a rescue one night. I woke up with the name Round-Up Rescue. It was just right. First of all, it sounded Texas. People in California have a certain idea about Texas. They think we're a bunch of dumb cowpokes. I wanted the rescue to have a name that captured the feeling of a good old western movie, but in the sense of rounding up animals to save them rather than drive them to the slaughterhouse. I wanted to change the way things were being done.

I very realistically began to assess just what to rescue. The answer was right in front of me of course, the pit bulls. These were the bulk of the intake and the majority of who wound up in Room 132. The CCSPCA had reneged on their free spay and neuter for pit bulls promise once their fundraising drive was over and the big expensive high dollar hospital was up and running. I could sense trouble around the corner. Without a sound plan, we would soon be overrun with even more pit bulls.

First thing on my list was to make an appointment with Sergeant Bill Long, the director of Coastal County Animal Care and Control. Everybody called him 'Doc', but he was no medical doctor. Legend had it that he used to drive a cab back in the hippie days. On one rainy night, he pulled over to save a tiny starving wet kitten and began his animal career. Today, he was the head of one of the richest most powerful animal care and control organizations in the country. He was often sought after for his opinions on lowering euthanasia, low-kill shelters, animal population control, pit bull fighting and any other hot media topic relating to animals. Whenever an animal story was being covered, Sgt. Long could be seen on the 6 o'clock news planted in front of Coastal County Animal Care and Control. Who would have ever dreamed the kindly ex-cab driver who pulled over to save a little kitten would someday be responsible for the callous mass murder of thousands of defenseless animals in one of the wealthiest regions in the United States?

I had written up a plan to save the adoptable pit bulls and presented it to Sgt. Long in our meeting. My idea was to house up to six pit bulls whose time had expired at the shelter and were scheduled for euthanasia. These dogs would be outright adopted by my rescue and were dogs who'd managed to pass all of the criteria to be made available for adoption by the shelter. Round Up Rescue would adopt the dog about to be euthanized due to space. As it stood presently, the animals were put on the euthanasia list and then offered to the CCSPCA, basically a formality since the CCSPCA rarely if ever accepted any pit bull breeds from CCACC into their program. Since the CCSPCA relied most heavily on their caveat to only take in pit bull breeds with a history of being owned, those poor dogs and puppies picked up as strays currently fell through the cracks in the system. And the cracks were getting bigger.

My strategy was to train and further prepare these dogs for adoption into responsible and qualified homes, something like a fun and healthy boot camp for pit bulls. Their curriculum planned for lots of activity, both leashed and group and intensive crate training. Doc absolutely loved the idea! He had only one reservation. He did not like the idea of the dogs living outside the CCACC campus. He suggested we find a place to house the entire Round Up program on site. I could not believe my ears. This was absolutely fantastic, beyond my wildest dreams.

Doc suggested I go forward with the rescue and obtain my 501©(3) non-profit status. Once that was in order, he wanted to schedule another meeting. For now, he would begin readying a space for Round Up Rescue right inside CCACC. He went so far as to suggest I bunk with Robin Twine of Jaildogs, the custody dog program already in house and under CCACC's protective cover. Robin shared an office with Colleen. I had to suppress a little tiny smile at that idea. It would never work, but I kept that knowledge to myself.

Robin and Colleen were the decision makers regarding the green volunteers and most everything dog at CCACC. These two ran the volunteers even though that duty fell under Jane Everly, the volunteer coordinator's job description. Colleen and Robin's office became a gathering place for volunteers and staff to hang and discuss the dogs at the shelter among other topics. I did things a bit differently, so I wasn't usually invited to join the pack. It never mattered much to me. I would attend meetings from time to time and would bring Girl along. She would place her paw on my arm and look at me as if to say, 'hey, I'm your friend." I was very lucky indeed to be with my best friend, Girl. I was interested in finding a way to save some of these dogs and if attending these meetings would save lives, I was in. I knew Doc's suggestion of sharing an office with these two wouldn't work for long before some horns would lock. I knew enough to try and keep these thoughts to myself for the time being. Looking back today at Doc's idea, I can't help but laugh out loud.

I got to work immediately setting up the non-profit. There was a lot to do. I had become close with several of the green volunteers while dog walking and felt we shared the same sentiments about the dogs we were caring for. I asked three of them to become board members. I was pleasantly surprised when each agreed. We set about writing out mission statement and came up with a great commitment of purpose that remains the same today.

It reads: "Pit bull dogs are dying in Coastal County because there is no place for them to go and we cannot live with this any longer. Affectionate, adoptable pit bull dogs are being euthanized simply because there is not enough room at Coastal County Animal Care and Control to house them until they can find loving, responsible homes and there is no private animal shelter in Coastal County willing to take them. We are a group of concerned CCACC volunteers who have founded Round Up Rescue in order to take positive action in response to this tragic situation.

Our Mission Statement:

1. To save good-natured, affectionate pit bull dogs from euthanasia by sheltering, training and preparing them for a lifetime of loving pets.
2. To offer training programs for prospective adopters.
3. To create a foster family network for puppies and dogs waiting to enter the Round Up Rescue training program.
4. To educate the public through media as well as instructional and outreach programs.
5. To provide a model of a positive hands-on solution for other shelters and communities to follow."

Colleen was busy helping to found Big Top Pit Bulls, a group reflective of green volunteer ideology. Big Top was comprised of women who were the end all be all when it came down to pit bulls. Colleen never made any bones about her feelings regarding the pit bull breed and how to train and treat them. In Texas, this kind of attitude is called 'your way or the highway'. She expressed more than once or twice she didn't feel I was well suited to rescue this particular breed. Once, Colleen asked me why I had chosen to rescue pit bulls. Why had I not chosen another breed like German Shepherds This struck me as being odd. She knew Mookie was a GSD. Looking back, I realize Colleen didn't get me. It wasn't and isn't about the breed with me. It was about saving lives.

When I become too sure about something, a little too 'know it all', I cease to learn. I get cocky like the next guy when I feel a sense of achievement or get a surge of progress. Everyone loves to excel, to shine at something. That's been my common denominator with the pitties, our outright hamminess. When I start to hear myself go on, I try to listen to myself and reel myself back in a little. That is when I fall prey to error and begin to sound like just another green volunteer. With two strong pit bull groups currently being formed to rescue dogs, we should be able to save many lives. That would be the thought.

One day, Colleen mentioned a dog in Room 116, Portia. Portia had amazingly been adopted by a family who'd seen her photograph on the website. Portia was one of these big black and white American Staffordshire girls who'd been picked up running the streets. She really didn't have much going on in the looks department, but she had something special that had appealed to the family who came in to adopt and share their home with her. This was a nice affluent family from a neighborhood populated by family-type dogs, Golden Retrievers and the like. I was surprised more than anyone else about Portia's adoption. I was confused at first when Colleen began speaking of the adoption and referring to Por-tee-ah. Even though I had taken her photo, I couldn't place the dog Colleen was referring to. It finally dawned on me that she was talking about Portia.

The downside of starting a rescue at CCACC was attending so many meetings. First, there was the initial meeting with Doc. Then, I had a sit down with Deputy Jill Burns, Doc's assistant and the Deputy Director. She was insistent that I meet formally with Colleen as the Animal Care and Control Supervisor and resident pit bull laureate. I was working full time and had my own family of pets to care for, not to mention my volunteer duties and commitment to keep up with the website and photos. I had finally seen some progress in that work and was hesitant to relinquish the website duties until the system was surefire and steady. Finally, I was trying to assimilate all of the required paperwork to launch the rescue as a 501©(3) non-profit corporation licensed to operate in the state of California. It was certainly time consuming trying to manage all those plates without factoring in the meetings. I couldn't help but be a bit resentful at the cost of valuable taxpayer money used to pay people to hold so many redundant sit downs. Burns was infamous for her mandatory meetings, often likened to an intense grilling by a military tribunal.

I was new and I knew it, though. I was willing to learn. No one comes to the table an expert. We must all start somewhere. Colleen loaned me the Colby book on pit bulls and another book written by an illiterate North Carolina dog fighter who started every sentence with "me, myself, I always…" I am astounded by the grammar used by some of these pit bull folks, but once past the English snafus, the content has proved to be useful in assessing so many of the incoming requests for dogs in our program. I am referring more to the applicants rather than the dogs. I am also surprised at the inquiries I still get from people interested in using the dogs for foul play. If the letter or application I get is grammatically flawed, a red flag goes up. Call that a throwback to the education I received from Mr. North Carolina. It conjures up all kinds of scary thoughts for me, myself and I.

I do have a prejudice against dog fighters. I have extreme prejudice against them and against backyard breeders. The dog fighters don't need a preamble. It's just plain wrong. Don't give me that culture rap or 'they don't know any better' crap. Everyone knows right from wrong and hurting any animal is wrong. That is as clear a fact as there is in this world. How any human being can take a wonderful creature of God and torture them in blood sport for monetary gain and a creepy thrill is against God, is against nature and is against the law. I don't get it. A thinking and civilized human being does not engage in cruelty for entertainment. Anyone who participates in any form of animal cruelty is a backwoods inbred loser who deserves whatever he winds up with, whatever that might be. I believe there is a huge payback at the end of the line for these folks whether in this world or the next. There simply has to be.

As for the breeders, now is the time to hold a moratorium on breeding. There are enough for now. It's like responsible pollution, responsible arson or even responsible murder. I get so many calls from vet offices asked to euthanize a litter so the breeder can keep their line perfect. Let's think about giving these dogs a break for a couple of seasons, why don't we? I get so tired of hearing someone wanting to have just that one litter, because they want to see the puppies or some other nonsense. Sex isn't fun for animals the way it is for people. Anyone who's ever witnessed two cats mating will agree. Rowdy Cowgirl has never been mated. She has the most pristine underbelly and is the happiest dog. If an unaltered male looks sideways at her, she's like, 'hey, bud, don't you even get any ideas!'"

I finished Colleen's books. At times the dogfighting book made me sick to read, but I read it just the same, cover to cover. I even copied some of it for my own personal use. The

Colby book was a turn off as well. Especially when I found out the operation relocated to Texas and parlayed their corporation internationally, their nasty fingers in worldwide dog fighting.

I pity those who've never experienced the bond that comes from being kind to animals. I have met a lot of people during the years. I've met good people and bad people. Not all of the bad people are one-dimensional characters profiteering from the pain and discomfort of animals. One of the biggest jolts would come from the crowd I thought was dedicated to saving animals. It's hard to keep one's focus amidst the politics and personalities one encounters when involved in animal rescue. I have been able to maintain clarity due to one strident and difficult measure and this would cause me to break many friendships and relationships. When it gets down to the wire, my choice has always been the side of the animals. Every single situation I've ever encountered has led to this simple choice, to take care of the animals or to turn my back on them. Every decision I have made in regards to Round Up Rescue has held true to this one premise, that the animals must come first. That is a promise I hold very close. There has never been confusion or anguish when I consider my personal mission in making decisions. Looking back, I realize I might have made a different call based on information I've gathered along the way, but at the time, I made the choice I had to make. My reward has and always will be the incredible bond I've been blessed with.

As I waited for the paperwork to return from Sacramento, I became involved with Dante Peterson of the group, Friends of Coastal County Animal Care and Control. A sideline opera tenor, Dante had attended the same mandatory orientation class at the shelter when we both began our volunteer training. As fellow dog walkers, we'd become friends. In fact, Dante had recently set up the Friends as a non-profit corporation and helped me with the paperwork for Round Up. Figaro's, a popular sidewalk café in the Italian tourist section of town had generously offered us the use of their restaurant for a fundraiser. We met with Figaro's manager and made plans to hold the function in the spring. We'd discussed the importance of hiring a dog trainer at CCACC and decided to focus the efforts of our fundraiser for that purpose.

The minute my paperwork arrived to qualify Round Up as an official non-profit corporation, a horrible and tragic event occurred that would change the way dogs were treated from that moment on. On the afternoon of January 26, 2001, I was walking the Akitas when the radio program I had been listening to was interrupted. An excited voice announced that there had been a dog attack in San Francisco and a woman had been severely mauled. I expected to hear an address in the hood, but the attack had happened in a high-rise apartment building in the very upscale exclusive neighborhood of Pacific Heights. The person who'd been attacked was thought to be dead. This was incredible. The story began to unfold throughout the rest of the afternoon and that evening. It became a nationwide event.

A young teacher and girl's lacrosse coach, Diane Whipple, had been in the process of returning to her apartment when the guardian of two Presa-Canarios was leaving her own apartment with the two leashed dogs. What happened next has never been resolved due to conflicting testimony, but the dogs' guardian lost control of the dogs. The male dog, Bain, mauled Diane Whipple to death. When the police and animal control arrived, Bain was immediately put to death. Hera, the female, was taken into custody at the local pound where she would live out the next year and a half in a dark kennel while awaiting the outcome of the trial procedure.

What happened that afternoon changed everything for dogs, for dog guardians, for rescue organizations, for shelters, for renters, for landlords, for homeowners, for insurance companies and just about anyone else in the state of California who had anything to do with a dog over 35 pounds. Panic swept the entire country. Every news story had a bit on the tragic incident in Pacific Heights. Talk radio was filled up with programming dedicated to the Whipple incident. The attorney for Whipple's partner built himself a tv career around the incident. I still see him piping in on any late night panel show with a microphone and a camera. The mayor of San Francisco's future wife and future ex-wife, Stephanie Guilfoyle, jumpstarted her assistant DA job into a blossoming court tv career. She'd flubbed up a couple of dog fighting cases while assistant DA in which the dogs were given back to their dog fighting owner!

At shelters all over the state and country, pit bull adoptions came to a screeching halt. This was no different at CCACC. Room 116 became a virtual morgue. The pit bulls were being euthanized as quickly as they were temperament tested and killed whether or not they passed or failed. It was a terrible time. It was genocide. People had ceased to adopt pit bulls or any dog remotely resembling pit bulls. You couldn't blame them. Each night as the evening news covered the horrific story, a terrifying animated picture flashed across the screen of a menacing brindle dog with razor blade fangs and jaws bared. I have never in my experience seen a real flesh and blood dog that looked anything similar to that image.

The dogs in Room 116 would stand there looking at the closing door without knowing why they were being excluded from human contact and possible adoption. I was knocked for a loop as well. An innocent member of society had lost her life like a scene from a horror film and now, innocent dogs across the country and throughout the state were being put to death by the truckload in reaction to widespread panic. The dog that attacked Diane Whipple had been Presa-Canario, a dog breed from the Canary Islands specifically bred for dog fighting. Pit bull is a reference term for dogs of the bull breeds and not even an accredited breed of dog at all. Pit bull as a breed doesn't even exist.

Billy Best of Best Dog Training had begun a contract

with CCACC when Debbie of Debbie's Devil Dogs ended her association and left town. Billy taught classes professionally in the side yard next to the facility. The classes were being offered as a courtesy to shelter dogs if accompanied by a volunteer. I felt completely helpless as all of the dogs were being euthanized. Like I always do, I decided to get up off my ass and do something. This is my nature. As Joe Hill said, "Don't cry, organize!" Well, I could still walk a dog. I could do that one small thing.

I decided to take Billy Best up on his free training offer. I made sure it was ok with Billy before showing up with a pit bull. I didn't know him very well and didn't know how he felt about pit bull breeds. Many dog professionals harbor prejudice against pit bull type dogs. One huge expensive dog boarding and day care 'ranch' here in Austin, Texas actually bans pit bulls! That tells somebody like me that somebody doesn't know what they're doing when they have to breed specify. Billy quickly laughed off my doubts. The wealth of his experience has been with shelter dogs of all breeds. This class began a long relationship between Round Up Rescue and Billy Best. I have never seen him turn away any dog and I have seen him help multitudes of dogs find homes and become exemplary canine good citizens.

Billy Best had worked for years with CCSCPA dog program. He'd been instrumental in trying to develop a kinder, gentler persona for pit bulls so they might be considered more adoptable. You might call him a kind of pit bull publicist. One of the programs deigned to lessen demonizing of the breed renamed the dogs St. Francis Terriers. The program was short-lived, but looked fondly upon by dog lovers. The St. Francis Terrier program might not have worked in the long run, but it was a brave and valiant effort that tried to effect change and find a solution in what still appears to be a losing battle.

Billy knew more about dogs than anybody I'd ever met. From that first day when I asked him if I could bring a pit bull to his class, I have been grateful to know Billy Best and his beautiful Belgian Malinois assistant, Tess. Tess was a brilliant dog trainer in her own right. She really knew how to push a dog's buttons. I immediately liked Billy and his approach. The day he welcomed me and my pit bull into his class kick started a friendship that has weathered the storm and saved many dogs.

I am ashamed to admit that I wasn't familiar with the pit bulls in Room 116 at this time. So many dogs had been euthanized in reaction to media panic surrounding the Whipple mauling. It was difficult enough to keep up with incoming dogs normally, but during these troubled times, it was almost too hard to take. I cannot describe how it feels to walk a dog you know is going to die. It's just very hard. On the Saturday class began, I got myself a leash and a collar, took a deep breath and went into Room 116. I mumbled the Lord's Prayer. On this day, the good Lord got one over on me and his name was Junior.

Chapter Seven
Junior

I Think About You
by Eliza Gilkyson

Junior

There, in the second kennel on the side next to Assistant
Deputy Director Jill Burn's office was a leggy, skinny, red-nose
male. He was nine months old according to his kennel card.
He was not all that much to look at. I didn't even read his card
to see what the volunteers had written about him. He looked
scared, but also eager to have a friend in this place. He was
covered in what looked like tar, as if he'd been tarred, feathered
and rode out of town like they used to do back in the old days.
He didn't even have a name. We went outside and joined the
class. I did not know much about dog training, but I did have a
sack of treats. I had heard a little about positive reinforcement.
I had tried it on Rebel at home, but he wasn't food motivated. I
bet Rebel could go for a week without eating. He is picky about
food and I suspect it's that Chow Chow in him.

The approved CCACC treat of the day was wieners
and cheese. I brought Hebrew National beef wieners and the
dogs really seemed to like them. I found Junior to be a willing
candidate. He was intelligent and had a high level of will to
please. The Hebrew Nationals were a hit with him, too. His
combination of eagerness to please and desire for a reward
made Junior a great dog to work with, even for a novice like
myself.

I have found that good training is based on patience and
timing. The timing part is always a work in progress for me, but
the dogs seem to get it despite my klutziness. The animals have
taught me patience I never dreamed I was capable of having.
They say that petting a dog or cat lowers one's blood pressure. I
didn't have to be sold on that concept. I feel it whenever I slow
down and spend a minute with any animal, anywhere and any
time.

We were placed next to a man with a big Russian
Wolfhound named Poppy. He was from the school of no treats.
I could see Poppy's nose twitch at the scent of our weenies and
cheese. I felt kind of mean, but I was sure Poppy had plenty
to eat at her forever home while Junior sat in his kennel at the

93

pound. I got over any pangs of guilt pretty quickly. The other trainer at CCACC used to ask us if we'd continue to go to work if the boss man never gave us a paycheck. "Why, hell no!" It's really a simple practice. I just gave Junior a treat and he'd sit there and be quiet. He caught onto the positive reinforcement very quickly. He'd sit there like a perfect little gentleman and I'd pop a weenie into his mouth like a Pez dispenser in reverse. Poppy's dad was having a harder time keeping her attention with military commands and he turned abruptly to me. "You are just feeding that dog!" He gave me a dirty look.

A little bit of knowledge is a dangerous thing. In my best Judy from 'Leave it to Beaver' voice, I said, "It's called positive reinforcement." Junior and I looked at each other and shared a secret grin. I gave him another treat. We had found our relationship, Junior and I. We have shared many smug moments since. He has a way of looking at you as if he's thinking the same thing you are thinking. Aren't these folks silly? Aren't I just adorable? Junior was a ham.

The next part of class was a bit of a coincidence. Billy introduced the idea of positive reinforcement. He explained to us the concept of rewarding desired behavior. If you want your dog to sit and be quiet, give him a treat when you see him sitting there quietly. If you don't have a cookie on you, most dogs will get the idea with a pat on the head and a 'good boy' or 'good sit'. Junior and I celebrated with another slice of weenie. When our class was nearly done, we'd learned a sit, a fair to middling down and the Billy Best 'off".

The Best 'off' is about the only explanation I can find when trying to understand why the CCACC and CCSPCA have such an unfounded and unrealistic take on Billy. My guess is they comprehend his style as negative training. If the powers that be were ever to attend Billy's class for themselves and witness his method firsthand, I believe there would be a few less dead dogs in Coastal County. CCACC and the CCSPCA consider a leash snap negative training and have bad-mouthed

Billy for negative training. A 'no' is considered negative reinforcement, so just about everyone in the business is guilty of negative training at some level. I have worked with Billy for a good number of years and ask all of the adopters in Coastal County to complete his basic obedience class before finalizing the adoption. I have never seen him harm any animal in any way. Billy has incredible dog instincts and reads dog language implicitly. I've seen him fix many dogs and we have worked together to keep a good many out of Room 132.

On the other hand, I've seen dogs adopted from these two institutions on choke chains and other questionable training gear and feel they might have fared better by attending a Best obedience class. Round Up Rescue's paperwork specifically prohibits the use of choke chains. Used the wrong way, a choke chain can cause severe damage to the animal. Personally, I've never learned the proper way to use a choke chain and don't plan on learning anytime soon. You can get a dog to do almost anything you want with a little patience and a cookie or whatever strums that dog's chord. It might be a trip outside or a cuddle with some of them, the ball with others or a warm look. It depends on the dog and it depends on the person. The ball is in your court.

To teach the Best 'off', Billy assesses the dog to meter his level of shyness or willfulness. For instance, Girl is a very shy dog who'd not been previously handled very much. Junior, on the other hand, was very willful and was all about being the center of attention. It's all about Junior. With a shy girl like Girl, Billy would take her leash and have me hold the treat at her nose. With Girl, I would barely whisper, "off", and give her a moment to respond. Here's where the timing is so very important. If the shy dog goes for the treat, all that's needed is a stern whispered "off". With Girl, that was all she ever needed. Girl loves food, any kind of food, so for her to refuse to take the offering into her mouth is a proper 'off'. To this day, Girl's 'off' is as strong as the day she learned it. I can throw a handful of treats on the floor and say 'off'. Girl will look and very systematically, turn her head away, never once going for the cookies.

Billy is a brilliant dog trainer, but the 'off' is his pièce de résistance! I am always amazed to see this big strong guy speak more softly than a butterfly to the sensitive dog. He loves dogs and knows just what will work with each one. I've never seen him get it wrong, either. The idea is to have your treats in your right hand and the leash in your left. While holding the treat with your right thumb and forefinger level with your shoulder, you say the words "take it." Move the treat from shoulder level to a few inches from the dog's mouth. You are giving doggy plenty of time to decide and allowing him to make a decision. He takes it, of course, and you then say, "good boy." Let him know he did something right, something great and something absolutely astounding. Bingo!

Then, again, repeat this step with 'take-it'. After puppy takes it and is again praised, it's time to separate the men from the boys. This is where Billy comes in. It's always best to have Billy issue the first 'off' since he will know whether a voice command or a leash snap is in order. Holding the treat level with the shoulder, say the word 'off'. Give the dog plenty of time to notice the change of commands. When lowering the treat, notice if your dog lunges toward it and repeat the word 'off' if needed. If he's a willful boy like Junior, you will quickly flick your wrist holding the leash. Your move is only swift enough to surprise him and you'll repeat the word 'off'. This snap does not hurt the dog, but again, is only to surprise him. Honest. I put a collar around my own neck and told myself to stay out of the candy. When I disobeyed, I snapped my own leash. The surprise is in the timing and insures that the command will work. You have a dog intent on pleasing you at this point. You have spent the entire class working toward a goal as a team. It is in your nature and the dog's nature to continue this upward slope toward success. Based on this concept, most of Round Up's adopters and their rescued dogs have begun long and wonderful lives together in a Best Way obedience class.

A good solid one time Billy Best 'off' will keep your dog from running out into the street and getting hit by a car, from licking up that deadly anti-freeze or chasing the neighbor's cat who might have jumped into the wrong yard. In a first class, often the participants are a little shy with the command. Billy will ask if they would hesitate if the dog were about to ingest poison. That always breaks the ice for even the shyest mom or dad and another dog learns the Best 'off'. With a little practice, each dog will turn their head away at the 'off' command and some, like Girl, offer a down in the bargain.

When you and your dog are learning something, to obey a command or to not pull on the leash, a special, silent bond is created between you and your best friend. You share a communication that needs no words. I believe with all my heart this is love. No one can tell me that dogs don't have that gene. Dogs like Junior, the hammy, pushy ones, want you to notice and reward them whenever they complete a task or do anything for that matter. Junior has a 'Different Strokes' look when he rolls his eyes like "what you talking 'bout, Willis?" The pay off for us straight men comes when we bridge the dog from food treats to the reward of ball, tug or Frisbee.

The more I worked with Junior, the more he reminded me of somebody. I just couldn't put my finger on it. It really bothered me. I'd comb my brain, but couldn't for the life of me recall who Junior reminded me of. His canine teeth hung down below his upper lip, which made him look rather like a crocodile. He was very thin and wiry. We suspected Viszla in the mix. One day, we were practicing our leash work, it came to me. Scred! He was a dead ringer for Scred, one of the old Saturday Night Live dirty muppets. I tried to look Scred up online and after much surfing, could only come up with one photograph. It was taken during the first season of Saturday

Night Live. I remembered when the second season started up and the regular cast members were talking about what they did during the hiatus. Scred and the dirty muppets were upstairs in a dusty file cabinet. The good muppets had their own tv show and had spent the summer making a major motion picture. Junior and Scred had a lot in common.

Scred was the troublemaker, the shit-stirrer of the group. I actually should have named Junior Scred instead of naming him Junior. It would have been the perfect name. From then on, every time he'd look up at me with those too long canines, I'd remember Scred and have to stop what I was doing to laugh. Even when he'd do something naughty, I'd catch myself laughing. He was a dead ringer for the naughtiest muppet. Junior had not only resurrected Scred. He'd permanently seared himself a place in my heart.

Junior and I set out looking to find him a good home. He had been captured as a stray along with his sister. He took care of her and got her safely to the shelter. She was put to sleep the minute her stray period was up. Junior passed his assessment tests and was placed up for adoption. He was a very smart boy, indeed. His kennel card read that he had been emaciated at intake. Someone had also noted to use a chain link leash as he chewed through cloth leashes. The vet tech, Carol, had cleaned Junior up and shaved off the tar spots.

I got permission to take Junior for outings to improve his chances of being adopted. I had to beg, but was willing to beg for Junior's sake. There is a lot of control in the shelter world. There is always a new rule being put into place and enforced. The bottom line was to walk out with the dog, a mantra I continue to use to this day. Each time I met with Colleen, she would ask the same questions over and over. She would always ask what my rescue's mission was. I couldn't figure out if she was forgetful or simply not paying attention. Each time she asked, though, I'd try again to explain that we wanted to find good homes for the adoptable pit bulls presently being euthanized for space.

Once, she asked my why I picked Junior. I didn't have a good answer. How do you explain what makes your heart beat? I just told her the truth. I told her I'd signed up for Billy Best's complimentary class and literally grabbed Junior from a kennel without forethought or afterthought. It was truly by chance that I had come to know and love Junior. He was smart and so responsive. He'd won my heart. I was committed to finding him a good home. I learned a lesson in the process that would benefit me later on in rescue. If a person would commit to taking one class with the dog they were thinking of adopting, they almost always ended up going home with the dog. You just don't want to give up on a dog you've taught to sit. Colleen went ahead and cleared me to take Junior on outings.

Our first date was on the Channel Two morning news program. Mornings on Two in Oakland is still my favorite show. Channel Two was one of the few news programs not breed specific and had a superb morning line-up. Ross McGowan anchored with his movie star good looks. On his side sat Tori Campbell and Frank Somerville. They were funny and genuine and always entertaining. Mark Pitta was the sports guy rounded off with Sal Castenada for weather and commentary. I'd channel surf from time to time to see what was going on nationally, but this local show always lured me back. They really held their own up against any of the big time morning shows. They had such a great mix of small town news combined with good-natured ribbing. I was surprised to hear them cover a major story and go for the jugular, asking questions the Katie Courics and Dianne Sawyers steered safely away from.

Frank was a vegetarian from age 12 and wouldn't hesitate to add his opinion after a distasteful story. Once, when they had footage of the Pamplona Running of the Bulls, Frank commented how terrible a sport it was. Those of us who love animals appreciate the bravery it takes to speak up for what you believe in. When I hear the usual awful stories about dogs reported on the news, I remember Frank. The dogs have a good friend at Channel 2.

Junior and I drove over early in the morning to appear on the program. While we waited to go on, the entire staff came by to meet Junior and admire him. One guy even donated $20 on Junior's behalf. I met a salty old veteran cameraman who freelances around the area. I would see him from time to time at other animal events. We got our cue to go on and boy, did Junior take his cue to heart. You would have thought he was going for an Oscar! When the lights went up, so was Junior! It was as if he'd been waiting for his big break all these years. He was a natural. He did every trick he'd learned from Billy and really wowed the news team and the crew. Frank even got up from his seat and said he was usually afraid of pit bulls, but "I'd like to pet him!"

When a pit bull has been trained and worked with a little bit, that dog can perform and show off with the best of them. The pit bull breeds are the showiest, hammiest scenery chewers in the dog world. Not to slight any of the other breeds, but I've seen pit bull after pit bull crave public attention. They are born to entertain. It's a shame they've been so misused. That says more about us as a society than their behavior as a breed. I have to say, I do not believe all of that ferocity should be attributed to bred-in behavior. From what I've seen, I suspect they are wired to respond to the cheers and noise of the crowd. They are so anxious to please, therefore so easy to train, that it's sheer joy to watch these dogs ape for the crowd.

After class one Saturday, Junior and I went on a one dog mobile adoption. Even though no one was adopting pit bulls, we didn't let that stop us. Junior and I would park our little table and chair outside a friendly pet store and have a mini-dog adoption. The people who work at one of our favorite pet stores, Nate and Julie, love dogs and pit bulls especially. In fact, they love them almost as much as Nate loves Tool and Julie loves Mary J. Blige. Both Nate and Julie adored Junior.

To this day, there is an 8 x 10 glossy of Junior under the glass countertop. That started a trend and soon the counter was filled with Round Up dogs. Junior's gets the most attention, though. He's reared up on his front paws and nose to nose with the camera lens. He has a look on his face like he's sucking on the world's most sour lemon. This was a familiar look for Junior when perplexed. I used to ask him, "Why the long face?"

I tried everything to get him adopted. He had learned so much from Billy. He would sit and heel for everyone who passed by our little stand on the sidewalk. When he'd see a stranger, he'd go out into the sidewalk and sit for them. He was such an attention getter. Once he had their attention, he'd perform. He would sit so erect with the best posture. It always got a laugh. He had the best posture I've ever seen in man or dog!

A professional photographer was doing some work at he shelter and had asked the volunteer coordinator, Jane Everly, if he could photograph some of the dogs. She volunteered her own dog, a pug, and asked some of us for ideas. I immediately suggested Junior. He'd already made his debut at Channel 2 and I knew he'd be perfect. The day came for the big shoot. It was the real deal with umbrellas, lights, tripod and the works. When Junior's turn came, he showed them his stuff. He was so terrific on camera. The little bit of training we'd done helped the photographer and his assistant get the most wonderful shots. Not only did Junior make the next edition of the shelter newsletter, but his photograph wound up in all of the water bills as an insert and in the voter's registration mailing as well. He became so popular that his photograph was even used as a baseball card for the San Francisco Giants.

We attended a local street festival. We were having a wonderful time introducing Junior around and soaking in the festivities. A local dog walking company had a booth at the festival each year and had asked us to attend. Junior met a lot of people and made lots of new friends. One lady was talking to me about dogs and had a small child by the hand. I was going on about who knows what and felt Junior pulling behind me on the leash. I learned a great lesson that day. The next thing I knew, Junior barked and snapped at the boy. While I wasn't paying attention, the little boy had been in Junior's space and the inevitable happened.

The mom was very understanding, but I knew what the seriousness of this situation. It was entirely my fault. Through my inattention, I had done a huge disservice to the pit bulls and I had jeopardized Junior's life. Now, I would have to report the incident to CCACC and Colleen. Dogs were destroyed daily at the shelter for less. In light of the recent Diane Whipple mauling, I knew Junior would be put to sleep. For a pit bull to snap at a human, at a child, was simply unacceptable.

I did the right thing. I took Junior back to CCACC and put him in his kennel, then called Colleen at home. I reported to her what had happened at the fair. I was sad. I knew they were going to euthanize him. Colleen had him pulled from the adoptables and placed back in strays while he awaited a new temperament test. Scott gave me a good chewing out after I told him what had happened with Junior. He surprised me by coming through for both Junior and me.

We made an appointment to speak with Colleen about Junior and what we could do to save his life. Scott and I never planned to have children. We felt the world was populated enough with kids and animals running around all over the place. Our thought was to try and do something to help the ones already here rather than add more to the mix. We approached the Junior situation as if we were adopting a child. We had a long talk with Colleen and after considerable debate, came to an agreement that we would foster Junior. This would be a special foster situation as the first Round Up dog. Junior would live with us on a day-to-day trial basis and would attend training on the weekends. No more festivals. Again, I begged. Again, I walked out with the dog.

We worked closely with Billy. Billy felt that Junior was not a dangerous dog, but just a bit willful. In fact, he felt Junior would excel at obedience work. After the initial basic classes, we signed Junior up for intermediate classes. By this time, Scott had taken over Junior's training. My prophecy had come true about people who attend training with their dogs. I was as surprised as Scott was that he and Junior would be the first living example. Junior became Scott's dog. They became inseparable as Scott and Fu Manchu had been. Scott had Junior heeling in no time. Junior became quite the show dog and shining example of what kind of work one can do with a dog like Junior. Junior loved training. He just radiated.

By default, Junior had become the first official Round Up Rescue dog. I was off to a good start with the rescue, but realized I couldn't adopt all of the dogs myself. During one of my meetings with Doc, he made the comment that I was going to wind up with a yard full of pit bulls. I admit, the thought made me a bit nervous. What in the world had I been thinking? What was I doing rescuing pit bulls of all things? I couldn't think of a more outlandish goal. Many nights, I went to bed and would lie awake with a million scenarios running through my head. Fear of the unknown just about did me in. Did I know enough to be taking these dogs out of the shelter and turning them over to members of the public?

The shelter clothes their fear of liability with seemingly caring terminology. The same sound bites become rhetoric each time CCACC was sought for public comment. Some of what wound up on the news was downright preposterous. Once, when commenting on a particularly gruesome incident, Doc was quoted saying a pit bull puppy who witnessed dog fighting would grow up to become a fighting dog. Nathan Winograd speaks about shelter directors being treated as experts in his book, Redemption. Considering some of the shelter directors I've met, this is a terrifying thought.

Mornings, I would get into my car and go on autopilot

with doubts crowding my brain. What kept me going was my busy schedule. When I walked a dog, it helped me set aside my fears and to remain centered. With the whole world seemingly berserk about the Whipple incident, I found that walking a dog helped me stay focused and calm. Only when I stopped to think about what was going on around me would the doubt and fear set in. How about surgeons and airline pilots? Do they allow doubt and fear to cloud their thinking? I remembered when I was a deejay at a college radio station. My stomach would turn over at the thought of screwing up on the air. It was 3 a.m. and probably no one was even listening. I gained a little bit of confidence the more I practiced. Once I became more comfortable at running the equipment, I began to have fun with the music.

The same ethic applied to me and to the pit bulls. When I was walking a dog, I felt good. They felt good. We shared something no one could take away from us. Everything was in its place and I was at peace with the universe. I didn't know it at the time, but I had been granted a very special gift. I was ever so slowly being granted the gift of faith. I continue to receive that gift today. Whenever I am feeling unsure or frightened about something, I grab a leash and walk my dog.

Like many others drawn to animals, I was abused as a child. I was very afraid and that fear manifested into anger much of the time. I am fortunate that my own anger has had a positive result. Today, I think of it as being violently passionate. I have been able, through my own experience, to connect with these dogs on a certain level.

Not all of the dogs in my life have come from abusive backgrounds. Some were just not handled much or were separated from their littermates at too young an age. Whatever their background, all of them wound up unwanted and forgotten at the city dog pound. No matter how sophisticated the shelter system, it is a frightening place for an animal. I get that and that's the reason this vocation has chosen me, like it or not.

I was about to learn the best of life's lessons and I was about to learn them from pit bulls. I started to trust my gut. I could be around a dog and just know in my knower that fellow was not out to get anybody. Billy once told me something I've never forgotten. He said, "The family pet doesn't just wake up one day and say, 'hey, I think I'll just kill my family today.'" It is not in their nature. Every time a take a class with Billy, I learn something new. Sometimes I learn about dogs and training and sometimes, I learn something about myself. As I attended more classes and walked more dogs, I began to question some of the opinions of those making decisions for these animals.

I love to encourage new adopters to attend Billy Best's obedience classes. I also ask that the new adopter practice leash walking for the duration of the foster period. Round Up has a strong foster to adopt program. I've learned that the dog, just like his people, needs to learn certain manners. Most of these dogs come from someone's backyard and were found running the streets by a neighbor who called animal care and control. These are other dogs just like Junior and Girl. They are dogs like Mookie and Rebel and Fu Manchu.

It was pointed out to me that my household was made up of three of the top biters according to Humane Society statistics. I certainly didn't set out to adopt biting dogs. I just happened to run into a Chow Chow, another Chow Chow and a German Shepherd before the pit bulls found me. I don't know the reason I wound up choosing the biters, but I don't believe it was accidental. I began to question these bite statistics. Who was keeping score? The same sources who decided breed and age on intake at the shelters were the same people who took down information regarding dog bites. I remembered the saga we experienced with Mookie and the post office and the inaccuracy of their information.

As in training or assessing, it's important to look at individuality rather than blanket statistics. It's good to gather information, but necessary to consider all of the facts. With these dog bite statistics, it's imperative to consider all of the data surrounding each incident. What was the dog's description? What expertise was being used to ascertain the dog's breed? What were the circumstances? Was the skin broken? Was the bit random or reactive? There are a lot of dogs being put down for bite related incidents. No one wants his dog to bite. There has to be a solution. Without properly investigated statistics, we are barking up the wrong tree.

The dogs I was seeing in the shelter were dogs under two years of age, usually unaltered and no training, if any. These dogs made up the major portion of killed dogs each day. By wit and chance, a very limited few would up on the available side. Commonly, these dogs got a walk outside once every two or three days. The rest of the time they spent running up and down their kennels, many going 'kennel crazy'. This wouldn't have been my first choice for a pet had I been one of the potential adopting families. It is not hard to imagine the worst news stories coming true when seeing a dog in this state.

Of the few people adopting at that time, most wanted a puppy from the puppy room. Most of these puppies weren't included with the others being featured on the CCACC website. Even to this day, puppies 6 weeks and under are automatically euthanized, no questions asked. These are otherwise healthy fat babes with sweet milk breath, the same age as countless puppies advertised and sold daily by backyard breeders.

A Canadian girl, Karla, was in charge of all puppies at CCACC. She was a green volunteer who'd landed herself in this position of power over puppies. Anyone familiar with Zimbardo's Stanford Prison Tests from the 70's is aware of what happens in cases of controlled dominance. Strange and unpleasant events unfold. People don't always set out to do bad things, but like the saying goes, 'power corrupts. Absolute power corrupts absolutely'. Over the years, Karla was allowed to make more and more rules concerning the puppy room and it's inmates. She was a self-appointed expert on puppy and dog behavior. I did learn some things from her, but nothing I could use with dogs. I would, however, get a first hand lesson about what can happen when someone is giving complete control and the abuse of that power.

Many puppies were being euthanized because they displayed common puppy qualities in relation to teething and headstrong play behavior. I saw many puppies destroyed because they lacked manners usually acquired from littermates and mom. By arranging a few playgroups in the puppy room, the volunteers could have learned a lot from the puppies. The puppies could have gained socialization both from humans and other puppies. Public interest could have been ignited with such a program in place. Who doesn't want to play with puppies? Everybody loves a puppy.

When able to simulate pack behavior with other puppies, puppies are allowed to teach one another dog language. Many of the behavior problems stem from the length of time spent interacting with littermates. I have seen so many puppies put down because the mother and or the father was aggressive. The argument was that the puppy would become aggressive. The jury is still out regarding genetics, but my money is on socializing these pups as often and as early as possible. If someone's parent exhibits low morals, does that mean the offspring will follow suit? How ludicrous when we apply the same criteria to humans as we do to animals.

I would later pull a pack of seven puppies from CCACC after two of their littermates and the parents had been destroyed for aggression. Word spread that Round Up was pulling the litter and the Craigslist pet forum was rife with the news. Many of the postings came from members of another pit bull group who've since been labeled as the pit bull Nazis. Suddenly, Round Up and me were seen as malevolent as the euthanized dogs and their keepers. How could these fat little fuzzballs be the spawn of such controversy and animosity? I just didn't get it. These seven dogs saw as much time together as I was able to arrange. They were each adopted out to loving and responsible homes.

All seven puppies graduated from Billy Best's puppy class. Today, all seven dogs are in the same homes except one girl who was re-homed when her family fell on hard times. Not one of these dogs ever showed the slightest sign of aggression and they are all eight years old today. As far as genetics are concerned, there is something to the argument. Five of the seven tore their hind leg cruciate, so there you go. The genetics did show up after all, but in their knees, not their behavior.

This one particular rescue has a long history of going after other rescues on public forums. This time, it was Round Up's turn, but over the years, they have continued to slam other groups who are trying to help pit bulls. One of the many hurtful comments posted by one of their members was that Round Up gives "sketchy dogs to sketchy people." This kind of public scathing hurts the dogs we are all trying to help. For a group who contends their main focus is education, it begs the question what is being learned from spiteful slurs? We are in the midst of an epidemic. It is a time we must work together to cultivate a better understanding of these breeds. Let's put our personal passions aside if those passions harm the objective.

Chapter Eight
Buster and Sue

It's Good To Be King
By Tom Petty

Topper and Vinnie

I received an invitation in the mail to attend a Puppyworks seminar at the Marin Humane Society outside Novato, California. The cost was upwards of $300 for the three-day event. On the roster were such dog luminaries as Terry Ryan and Leslie Nelson who'd been around for years and were well respected in dog circles. Trish King of Marin Humane was teaching a few classes as well, but the star attraction was to be Sue Sternberg of Roundout Kennels in upstate New York.

I had heard of Sue Sternberg. She is very controversial, especially with pit bull people and those of us who rescue them. She is responsible for the plastic hand widely used to test dogs for food aggression. If a shelter is using the plastic hand, they probably subscribe other Sternberg methods. It would be at this very seminar I'd learn other industry terms like 'whale eye'.

I once saw a beautiful dog running around Lake Madrid. He was probably part Rhodesian Ridgeback and had rich ruddy coloring with the telltale wedge head of a pit bull. Harold was a gorgeous dog. He gently allowed me to pick him up and lift him into the back of my truck. I knew he wasn't going to hurt me. He was just a big gentle boy. I took him to CCACC hoping we could help him find a good home.

Julie Chen, the same volunteer who'd almost fostered Girl, decided Harold had 'whale eye'. Because she had green volunteer status and bred sighthounds, she was considered quite the authority. He was supposed to have growled when an air conditioner repairman walked down the aisle by Harold's kennel. I'm not saying he did not growl, but the level of noise and clanging in that facility is near deafening. A dog's reaction should not be criteria for euthanasia. However, based on this and the words 'whale eye' written across his kennel card, Harold was put to sleep. Julie suggested with a smile, since I was close to Harold, perhaps I should sit in on the euthanasia. My jaw dropped open. I had no response. She intimated that she sat in on many of the euthanasias performed at CCACC.

Doc never misses an opportunity to refer to CCACC as being 'the best shelter in the world' whenever he's being interviewed. In a shelter reputed as being one of the best in the country, I could not believe they didn't have a better system in place regarding temperament testing. For such a formidable facility and the hub of some of the best dog minds in the area, I felt Harold should have had more thorough consideration. I felt the system let Harold down. I had let Harold down. I had picked him up that day with the thought that I was helping him by taking him to a place of refuge. Instead, I had driven him to an early death.

The Sue Sternberg flier was circulated widely. I was excited about attending the event. It would be like a vacation in October with lovely weather and the lush Marin Headlands providing the backdrop. I made plans to attend with Dante Peterson. We could discuss our non-profit work and bounce fundraising ideas off each other on the drives to and from the event.

I had received an email form the young woman who'd organized the affair. She was enthusiastic about Round Up's work with pit bulls and wanted to inquire about using some of the dogs in our program to be evaluated by Sue Sternberg. I forwarded the information to Colleen who refused, hands down. Usually when Colleen was this adamant, a control issue was involved. This time, though, she had a very good reason. Colleen was not a fan of Sue Sternberg's invasive assessment technique. This was the first negative reaction toward Sternberg I'd experienced. I had gotten caught up in all of the preliminary excitement and pushed aside my own instincts. I was learning another lesson about listening to my gut feelings.

The event was successful in number. There were several hundred attendees, many of whom had brought their own dogs. I was struck by the atmosphere in the larger room where we'd gathered for the first of the Sue Sternberg lectures. Another attendee commented she felt like a supermodel when she first walked into the room. There were very few men in attendance, but a strange sense of testosterone permeated the air. In other words, it was tense. The dogs were on short leads and it felt weird to me, like a Leni Riefenstahl film. My initial excitement began to dissolve.

Sternberg is internationally famous for having written several books on dog temperament and evaluation. Her teachings are so commonplace, that her name has become synonymous with temperament assessment in shelters across the United States and beyond. She exhibited her method for us over and over during the seminar. She will push the animal until she is fully satisfied the dog will not go off under any possible circumstance. The dog might have been pulled from a kennel, scared and confused in this strange noise environment. Sternberg's own former employees have referred to her technique as invasive, as if someone were poking you again and again while you were trying to eat or rest. Most people will turn and say, "hey, quit, you!" A dog will bark or growl in response and be labeled as dangerous.

Sternberg looked something like a gym teacher to me. She was sporty and athletic with short brown hair and a wide mouth she used to make funny faces and accentuate her points. She opened with a comedy routine about Starbucks and her chai tea fix. She was entertaining for a kennel person, however, I had the feeling I was at one of those mandatory comedy traffic school classes.

During the first session, she warmed us up with tales about her kennel and her cattle dogs. She told us they did what they wanted and everything in her house was chewed up. I could relate to the chewing. When Rowdy Cowgirl first moved in with us, she chewed up a Johnny Cash record and a Moby tape.

Sternberg started off with a speech about her style of evaluating. I perked up, interested in making new strides toward problem solving. According to her handout, Sue was

113

looking for a dog "who enjoys lots of stimulation" combined with a "high sociability index." She relied on a caveat that explained "love and training do not change heredity and basic temperament. Abuse and neglect are neither an excuse nor a cause for aggression."

She relied much on video to promote her program. To illustrate fence-fighting, she showed us a dog-eared old video starring an old shepherd called Buster. She used a tug on a long lead to get Buster wound up and excited. She made sure to note his showing of teeth and his tail up in the air. Old Buster was a good subject. He had some resource guarding issues with a toy Sternberg kept grabbing at and he wouldn't release. One thing for sure, Buster was way out of his league. I wondered why she didn't attempt to train some of those bad habits out of him. That alone would have been worth the price of my ticket. Was the answer to kill the dogs without looking for a way to correct these problems? Maybe Buster had never had a toy before and didn't know how to play games. Badass or not, Buster has made Sternberg a buttload of change performing over and over again in that glitch-filled old video tape.

The next part of the session was dedicated to evaluation. Up first was a young pit bull from a nearby shelter. This would have been a Coastal County dog had not Colleen wisely vetoed the idea of bringing CCACC shelter dogs to the seminar. When I had an opportunity to meet the director of the young pit bull's shelter later on that afternoon, I found her to be a lot like myself. She was newly introduced to the pit bull breeds and wanted to find some solutions to growing problems such as over-population and finding suitable adopters. She had brought a few of her shelter's dogs to the event in hopes that a world-renowned behaviorist like Sue Sternberg might help.

Sternberg gave the crowd their money's worth as she gave the young piebald pit bull the Sternberg once over. She sized the dog up before assessing him as a trial lawyer would go over a witness. She did stress to neuter young. Whenever

Sternberg referred to a female dog, she used standard AKC terminology. We must have heard the bitch word about a thousand times before lunch. In modern society, that term is politically incorrect. In fact, it's downright offensive and disgusting. I get the same feeling when I hear a racial slur. I sensed there was more behind Sternberg's vehement use of the term than kennel standard. The term reflects as much on the person using the word as it does the society allowing the use. Female dog is much more preferable and respectable.

Sternberg would predict how certain dogs would behave later in life had they not been euthanized. For instance, if the dog didn't pass her extreme temperament test with all of the prods and invasive manipulation, she was certain the dog would attack, perhaps maul and even kill. Why hasn't someone then written the definitive book on all dogs and their behavior and be done with it? We could all just read that book and fix all the dogs. There would be no more dog bites, no more maulings, no fearful dog aggression, separation anxiety and on and on.

The little pit bull puppy was playful and seemed like a normal dog. He was curious and had typical puppy traits. He wasn't a normal dog to Sue Sternberg. Her big thing was do your need me; do your want me; are you trying to get away: or, are we in this thing together. I have spent some time around dogs and it takes a bit of time to build a relationship with a dog. It took me months to realize I couldn't live without Girl and Mookie.

Sternberg recommended euthanasia for the puppy. When a big time expert like Sue Sternberg says a dog is going to harm a human being, there aren't too many options for that dog. If I hadn't considered the meaning of the word adoptable before, I had pause to think about it then. I remembered something vitally necessary to assess dogs. I'd gotten so caught up with what the pros were saying that I'd ignored what I had known all along. It was something the dogs had taught me and something I could not learn from a book or a seminar. It was all about the feeling I got from a dog in my own gut. It was my bond with that particular dog.

I remember people telling me I was crazy to take a pit bull like Girl out of a shelter when I didn't have background history on her. Even though she had been running on the streets and I had no idea where she was from, when she looked into my eyes, I knew Girl was a good dog. I knew she would try as hard as she could to do what I wanted her to do. That is something you cannot be taught. I had spent a lot of money for the seminar, but would come away with one valuable lesson. From then on, I would remember to heed my own instincts.

I wasn't able to speak to the woman from the little puppy's shelter again. I didn't want to know what was going to happen to the little boy who'd made the grave error of showing his nature, of playing full throttle, of not needing Sue Sternberg too much and failing the plastic hand prod test. I do not trust this test and think it quite cruel. Imagine poking some old hungry truck driver while he's getting down on his chicken fried. You're likely to draw back a bloody nub.

We had a slight break while Sternberg made some jokes. Everyone laughed a little too hard. Perhaps she was attempting to dispel the pall of doom in the room while we thought about the puppy being put to sleep. She went on about the Starbuck's chai and dropped a reference to MacDonald's where she takes dogs for a cheeseburger before she has them euthanized.

The next dog was a large female Rottweiler from the Humane Society where the event was being held. I must say, the facility was indeed a lovely place. Trish King was one of the staff trainers and well known in dog circles. She had volunteered the rottie for Sternberg to evaluate from their kennel. King sat with the rest of us in attendance while she held onto her little Cairn terrier, an over-aged Dorothy. She was an enthusiastic supporter of Sternberg, often leading the rest of the audience in bursts of applause. Sternberg has a near religious zealot following amongst dog professionals.

The Rottweiler was a typical rottie. I found out a little about the breed when I acquired a Rottweiler as one of my dog walking clients. I wanted to understand Rottweilers better and learned they were butchers' dogs and were trained to guard the meat. I've met more than one rottie enthusiast with a funny story about their dog and the dinner table. One fellow said his dog would sit by the table while he prepared dinner and not allow anyone near the food until the man gave him the release command. This dog even protected the food from himself, not allowing himself to eat until he got the go ahead from his master.

The Marin rottie was a beautiful girl, large and glossy as a healthy Rottweiler should be. Rotties share some of the same stigma and mythology attached to the pit bull breeds. People read something bad about them in the paper or see a story on television and attribute the behavior as a genetic characteristic of the entire breed. You never hear the story about the sweet rottie following her little girl to school. It's a nice story, but doesn't sell newspapers.

Sternberg went to work on the dog, prodding and poking her all over and getting no response. The rottie just sat there and let Sternberg do her business for the crowd. Sternberg let us know she was putting SCAN into effect. SCAN is her program standing for sexually mature, cautious, arousal and no signs of friendliness. Rottie was a prime candidate for SCAN according to Sternberg.

I wondered if Mookie, Rebel or Girl could pass the SCAN test. Mookie hated having his nails clipped and being brushed. I would clip his nail and he'd bite the air. The bite is an air snap and not a real bite. I knew it was a game Mookie played with me. He would never have bitten me. I knew that. He was a dog who'd come to us with quirks. Maybe those strange behaviors were acquired from the treatment he'd received from the Rastas. Maybe Mookie did not get to spend the required period of time with his littermates necessary for a socially well-rounded dog. Whatever the reason, he had those quirks, so Mookie and I made a game of nail clipping. It became our practice to brush and air bite. It might not be the standard taught in obedience, but it worked for Mookie and it was fun for us. It became part of our routine and our special bond.

Rebel is fond of a prod. In fact, he hikes up his short little leg so that the prodder can have better advantage. When he's done, he simply gets up and moves away. Rebel's always been his own little red man. Girl loves to have a good prod above her hip beneath her rib cage. She'll even turn and give you a good show of her canine tooth as she curls up her lip in ecstasy. It's scary looking the first time or two, but it's Girl's way of acknowledging that you've found her spot. With just these three dogs and their funny habits, it's awe inspiring to consider all of the other dogs out in their world and their special peculiarities. Each dog is an individual and has complexities as do we humans.

The female rottie took her prodding with an indifferent attitude. She had no reaction one way or the other. The only one who had any reaction was Sue Sternberg. The more the rottie sat and did nothing, the more Sternberg got her own panties in a wad. It was kind of funny to see a grown woman poking away in a frenzy and the big dog laying there ignoring her. Finally, out came the plastic hand and the bowl of dried kibble. The rottie didn't even seem to care about the bowl of food. All in all, the dog was just sort of there. When Sternberg finished with her assessment, she dropped her head dramatically and said she was forced to recommend euthanasia for the dog. She said this dog had the capacity to hurt someone and her findings led to euthanasia as the only option.

The enrapt audience gave her a rousing vote of encouragement. I felt like a leftover SDS at the Republican National Convention. I had been raised in the south during the civil rights movement and was no stranger to lynch mob mentality. It terrifies me to this day. What in the world was this

118

seminar I'd found myself in the midst of? Trish King assured
Sternberg that the Rottweiler would be exterminated. There
was a collective sigh of relief as members of the crowd reached
down to pet their own closely harnessed dogs as if to say, "good
dog. You're a good dog. We are safe."

Trish King conducted a seminar a few years later
at a local city pound. She was reported to have opened her
workshop with a statement that she did not like Rottweilers and
that she was afraid of them. Now, I don't know that many rotts,
but I see them walking with their people at parks and on city
sidewalks. I am always amazed to see their big German butts
happily bouncing alongside while looking up at the person
holding the leash. I'm sure the breed has its share of unruly
citizens as do all of the breeds, but I've been lucky enough to
witness the good citizens in my travels.

When we broke for lunch, Dante and I ran into a guy
who'd previously worked in the kennels at CCACC. He offered
to show us around the Marin facility. We gratefully accepted. I
was surprised to see such a low number of cats and dogs in the
adoptable section. In fact, there were not that many kennels
and spaces for adoptable pets. If memory serves me correctly,
there was more square footage in the plush gift store where
I'd purchased some expensive Premier gentle leaders than the
adoptable area.

He showed us the crematorium where people could
bring their own pets to be cremated after they'd passed on. It
helped raise money for the shelter, but was also used to cremate
the shelter's own euthanized animals. We traipsed back to the
kennels nobody else sees in shelters. The donating public is
usually only aware of the few cozy hotel style digs, such as the
lobby in CCSPCA. Most of these dogs end up with their lives
depending on the say so of one person. At CCSPCA, most
people don't see the animals behind the scenes. For wealthy
organizations that have the opportunity to effect change, this
just ain't right.

In the far corner of the stray section sat the female rottie we'd witnessed fail the Sternberg assessment. Next to her was the hugest pile of steaming diarrhea I'd ever seen. It was fresh and wet and stunk to high heaven. There was even steam coming off the top. She had the same look of disinterest she'd worn throughout her episode with Sternberg.

I said 'hi' to the dog. She turned to look at me, her tongue hanging out. She seemed to be one of those dogs that likes to just lay there and hang out. I sure didn't get the feeling she'd like to kill me or anyone else for that matter. She hadn't even expressed an interest in killing Sue Sternberg when she was being assessed. Dante let out an audible "awww" which expressed perfectly how we felt. Here was a dog that had been condemned to death because she'd failed Sue Sternberg's test in front of the paying crowd. The crowd had been more than enthusiastic that the dog was condemned to being put to sleep. The entire time she'd undergone the incredibly over-stimulating evaluation, she'd had to go potty. Not only was this poor dog not exercised properly before being pushed and pushed hard, her insides were about to explode with diarrhea. I saw that with my own two eyes.

What kind of a dog trainer doesn't let a dog have a chance to go outside and poop before enduring as grueling a test as the Sternberg assessment? What kinds of experts were these people anyway? We had spent good hard-earned money to learn about dogs and what makes them aggressive. All I'd learned so far was how to kill 'em. If I had my doubts before, they were confirmed now after seeing this poor girl would was about to die. I am wrong about things from time to time, but I am willing to admit when I am wrong. I do have a pretty good gut feeling about dogs. The signals we learn from behaviorists and books are certainly worth noting. A dog will usually tell you what they are feeling if you're watching and listening. I have found in my experience that dogs are quite clear in their communication with us. My own errors took place when I was

120

not focused and allowed my thinking to become clouded.

This dog was going to be killed because her signals were incorrectly read. Sue Sternberg is an ambitious and powerful person. Even CCACC used her methods. Trish King had assured Sternberg that the rottie would be put to sleep. Everyone was safe. How many other animals had been unfairly euthanized due to an improper assessment? How many other Sternberg seminar graduates were reading a dog improperly and influencing shelter temperament tests? I do not care to venture a guess. There is a huge misconception that euthanasia is the only solution for the overwhelming population of unwanted animals. This is tremendously wrong. All it takes is one person who is willing to look for a solution and I was about to go looking for that solution.

The CCACC attendees learned a great deal from the seminar that weekend. Two shepherd mixes from the adoptable side, Vinni and Topper were put to sleep for food aggression by way of the plastic hand the following week. A little bit of knowledge is a dangerous thing.

Chapter Nine
Mr. Burns

Lost Cause
By Beck

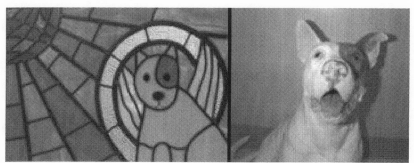

Patch

What child didn't grow up influenced by Disney pictures like 101 Dalmatians with evil characters like Cruella DeVille? I'm more visual and imaginative than most, which has benefited my writing and filmmaking. The pictures I hold in my head are luminous and vivid. Truth fascinates me. Truth can be so much more powerful than fiction. I'm often stumped to come up with an imagined story more intriguing than reality. It is a hard thing to create characters as interesting as those people who cross our paths. In my own life, I am always encountering people much more strange than the one I read about or see portrayed in a film.

I can't say why people enter the field of animal control. I have met some wonderful folks who are paid to take care of the city or county animals. Some of these people literally do their good work in secret; having been threatened with their jobs should they rock the boat. One sweet worker at CCACC sneaks blankets and toys to the animals in secret. She has been repeatedly warned by Deputy Jill Burns not to waste time and money with 'extras'. She is not the only CCACC employee forced to fly under the radar in fear for her job.

I first met Deputy Burns when I found Angel Divine when I'd asked the counter person to forward my contact information to the new adopter. She transferred my call to Deputy Burns, who in turn, put Marty in touch with me. From the day he returned my call until the day he passed away, Marty and I remained good friends. He has been gone from this world for a while now and Angel lives with her other dad, Russell, Marty's partner in Phoenix, Arizona. Russell sends me funny pictures of Angel Divine weekly and they are active members of our online rescue playgroup. This was the last nice thing I can ever remember Deputy Jill Burns doing for me, for anyone or for any animal.

Deputy Burns had come from another animal control down the coast a couple of years before. Legend had it that the other shelter was so happy she was leaving, they threw her a big going away party and neglected to invite Burns herself. She was a funny looking little woman with cropped steel grey hair brandished with a braided tail in the back. The staff referred to her as Mr. Burns behind her back, because she was a dead ringer for the character on tv's The Simpsons.

You wouldn't believe a character as awful as Burns in fiction. Maybe in a comic strip, but even in comics, one needs dimension. Some good and some bad is necessary to make the character believable. Even Nurse Ratched in One Flew Over the Cuckoo's Nest was multi-layered with a couple of good qualities. I was taking photos of the cats one day when I first started volunteering at the shelter. A man, looking at the cats, was removing the kennel cards and clipboards from the kennels. When he'd replace them, I noticed there were being hung up in the wrong place. I finally said something to him and he flew off the handle. Animal care and control attracts strange types even as potential customers. I tried to explain the importance of keeping the correct chart with the right kennel. That sort of mix up could result in an animal being medicated improperly or even worse, a mistaken euthanasia. He marched out and complained. Next thing, I was called immediately over the loud speaker to report to Burns' office. This was my first of many future 'visits' with Burns.

Burns is a classic passive-aggressive person. She started her tirade in a strange calm voice. "The public must always come first," she said, her words carefully metered. "No ifs, ands or buts." I tried to explain the serious nature of mixing up the kennel data, but she just stared back at me with her weird smile. She maintained her position, even while she seemed to consider the dangers involved. Deputy Burns replied that my argument was irrelevant. I was astounded that more care wasn't being taken to insure the city's animals had the best treatment.

Everything I'd learned from volunteer orientation throughout training professed what a great shelter CCACC was. The world 'care' came before the word 'control' even in the title. How could the potential loss of an animal's life be so insignificant? Jane Everly, the volunteer coordinator, had warned me about Burns. Jane had lost many an argument with Burns regarding animal welfare. Everly, as did each department head at CCACC, met weekly with Burns to report her entire schedule by the hour. Everly was grilled regarding her every action throughout her workweek. To sum up, Burns would then offer a psychological briefing while commenting on personal flaws such as Everly being too emotional. By the time Burns was through with her, Jane would be wrung out like an old dishrag.

My own first meeting with Burns wasn't so awful if you take out the part that animals' lives are irrelevant. I remember commenting to Jane afterward that I couldn't believe Burns did not appear concerned in the least at a possible mistaken euthanasia. Jane had responded that it would be wise for me to never disagree with Burns on any issue. Burns was known to never back down, ever. In fact, Burns would badger away until her opponent was confused, exhausted and broken down, very Manchurian Candidate and very dramatic. To think of valuable taxpayer dollars being wasted on these useless meetings is unacceptable. I'd run into her kind all my life and I knew the day was coming when we'd lock horns. For now, I had work to do and planned to fly low as long as I possibly could.

She'd be all smiles with a big, "hello, Cindy" in the hallway or main lobby as if she were the queen of the Neches River Festival sashaying through town on a float. I'd respond in kind and we'd continue on our separate ways. I was more sensitive to Jane's dealings with her after my experience. She was constantly on Jane, calling her to task for every decision made. Jane had been given an extra position, Media and Outreach, in addition to her full time Volunteer Coordinator duties. Now, Jane had two full time jobs for the price of one.

There were hushed rumors over the years I volunteered at CCACC, but no one was ever brave enough to vocalize their complaints. First, Burns had Doc's backing. Secondly, Burns was cagey, too smart to do anything anyone could nail her on. She was a master manipulator and never left a paper trail. She would have department supervisors carry out her instructions, taking extreme care that the trail would not lead back to her office. As example was the case of the small kitten killed while in transport by animal control officer Johnny Jay.

Johnny Jay was an enormous ACO who'd been rumored to look the other way involving known dog fighters and their illicit activities. One Sunday, Dante Peterson was doing a ride-along with Jay. They received a call about a stray kitten. They picked up the kitty and put him in one of the kennels in back of the van. Before driving back to the shelter, Jay stopped off at a fast food drive-through restaurant for a large lunch. His driving was so erratic, speeding and making hairpin turns, Peterson could hear objects being tossed about in the back of the van. He heard the sides of the van's walls being hit. When they arrived back at CCACC and opened the back to retrieve the kitten, the little animal was dead.

Peterson reported the incident to Deputy Burns who instructed him to write the incident up in an official report. In order for Officer Jay to be properly reprimanded, certain mandatory steps must be followed first according to Burns. Peterson completed the report and filed it with CCACC. The supervisors had their weekly meeting at which Officer Jay's direct supervisor, Captain Debbi Latrell, was in attendance. After much debate and several meetings later, Officer Jay received a slap on the wrist and continues to draw a paycheck from CCACC to this day as an animal care and control officer.

Why not approach the media with these problems? Why not report these issues to Doc, the director of CCACC? He answers directly to the mayor and holds the power to effect drastic changes regarding the way the city's animals are being treated. As I write this today, the media has yet to report any wrongdoing at CCACC in regards to animals and their treatment. If the story isn't a fluff piece or covering some horrific mauling, the public is kept safe and protected from any knowledge of misdoings at the city shelter. The media's stand is to continue to perpetuate the myth that CCACC is the world's best shelter and backed up with Doc's miraculous live release numbers. To this day, I have no idea where he got those numbers. What happened to all of those stray animals that never made it over to the available side? There is no representation in CCACC statistics.

A look at the Berkeley shelter illustrates the difference. On any given day, each kennel in the city of Berkeley's animal care and control is full of barking dogs looking for a good home. This shelter houses around 50 kennels in the adoptable section. The available kennels at CCACC are rarely full. In the past few years, I have checked their available numbers, which average six or seven dogs for adoption. Where are the ones who don't make it over from the full stray side? The answer is they have been euthanized, but Doc's record keeping has cleverly disguised these numbers.

I tried to go through the proper channels when forming my 501©(3). This meant tons of meetings with Colleen and Deputy Burns. Besides running my private dog walking business and my volunteer work, I was trying to manage all of the spinning plates necessary to form a non-profit corporation. This did not leave much time for meetings; however, I did try my level best to comply with their demands. I kept Colleen and Deputy Burns up to date with Round Up Rescue and its plans. In meetings with my own board, I was warned to be wary of my dealings with CCACC and to take any of Doc's promises with a grain of salt.

It was hard not to trust Doc. You wanted to believe this kindly roly poly fellow with his jovial demeanor. I, like most other people who met Doc or saw him interviewed, was caught up in his spell. Extremely charismatic, he inspired belief that we could find great solutions for these animals and save many of them. I didn't need too much inspiring. Here I was all ready to go out and save pit bulls in a climate where most people either hated them or wanted them all dead.

Doc had landed into the position as head of CCACC when CCSPCA didn't want to be the city dog pound anymore. CCACC was created and Doc appointed as the director. Before the 1994 adoption pact was created and the CCACC was formed, CCSPCA had even sold animals to research for experimentation. The organization had a ways to go before their image was salvaged. I told my fellow board members that I would be careful, but I really believed that Doc was on the side of the animals.

Going into these redundant meetings with Colleen to exhaust the same topics, I began to wonder if she was even listening. She had forceful ideas about rescuing pit bulls and would strongly encourage me to observe her temperament tests. I tried to make myself available as scheduling would allow and was able to get a basic idea of how she operated. I learned more about her rescue group than I did about the pit bulls. The meetings had a tendency to drone.

Colleen's views were different from my own and from the viewpoints of people I'd surrounded myself with. She vacillated between wanting to save an animal one day and being inaccessible on another day. A dog called Patch was a shelter favorite at this time. She was one of the best dogs I'd ever met. Everybody loved her. She was a big, fat female about 8 months old. Her kennel card read 'pit bull', but she was one of a kind. She was cow spotted with rusty red markings. Everywhere else, she was pink. Her nose was pink with rust freckled pigment and Miss Piggy pointed big ears. She was as silly and fun loving as she looked. When you'd go to pet her, she'd splay herself all over the floor on her back with legs sticking out in every direction. She loved everyone she met and didn't have a mean bone in her body. This dog was just not capable of anything bad. She had a wonderful soul and was a beacon of light and hope in an otherwise dismal place.

One volunteer, Diane, loved Patch especially. Diane was a green volunteer who came every day to walk Patch. She would take Patch to the park and had special permission to take her to events to try and find Patch a home. She had lined up a placement for Patch with Layla of Outer Space Rescue should she not be able to find her that forever home.

Deputy Burns had implemented a new ruling prohibiting anyone from rescuing an animal that'd been placed on the euthanasia list. This was in direct opposition of the Hayden Act. Senator Tom Hayden is the infamous ex-husband of Jane Fonda and former member of the Chicago Seven. When serving as senator from California, he had written a controversial document referred to as the Hayden Act. Among other strides to help animals, the Hayden Act expanded the stray time for in impounded animal. The bill also provided that a 501©(3) rescue could have an accredited trainer assess an animal, even if that animal had been slated to be killed. If the animal passed the trainer's assessment, the facility must release the animal in question to the rescue organization. This was huge. Before the Hayden Act, impounded animals had absolutely no defense against some inept worker who had decided the animal was vicious.

This was a hot and controversial topic. Certainly, no sane person our group supports turning loose a dangerous dog, but I have come across more animals than I care to remember who were not given a thorough and fair temperament test. My own respect for the bill is weighted in the right of each animal to have a fair and qualified chance. The Hayden Act bravely pioneered the way for some animals to finally have the opportunity they deserved. The bill allowed rescuers like myself to do the job we were chosen to do.

We took beautiful color photographs of Patch and pasted the posters all over the city. She looked like a big grinning pig in all of the glorious parks, coffee houses and pet stores. It was relieving to know that Patch was safe. Even if she was not adopted from all of the exposure, she had a safety net with Layla's Outer Space rescue group. Layla had placed a c.i.p. or call interested party on Patch with the front counter at CCACC. This was referred to as a hold. Layla would be called immediately when Patch's time ran out. I put the last of the posters up on top of Bennett Mountain at the dog park. Her face took up the whole 8 ½ by 11 inch colored paper. I kept turning around to look at her happy face as I returned to my truck parked down the hill. This was why I wanted to help animals. This is how it was supposed to work.

I backed my truck down the hill and looked once more at Patch's poster. The sky that day was as blue as a Microsoft Windows screensaver with the brilliant horizon and bright green grass, a perfect day. I drove back to the shelter and saw Diane sitting in front of the building. She was crying. A staff member sat beside Diane and was patting her on the back. They looked so sad and hopeless. Something must be terribly wrong. Diane was heaving and sobbing so hard, she couldn't speak. I asked what happened and the staff member told me Patch had been put to sleep. Colleen had put Patch down that afternoon. I couldn't believe my ears. The shelter wasn't even that full. Patch had somewhere to go. All these facts swirled in my head. I later found out that Colleen had been angry with Layla over something. She had retaliated by killing Patch. That should never have happened. I began to understand the meaning of the word 'control'. Patch had fallen through a crack in the system of the 'best shelter in the world'.

I was crushed. There is a page dedicated to her on my website. Her sweet face still shines with hope and life, which was stolen from her that sad afternoon so long ago. Diane couldn't volunteer for a long time after that. She made a stained glass of Patch's face in tribute to her. This dog should never have been killed. When I think of Patch, I think of how that sweet dog should be with her happy family. She should be alive and running to the top of Bennett Mountain with a pack of other dogs enjoying the park. That is what God created this beautiful girl for, not to be killed in a cold and unfeeling chamber and packed up in a garbage bag. It's a scar on our society when we human beings permit healthy, happy animals as innocent as Patch to die needlessly and alone without dignity.

After Patch, it was especially hard for me to attend the meetings with Deputy Burns and Colleen. I found myself explaining over and over why I wanted to save pit bulls. With me, it wasn't the breed of the animal, but the needs of the animal. One morning, two baby pigeons were brought in to CCACC. A person had found them and trusted the shelter to care for the birds. They were fat and didn't have one feather between them. I had never seen anything so silly. They looked like plucked chickens, meaty and healthy and full of personality. Looking at them, it was easy to believe how they'd fallen from their refuge. I couldn't imagine anything more interesting and quirky than these two baby pigeons.

The pigeons had been brought to the vet room for euthanasia. CCACC euthanizes all pigeons on intake. How criminal for such a wealthy city to kill these precious birds. Wasn't there some group in this district to help wildlife? I was informed that the shelter down the road, another privately owned SPCA, took all of the other wildlife, but not pigeons. A flock of pigeons roosted in the warehouse across the parking lot from CCACC. Every day when I would leave the shelter, tired from fighting the fight, the last thing I'd see would be this magnificent flock of pigeons. They'd light on top on one roof, then one would take off and they'd all follow and land on another rooftop. One would take off and they'd all be off and running again. I love birds, but of all the species, pigeons have the loveliest flight pattern. It's mesmerizing. Many nights in the cold fog, they would remind me something greater was at work in the universe.

I got on the phone and started calling around to try

and save these pigeons. I found a great rescue group in Marin County call Marin Wildcare. The lady on the phone said, "sure we'll take those pigeons." She went on to say they would rehabilitate them and when the time was right, release them back to the wild. I was so excited. Those pigeons could live and also enjoy life in the glorious Marin headlands. She told me to have them there at the facility by 5 p.m. that afternoon and gave me directions.

I went to Captain Debbi to see what hoops I needed to jump through to get the pigeons to Marin Wildcare. Most of the officers were sitting around the large table eating and reading the newspaper. Captain Debbi raised her mullet haircut from the newspaper long enough to tell me everything had to be cleared through Deputy Burns. She said Deputy Burns had to authorize any animal transport that was not pre-delegated as a regular daily delivery. A Project 20 volunteer took care of the current wildlife daily transport as part of his duties to work off community hours. Project 20 was a civic funded plan that allowed the public to cancel tickets and the like through a work release volunteer program. Richie, the guy who made the daily wildlife run, was a fellow Texan I really liked. He'd done time in the state pen and was a colorful character. Like many ex-cons, he was a fan of pit bulls and we had hit it off.

Since pigeons were not included in the daily rescue transport, the only chance for these babies was with Marin Wildcare. I volunteered to speak to Burns, since no one in the squad room wanted to take her on. I wasn't too excited about meeting with her either, but this was a life and death situation. I used the mantra I would use to this day to get through tough times. Do whatever you need to do to walk out with the dog. In this case, it was baby pigeons and I was prepared to do whatever needed to be done to save their lives. I was committed to walk out with those baby pigeons, even if that meant a meeting with the dreaded Deputy Burns.

I called Burns. She was always in her office during work

134

hours. You could say that about her. Usually, she was either in a staff meeting or a meeting with a member of the animal connected public, but she was almost always in her office. Most of the staff and many members of the rescue community have a horror story or two about meeting with Burns. Some even went to Doc for help after one of these encounters. Doc never, to my knowledge, came to anyone's rescue. A few staff members went so far as to apply to their union representative for help. Unfortunately, the union guy is a close colleague of Doc's and would relate the complaints verbatim so that Doc could run damage control. The staff member would be called on the carpet and dressed down by Burns and Doc. One staff member who'd been sold out by the union rep sought legal representation after she'd lost her job. The attorney couldn't believe what was happening to these people in a government agency. The employee won, if you want to call it that, and was reinstated to her former position as an animal control officer.

Burns agreed to see me and told me to report to her office. I promptly arrived and expressed my concern about the baby pigeons. I asked if perhaps they could be transported to Marin Wildcare. First, Burns said they could if one of the ACO officers would agree to do the transport and if the ACO schedule was open. This was good news. I had just left a roomful of unoccupied ACO officers. She even called Captain Debbi while I sat in her office and asked if one of the officers could transport the birds to Marin. Captain Debbi asked out loud if there were any free officers. Every single ACO replied that he or she was busy. This was at straight up 12 o'clock noon.

Burns hung up the phone. She said how sorry she was, but there were just no available officers to make the run to the sanctuary. I asked her if I could please take the birds. Whatever it takes to walk out with the dog. She again expressed how deeply sorry she was, but liability prevented her from allowing me to do the transport. I told her I was recently cleared as a

501©(3) non-profit and had current automobile insurance. This should free her of concern. She again apologized, but simply couldn't allow me to take the birds. I was near tears, but held back. Instinct told me to keep my emotion in check. I couldn't let her see me weaken, just like in the wildlife world where a sign of weakness is a death sentence.

I tried for an hour to change her mind, but she was as rigid as a cement block. Finally, she agreed to think about it and get back to me by that afternoon. I made sure she had my cell number that was strictly used for emergencies. I had to run by the house and check on my own animals, plus still had some dogs that needed walking that afternoon. She promised to contact me as soon as she came to a decision. I waited and waited to hear from her that afternoon, the memory of those precious little birds in my mind. Finally, around 3 o'clock, I called her office and got her voice mail. I didn't hear back and tried again at 4 p.m. I got the voice mail again. With traffic, I would need to pick the birds up now to get to the sanctuary by five.

I checked my email and there was no message from Burns. I checked the home phone again. Still nothing. Finally, there was a message at 5:25 p.m. Burns curt voicemail stated she was curious whatever happened with the two birds. The sickly sweet tone of her voice was nauseating. I got a bad feeling in the pit of my stomach. She knew good and well what happened to the birds. I was their only hope. It seemed like no one else at the shelter that day cared one way or the other about them. Two healthy fat babies had been lost for no good reason. I cannot comprehend what circumstances allow for this kind of loss. What difference would it have made to anyone if the birds had been saved? I know a lot of people do not like pigeons. I've heard them called ugly things like rats with wings. I have to feel sorry for those people who have never enjoyed watching them take the sky as they slap the wind with their wings. I later created a rescue to save the pigeons of Coastal County called

'A Wing and a Prayer'. Pigeons are the pit bulls of the bird community.

I got a strange call the next morning from the shelter. I was alarmed when my cell phone rang. It was Dr. Ralph, the CCACC veterinarian. Dr. Ralph is a former rodeo vet and not a very friendly doctor. Dr. Ralph was well known in area vet circles as having graduated at the bottom of her class. She once amputated a cat's paw for a malady called slipped skin. The actual cure for slipped skin is a poultice of sugar and water. Ralph had just chopped off the paw. The vet staff at the adoption facility where the cat wound up called it medical malpractice. This same facility saved many cats Ralph had diagnosed with heart murmur. When re-checked at the adoption hospital, heart murmur was undetected every time. The suspicion was that heart murmur was listed as an excuse to euthanize.

This morning, though, Dr. Ralph and I were on the same side. She was livid. She asked me why the two baby pigeons had been left overnight in the CCACC squad room. I had no answer for her. I was as shocked as she was. I told her the birds had been brought to the squad room the previous day when we were trying to arrange transport to Marin. The last time I had seen the birds was when I left the squad room for my meeting with Burns. I explained about my meeting and how Burns had put the matter on hold until she was to get back with me later in the afternoon. When I had left CCACC the previous afternoon, the two birds had still been under the care of Captain Debbi Latrell and the ACO staff. The birds had been in perfect health as far as I could tell.

Dr. Ralph then told me the birds were discovered dead of exposure in the squad room this morning. I could not believe the birds had been left to sit on that table all afternoon unnoticed. Call waiting beeped. I answered the call from Burns herself. Her voice was dripping with sweetness just like when she greets you in the common areas at CCACC. "Oh, Cindy, I just found out about the little pigeons. I just wanted to call and let you know we are going to get to the bottom of this and find out what exactly happened."

I was silent. All she'd had to do the day before was allow me to carry the birds to Marin. They could have been on their way to recovery. They had been so healthy and alive. Now, they were dead of exposure. Everything about this was wrong, wrong, wrong. There was no excuse. Burns was to blame for this. Here was someone who had the authority to kill with a whim. She would authorize an ex-con to run animal daily down the coast, but wouldn't let a 501©(3) accredited organization carry two baby pigeons to a sanctuary. Due to her warped control issues, two more innocent animals were dead.

It's hard to keep acting as if all is right with the world. I was beginning to understand the elements of survival in this arena. The ones who were able to maintain on a daily basis were the ones who chose politics over animals. There was no way I could do that and keep on doing what I was doing. I knew it then and I know it sure as shooting now. With every decision made in rescue is the question of the animals or the politics. In each instance where I'd be forced to choose animals rather than politics, there would be trouble. I had begun to get a bad name in certain CCACC circles. I had finally realized that not everyone involved cared about helping the animals or finding solutions. It was so very clear to me when I looked at the innocent face of an animal whether a baby pigeon or an unwanted old pit bull. When their face met mine, I knew what my choice had to be. There wasn't a choice. Neil Young said it best in the words of "Ohio".

National Pet Stores had several locations in Port Harbor. One of the branches in a very upscale neighborhood asked if they could make Round Up Rescue the recipient of their Christmas Drive. I had forgotten completely about it until one day when I got a call to come and pick up the check. They had raised over $2,000! Nobody was more surprised than I was. I never dreamed they would raise that kind of money. The manager and employees really loved pit bulls and what we were trying to do. They had wanted to help and boy, howdy, did they help!

I thanked Shawna and the crew for all their hard work. Shawna mentioned she'd received a call from Deputy Burns at CCACC. The conversation had escalated into Burns shouting at Shawna. It seemed a customer had thought the pet store was raising money for CCACC, namely the pit bulls. Not a fan of the dogs, the woman had complained to the shelter.

I was waiting in the CCACC lobby for an adoption appointment later that afternoon. The process was and is a lengthy one. I had learned to bring something to read. I looked up from my book to see Burns standing right in front of me, hands on hips. She lit right into me. "Just what do you mean posting notices all over town stating you work for CCACC?"

I was speechless. I had never posted anything of the sort. Burns went on that she'd received complaints from the public that National Pet Stores was taking up a collection to save CCACC pit bulls. "This is against regulation," she said.

I knew of other rescue groups who raised money to help animals. Why was it suddenly forbidden? Again, I tried to reason with Burns. However, there was no room for discussion while she was driving her point home, mind already made up. The posters had only stated that all donations went toward helping rescued animals at CCACC, the same exact wording in our mission statement. Even though she'd been given multiple copies of our statement, today, she was behaving as if she'd never heard of Round Up Rescue. I was pretty shocked at her outburst, especially since she'd chosen the main lobby to hold forth. It was embarrassing. She even asked how much money we'd raised. I was so shocked at the ordeal, I told her the amount! Looking back, it was none of her business and did not concern the members of the public and staff who bore witness to the spectacle.

One could never gauge just how Burns would act on any given day. She could be your very best friend or ice cold. The day Patch was exterminated had been a sad day for those of us who'd been involved in finding her a way out of CCACC. I remember sitting in the lobby when Burns happened to walk by. She seated herself beside me and asked how things were going. I knew enough to keep it light and answered accordingly.

That day, though, Burns had been upbeat. She had a suggestion which would, if put into effect, save a lot of dogs. She suggested we spotlight one of the pit bulls. We could pick a dog that really stood out, a shelter favorite. We could take this dog to training, to local events; to news broadcasts like I'd done with Junior and whatever else might help that dog find the right home. Boy, what a great idea!

I asked her how we could put such a plan into action and her mood changed. From a caring colleague who wanted to help the animals, she told me I was playing with the big boys now. She used the exact words. Not to split hairs, but she and Doc were city workers after all. It wasn't like they were the Rolling Stones. Burns informed me that I would need to work up a proposal and schedule a meeting with CCACC department heads who would be affected by said plan. I kept my thoughts to myself as I wondered how the spotlight proposal could save lives. The goal was to walk out with the dog and to walk out with the dog; I would need some agility to jump through the necessary hoops.

I stopped by Doc's office to check his availability. After penciling in a tentative time for a meeting, I requested that same window with Burns, Volunteer Coordinator Jane Everly and the new Animal Care and Control Supervisor, Lt. Zed Dane. Colleen had taken a position at another county shelter. Her departure had been sudden. There was some scuttlebutt around CCACC, but no one knew the whole story why she'd left so abruptly. It was suspected that her leaving had something to do with Burns, but no one knew for certain.

Dane had been a volunteer when I started volunteering at CCACC. He had gone from volunteer to hired kennel attendant. I'd always thought this was strange since he had formerly been a veterinarian. He was a tall studious looking fellow. Always soft spoken, he moved quietly among the animals. That is so important in a facility full of scared creatures. You can see the fear on their faces when people slam the big metal doors and gates. I looked forward to Zane as the new Animal Care and Control Supervisor. It looked like a new day was about to dawn at the shelter. I could see a ray of hope on the horizon.

I worked hard on the proposal for the next couple of weeks. I spent every spare minute on it between walking the dogs, volunteer and rescue work. I wanted the proposal to be sharp and professional so everyone would vote to support the plan. By the time I was finished, I was quite pleased with the effort. I noted in the first section the difficulty of finding good homes for these dogs due to public fear and lack of knowledge about pit bulls. The proposal acknowledged the diminished resources and the scarcity of organizations willing to rescue these breeds. Training was a mainstay of the plan, which didn't attempt too much by suggesting we try and save all of these dogs. The plan maintained a focus effort of concentrating on only one dog at a time.

The idea of setting aside one kennel for the spotlight dog opened the next part of the proposal. Round Up Rescue would take the spotlight dog to training and pay for that training. We would post the dog on our websites and appear on local television programs. The dog would attend local city and neighborhood functions, which are held most every weekend. We could take the dog to mobile adoptions sponsored by our own and other rescue organizations. This in itself was landmark. Most rescues are working in the 11th hour to save animals from euthanasia and have very little time to network with other rescue groups. If we worked together, we could save so many more animals.

A similar, more informal plan already in effect at CCACC had proven itself to work. Currently, an adoptable dog would be held aside in an extra kennel while awaiting potential adoption. This had been Colleen's personal program and was pretty much a one-man show. It was hit or miss and only geared into action when Colleen selected a dog she liked that had run out of time. She would randomly move a dog around the shelter to buy him more time. She might put him back in the stray side or with the custody dogs while she looked for someone to foster. It was a valiant effort, but could have been much more successful and could have saved more lives. Colleen's plan had no room for input; however, it demonstrated there was a degree of wiggle room at the shelter. With a plan and some strategizing, we could work together and preserve the life of at least one dog at a time....the lifeblood of Round Up Rescue. The Spotlight Proposal borrowed quite a lot from Colleen's effort. Should the shelter become filled, Round Up would legally adopt the dog from the shelter.

The downside was explored as well. Due to some of the work we were doing, Round Up had begun to receive some serious qualified inquiries about adopting dogs. Unfortunately, two of these dogs had been euthanized before the interested families had a chance to meet those dogs. We suggested utilizing the television monitors in lobby to feature streaming video of the dogs at play. I volunteered my own time and equipment to create the videos so the shelter wouldn't have to shoulder any financial burden.

The plan outlined further ideas for in-house training so that new adopters who didn't meet the stiff requirements of having pit bull experience could qualify. Finally, the plan summed up on a financial note. Not one of our ideas would cost the city one penny. In fact, should the proposal be instated, CCACC could help other shelters find viable solutions for this epidemic problem. This shelter could actually become the best shelter in the world. It would certainly increase the shelter's donations. People love to see their government at work.

A few years before, a beautiful German Shepherd had been killed when used as bait in a dogfight. The public outcry was immense. The community donated over $75,000 in the name of the dog to help end dog fighting in the city. The money was never used. In fact, no on could figure out whatever happened to the fund. Like so many affairs connected to animals in Coastal County, the public was kept in the dark regarding the truth. The fund to stop dog fighting in the tragic German Shepherd's name became just another topic of speculation whispered among the staff and volunteers. In my first meeting with Doc, this fund had been dangled like a carrot as we discussed the formation of Round Up Rescue to help the pit bulls.

On the day I was to present the proposal, I arrived in the volunteer room early. I wanted to be fresh and alert so they would buy the plan and we could start saving dogs right away. I was nervous and apprehensive, which always affects my stomach. I braced myself and chanted my mantra. This time, I could potentially walk out with a lot of dogs.

Everyone started to filter in, proposal in hand. Jane smiled a secret smile at me for support. We were all in place except for Doc. We made small talk while we waited. Finally, after another 10 minutes, Doc arrived. He had his proposal folded in one hand while taking off his suit jacket with the other. As he seated himself, Doc began to scan the proposal. He apologized and said he hadn't gotten a chance to look at it yet and would just read it over while we talked. This proposal had the potential to save the lives of many animals. If people were coming into the shelter to look at the celebrity spotlight dog plastered all over town, they would bring their friends and families. The adoptions could be greatly increased for all of the animals in the shelter. The more people you could get to walk in the door, more animals would be able to find homes.

It was simple. For Doc to fail to see the all around benefits of the Spotlight Proposal was short sighted to say the least. For anyone at that meeting to not have read the proposal was rude and disrespectful. I had made sure each person in attendance had a copy of the proposal a week before the meeting was scheduled.

As the meeting progressed, Burns and Lt. Dane asked me many questions. Most of their questions had been outlined in the proposal, but I expounded as best I could without sounding redundant. Most of the questions pertained to shelter liability, naturally. As I had carefully outlined, nothing other than setting aside a kennel for a deserving dog would be changed from the way the shelter was presently being run. We just wanted to give that one dog a chance and make sure he would not be euthanized before he had an opportunity to reap the benefits of the program.

Advertising is a strong tool. When people have a chance to see a good dog, trained and well behaved, it helps to dispel many of the bad images the media has force-fed them. We don't see those hundreds and thousands of nice dogs being killed every day, but only that one untrained one who made the headlines.

Doc folded up his proposal and chimed in. We all turned our attention to him. He thanked me for all of the obvious hard work and thought which had gone into the proposal. Then he said something that still makes my flesh crawl. He said he had a proposal for me. Why not spotlight one, even two dogs at a time? I perked right up. This was more than I'd hoped for. He elaborated that CCACC was going through an initial stage of restructure. This proposal worked in concert with the renovation being planned.

First, there would no longer be a pit bull room. All of the dogs would soon be grouped together in kennels regardless of breed. On the surface, this was a great idea. I could see by placing dogs of all breeds together how some of the mythology and unfair prejudice against pit bulls might begin to slip away. Burns, Everly and Dane responded positively as well. Jane was always trying to debunk the bad press given to pit bulls. She thought this would send an excellent message to the public that all dogs deserve a good home.

Then, Doc dropped his bomb. He said, "yes, let's spotlight two dogs at a time for as long as it takes to get them into an approved home. All of the other pit bulls in the shelter will be euthanized. This will cut down on the cost of keeping the full kennels clean on a daily basis." I couldn't believe my ears. Maybe I didn't hear him correctly. Had he actually proposed the senseless killing of hundreds of dogs without a temperament test and even the slightest chance of finding a home? He said yes, that I had heard him correctly. Even Burns looked a bit shocked at his revelation, but immediately jumped to get his back. She made a halfhearted attempt to suggest some sort of compromise between Doc's bombshell and the Spotlight Proposal. I couldn't see it. Even though I am all about solutions and compromises, I couldn't see it. There was absolutely no way to merge his plan with mine. One was about living and the other, about killing.

Doc went on to say that was the plan, take it or leave it. I finally got what everyone had been trying to tell me all along about Doc. I did not know if the wet kitten story was fact or fiction, but if he came upon a kitten in the rain today, I don't believe he would stop at all. If the kitten were a pit bull, he would most likely run over the dog.

I left the meeting with a heavy heart. I had learned a hard lesson. The two people in charge of CCACC operations were not interested in helping animals. At least, not when those animals were pit bulls. I continued to move full speed ahead with the rescue. I wouldn't allow this setback and all of the wasted effort to impair the good work we were trying to do. We had a sound plan, the spotlight program being only one of several ideas. During the next few months while planning and strategizing for Round Up Rescue, I would no longer expect support from CCACC.

I attended a fundraising party for Layla's group. There were many other local animal groups represented at the affair and I had a chance to meet some interesting people. Many of these people would become good friends to Round Up Rescue as well. I met one lady who rescued Northern breeds. She was inquiring about my rescue and the trials of forming a 501©(3). I had learned to be a bit cautious about our mission to rescue pit bulls. Even in the dog world, not everyone was a fan of the pit bull breeds. Most people made the same comments. They either said, "you are so brave" or "why did you pick pit bulls to rescue?" I always had the same answer, "because they are the most likely to be killed."

My new friend was different from the usual people I met. She was very supportive and said she admired our group for taking on such a huge challenge. I told her of my recent meeting with Doc at CCACC and what a shocking experience it had been. She then told me of a similar experience. She had been called at home to come in for a meeting with Deputy Burns. This woman is a very nice California native with a calm and pleasant demeanor. She was completely sideswiped by Burns. The meeting turned into a grilling with Burns turning on the woman the minute the door closed. Burns wanted information about another rescue. The woman was surprised, but refused to divulge private information about another party. Burns became enraged and threatened her. Burns told her to either come forth with the requested information or Burns would see to it that she never rescued another dog from CCACC. In fact, Burns threatened to kill all Siberian Huskies that entered the shelter.

This was huge. I couldn't believe a director of a city agency tipping the pay scale at a hundred grand was able to treat a member of the public in such a manner. To use threats and wield her power over innocent animals sounded to me like something out of a third world country. This could not be allowed, especially coming from a sophisticated city shelter. I suggested she go public with the information. She was absolutely terrified. She knew of situations where Burns had indeed retaliated by using the animals to get what she wanted. The woman loved the dogs she was trying to save and wasn't prepared to take the chance of losing even one. Burns was using her power to kill the very animals that the taxpaying public was paying her to protect.

Unfortunately, most rescue people felt the same way as my new friend. People in rescue are just normal people who are frightened of confrontation and cruelty. Most try to do their good work and fly beneath the radar. I was scared, too, but also willing to look the beast in the eye. I was naïve. I had no idea how far reaching their power was. I didn't have a very solid take on how media perpetuated the myth that CCACC was the world's best shelter and would print or report nothing less than stories which glorified the facility. Sometimes, I wonder if I should have chosen the path most trod and worked behind the scenes.

Deputy Burns had a strange side. I began to study her as you would study a character in a novel. I noticed a pattern to her behavior. If, for instance, one were to take on a particular animal to help, Burns would confront that person who might be a member of the public or rescue person. When the person would stand up to Burns, they would lose the battle every time. Burns would exhaust every avenue to prevent that person from walking away with the dog. I noted in some rare cases, if the person were to appeal to Burns' knowledge and expertise, that person would walk out with the dog. This was important and would serve later to save animals.

A chicken showed up at the shelter with quite a story. It seemed someone had attached the hen to a bunch of balloons and released her into the air. She became an instant celebrity when the media got a hold of the story. Everyone began showing up at the shelter to adopt her. This facility has a number of chickens at any given time, many of them often euthanized. Burns stepped into the frenzy and claimed the job of selecting the lucky lottery winner who would go home with the chicken. This was not her job description, but the cameras were rolling.

The day was set for the drawing with heavy advertising. Something like fifty people showed up to see who would draw the lucky number. This meant 49 people would go home empty handed with their feelings hurt. People wear their hearts on their sleeves where animals are concerned. It's prudent to remain aware of this when involved in rescue work. CCACC had an opportunity for good press and there happened to be seven other chickens in the small animal section at the time. These other chickens didn't have the benefit of a tv camera. Some of the staff and rescues suggested that the public be made aware of the other chickens. This incident is only one of few when the public, rescue community, CCACC and the media worked together successfully to save animals. Wouldn't it be nice is we could repeat that performance from time to time? How about every day?

One of Round Up Rescue's short-term goals was to hire a dog trainer for CCACC. We had met with Doc and Deputy Burns several times with Dante Peterson and the Friends of CCACC. Everyone seemed to be on board regarding the need for a full time trainer. Dante's group and Round Up were still working on the big bash to raise money specifically for this purpose. The idea of working with the dogs to eliminate some of the hyperactivity and behavior issues that landed them in CCACC was certain to improve adoption numbers. A good trainer could make a huge difference at the shelter and in the community.

Dante and I met with the manager of the sidewalk café to proceed with the fundraiser. She enthusiastically offered us the café and catering! The event would be held at a very busy tourist part of town. The weather was almost always sunny and the tables always filled with customers like an impressionist painting. We busied ourselves with soliciting items to be sold through silent auction. Once we started, it was quite easy. Weekends at lush resorts and spas, tickets to the opera, ballet and symphony were donated. There were boat rides, dinners at local restaurants, paintings, facials and makeovers. Local animal-loving entrepreneurs stepped up to the plate with gusto to help raise money to hire a trainer.

I had a brainstorm for one of the items. I took a photo of a little girl in our rescue, Tish. Tish had come from the custody area at CCACC. Custody dogs and other animals were held while their owners were in jail or might be awaiting trial for cruelty and other cases. Tish had been picked up in an abuse case. She was covered head to toe with gunk. She had a horrific case of demodectic mange, so bad that her entire scalp had turned black and was covered in a sticky, sickly ooze. Lt. Dane had told me to forget trying to help Tish. He said she was one who was just too far gone to help, but there was something about her that got to me. I couldn't just walk away and forget about her.

She had the tiniest little under bite from a boxer gene, I guess. She was on the littler side and under all that nastiness, looked like she'd started out as a white dog. I told Zane I was pulling Tish. She was spayed and all doctored up, meaning, they gave her a dose of everything they had in the medicine cabinet full of toxic pharmaceuticals. Dr. Ralph said she had no idea what was going on medically with Tish, so she just gave her a dose for whatever she might have and in some cases, two doses. I had lined up a foster home with a young lady who loved pit bulls and wanted to help. She was only 13, but her mother said they would foster Tish. The day we met and took Tish to the park across the street from the foster's home was a day framed in gold.

Tish literally seemed to heal before our eyes! She still

suffered effects of the mange, but her will to survive and maybe even thrive radiated from her. It was what I had felt from her back in that dark kennel. She would look at me through the bars like, "help me, please. I won't let you down. You'll see." I did see it and I couldn't believe it.

Tish was a perfect dog. She never pulled on the leash, always had a smile on her little rose-flesh colored lips and a happy bounce to her step. Her under bite gave her a quizzical look. She was tiny and we called her our teacup pit bull. Once she was healed, she was indeed white with a big fawn spot on her side. She could have been a distant cousin of Girl's.

I created a poster modeled after the well-known Mastercard commercials running at the time. On the bill was a list of items along with a price tag. For instance, a donated leash and collar, value of $24.95 and where to purchase. Next was a dog bath and grooming, $70 with the name of the facility who donated the spa treatment. Listed was cup of coffee and cookie to share with Tish at a local dog friendly coffee house, $5. We included a walk at the park to try out the new leash ending with a photograph of Tish and me watching the sunset. Written next to the photograph was "watching the sun go down with a rescued pit bull.......priceless!!!"

'A Day With Tish' ended up being the most popular item at the event. People were bidding and talking about spending the day with Tish throughout the rest of the festivities. It was a great day. To see all of the pit bulls we'd rescued with their new guardians at the event was priceless as well. The dogs were all very well behaved. Most had already graduated from a Billy Best obedience class and were showing off some of their good behavior. One of the new dads, Todd, who had adopted Madeline, still tells the story of Junior at the dessert table. Todd happened to look up during the middle of the day to see Junior straddling the table nose deep in lemon meringue pie!

It was a wonderful day all around. We ended up raising

over $5,000 toward hiring a dog trainer at CCACC. Dante gave Round Up half the money, which we immediately began investing. We took dogs to training classes and jumped up adoptions. It is amazing what a little obedience work can do.

Throughout the course of meetings between Doc and Burns, Dante and myself, some roadblocks begun to stifle our progress. Doc and Burns claimed that the shelter could not hire anyone with donated funding. Doc was adamant about this issue. Absolutely no city worker could be paid by outside funding. The money had to come from the budget. This had, according to Doc, always been the system in place and could not be changed. This would be particularly interesting to note in the future when I became more acquainted with Doc's manipulation of that same budget, not to mention the mysterious outcome of the funding raised for the mauled German Shepherd.

No one was more surprised than I was when it was announced that renowned dog behaviorist, Lydia Bench, would be joining CCACC as the head of the dog adoption program. None of us had heard of Bench, so we began researching her background. I had seen shelters hire famous dog trainers before with less than shabby results. Every dog Round Up had rescued had been on the euthanasia list, turned down by CCSPCA. Another renowned dog behaviorist ran the CCSPCA dog behavior department. She'd also been hired on the merits of writing a book. I even tried to read it. Besides being incredibly boring, I wondered why would I should finish a book written by someone who turned away the very dogs I wished to rescue.

My fears were justified. Bench had absolutely no experience with shelter dogs or pit bull breeds. I was nervous. When I later found out her salary was $65 per hour, I was amazed and appalled. Why would a shelter spend that kind of money on someone without shelter dog experience? With 75 percent of the shelter's intake dogs being pit bull breed, what were they thinking? It was later discovered that Lydia was a personal colleague and acquaintance of Deputy Burns. This explained a lot.

At this time, mandatory budget meetings were being held once a week at CCACC. The staff was repeatedly notified to tighten up and warned of potential layoffs. Bench's hire seemed luxurious to more than a few of us. At one meeting, Doc pointed out the shelter had no budget for flea deterrent. At a meeting the next month, he disclosed there was no budget for food! For a shelter in such an affluent community, where was this money being appropriated? When considering the rendering truck still paid to retrieve each day's killed animals, something was way off. Something was not adding up.

Some of us, the staff, volunteers and other rescue groups, were beginning to become concerned with the decision making at CCACC. Burns rule which prohibited saving an animal scheduled for euthanasia was illegal under the Hayden Act. Rather than take her to task over the issue, I decided to strategize and plan. As the adoption pact stood between CCACC and CCSPCA, animals considered adoptable were first placed on the euthanasia list and then offered to the CCSPCA. CCSPCA looked for a reason not to accept the animal and could usually find an escape route by using behavior or illness. It was not a difficult feat for a policy-wise shelter rep. All of these cats and dogs dying in one of the wealthiest areas in the United States and it was common practice for CCSPCA to travel far and low to seek out 'adoptable' animals to 'save', 'adoptable' meaning smaller and purebred cats and dogs.

By placing a 'hold' on every single adoptable pit bull, I tried to save the dogs that would be left with no option once their number was up. Under Burns' decree, the dogs would be automatically euthanized after being turned down by CCSPCA. Even though her ruling was illegal, who had the time and fortitude to question her authority? After I started placing holds on all of the adoptable pit bulls, the gloves were officially off between Burns and myself. She didn't like it one little bit that

I had come up with a solution bypassing her authority. She was the kind of person who took it personally and felt challenged when not in complete control. Soon she was demanding more and more meetings with me. I tried to accommodate her at first, but eventually had to respectfully decline. There just wasn't enough time in the day. I also had to earn a living and run my rescue. Unlike Burns, I didn't make $99,000 a year.

I cannot begin to describe what a meeting with Burns is like. You enter the office while under the assumption you are two individuals looking for a way to help the animals. The glass walls allow for a visual to the hallway, so the comings and goings of personnel and animals can be monitored. The opposite wall features picture windows with a view of the side yard. Inside her spacious digs sits the crate her two dogs share.

If you disagree on any level with Burns, she turns the affair into a psychological inquisition. She'll sweetly say, "Cindy, may I offer you some personal advice?"

After several meetings going south after I allowed the personal advice offer, I began telling her no, not interested. The first few times she solicited personal guidance; the meeting would spiral into hours of private character evaluation. Common topics would be fear, family information, how to change one's personality and other completely inappropriate areas she hadn't the education or training to broach.

My heart went out to members of the unsuspecting public who'd been called to meet with Burns. Survivors of her interrogations often came away feeling violated and describing symptoms of post-traumatic stress disorder. Many of us involved in rescue work feel things deeply. Many of us have emerged from challenging backgrounds. For a person in power to exploit this vulnerability is harmful and downright mean. Burns was tenacious. Even when I'd refuse her offer of psychological advice, she'd continue to offer 'help' throughout the rest of the lengthy meeting. I would change the subject to a broader topic and attempt to remain focused on the animals. If

I had slipped and divulged some childhood tidbit, I guarantee we'd still be in her office right now.

I don't have anything to hide from anyone, but the good people of Coastal County were not paying her to figure out what happened to me in the third grade. We were in that office to discuss ways to handle the pit bull problem. I did have a rough childhood, but it has strengthened me for the path I've chosen to follow and I regret nothing. It's not an accident I rescue pit bulls. I feel an affinity with all animals, but especially those animals misjudged and misunderstood by society.

I admittedly have a fear of some women and I've run across more than a couple with traits resembling Burns. The world is unfortunately filled with people like her. There are strong women in positions of power who use that power to manipulate. I look at this practice as a sickness. Power corrupts and absolute power corrupts absolutely. I wonder what my old government teacher would have to say about Burns. He had shared so much with our class about the obedience to authority shock test and Nazism. He would have had a field day with Burns.

Now that I'm far away and don't ever have to sit in the hot seat again, I am relieved. To know that some poor unsuspecting soul is in there right now in my place, though, is very sad. Even though I am thousands of miles away, it terrifies me that this woman still has the power to hurt so many people and kill so many animals. And she is being paid to do so.

Chapter Ten
Round Up Rescue

Devil Went Down to Georgia
by Charlie Daniels

Stevie Ray

Based on the live release numbers Doc provided to the media, the shelter was believed to save more animals' lives than it actually did. Walk down the main hallway on any given day and peek through the door at the stray kennels brimming with unwanted barking dogs. The adoptable side is usually two thirds or so empty with only five or ten available dogs for adoption any given day. These are not just pit bulls, but all breeds. Anyone can monitor the number on a daily basis by using the Pet Harbor website. By comparing stray animals to the animals available for adoption or the CCACC website, the numbers can be accurately assessed. Those numbers never jived with Doc's statistics.

All those dogs dying on a daily basis is too much to try to conceive. Long ago, I saw a little brindle puppy being led down the hallway by a blue uniformed kennel worker. The dog was looking up at the stranger as if he'd made a new friend. What I saw on that puppy's face was hope, tongue hanging happily out, his tail was just a wagging. The little dog walked down the hallway looking at the other dogs on either side as if he were being taken outside to play. He walked with his new friend into Room 132. This was his last time to go anywhere. That image haunts me to this very minute and it breaks my heart.

Besides Junior, one of the first dogs I rescued under the Round Up umbrella was Stevie Ray. He was named after Stevie Ray Vaughan, the brilliant guitar player and singer-songwriter from Oak Cliff, Texas. His shelter name was Zeke. He was on the adoptable side for two months, meaning every incoming dog his age, size and breed was temp tested against Zeke. There was a reason for this. The questionable test was very hard to pass. A dog would be pulled from his kennel, put nose to nose against a strange dog in a dark hallway. Even if the resident dog had passed the test many times, should he show any fear or aggression, he'd be pulled from adoptables and placed right back on the stray side. Most didn't make it out again. They term it 'kennel crazy'. Since not every dog likes every dog, many good dogs fall through the cracks by use of this system. Many people live their lives with great dogs that don't love every single dog they meet.

The other reason there were not enough good dogs to temp test was the cap at only allowing six pit bull dogs for adoption at any given time. Most shelters don't want to look like a houseful of pit bulls. All over the country, shelters are full of pit bulls. A good shelter is the one who gives all worthy dogs a chance at adoption based on sound temp tests rather than breed. A good shelter doesn't have empty kennels. CCACC always has empty kennels.

During Zeke's time, Doc had quietly begun implementing his 'keep it small and clean' plan. As he'd mentioned in the spotlight proposal meeting, Room 116 had indeed been changed from the pit bull room to just another room of dog kennels. Every breed was mixed in. Word had it that Burns had something to do with the move. Supposedly a pit bull in Room 116 was barking too loud next to her office and she ordered the dog moved back to the stray section.

I noticed fewer and fewer pit bulls in the adoptable side and from that time on, never counted more than four adoptable pit bulls at any one time. Colleen had unexpectedly broken with Big Top Pit Bull Team after a row with their president. Even though she'd been pestering me to finalize Junior's adoption, Colleen suddenly left CCACC and forgot all about Junior. If I'd not gone to the front counter and brought it up myself, Junior's file would still be floating around like a stray dog running around town.

When Zeke grinned, he was dead ringer for Stevie Ray. He looked like he had a big jawbreaker in each cheek. He was buff colored and part Shar-Pei. I would reach down to pet him and always laugh at his funny coat. He was covered in short fur with a long hair ever so often placed about an inch apart. It resembled a Tex Avery cartoon when the fleas would run up and down the dog's back and hide behind the large animated hairs as big as tree trunks. He was a funny and sweet boy.

Stevie Ray and I walked all over the city. At first, he really pulled on the leash, but I was determined to train him on a flat collar. I'll never forget our first breakthrough when a dog approached us. Instead of pulling on the leash and acting crazy like 'gotta meet that dog, gotta meet that dog", Stevie sat for a treat and looked up at me. My heart just soared. Stevie had gotten it. He was very proud of himself, as he should have been.

Room 112 is the contagious disease room. This is where I'd found Tish. The diseases usually range from demodectic mange or kennel cough to any number of easily curable maladies. Demodex is not contagious to other animals or humans. It affects dogs with a weakened immune system and usually transmitted from mother to pup. It's nasty to look at and usually evident from loss of fur or scaly, scabby spots. In fact, as I've gotten more familiar with holistic treatment and namely homeopathy, I've found that demodex is generally outgrown and requires no treatment. Most vets don't want us to know this. I have used toxic dips and oral drops, but today rely on a solid raw diet and homeopathy to cure almost everything that comes across Round Up's path. When considering how simple it is to cure demodex, I am horror stricken to think about these Room 112 dogs being routinely killed even today at CCACC.

For the next two years, I placed a call interested party or hold on every adoptable dog in Room 112 with demodex. Each of these dogs is now living in a good home, trained and a happy member of their family and community. One dog in particular had fallen through the cracks as do so many at this shelter. She was a backyard dog and not really a standout. She was all black with a white blaze on her chest. She had short spindly bow-legs.

I got a late afternoon call from Lt. Dane. He asked if I would be interested in taking her. If I didn't pick her up in the next hour, she was going down. I was driving and had no latitude for finding a foster home. I had to scramble to get her into a vet hospital who boarded dogs at the last minute. It wasn't my favorite, but the usual facility where I boarded couldn't take in a sick dog. I had to write a personal check to get her from the shelter, because the rescue was tapped. Rescues pay the same as the public for animals, but CCSPCA, even though a multi-million dollar corporation is charged no fee to pull animals.

When I picked her up, I fell in love. She had a tiny knot on her head, which they'd called demodex and landed her on the euthanasia list. She had rubbed her head against something when confined outdoors at her previous home and had developed the bump. Pit bulls and all dogs in general make terrible outdoor pets. They want to be indoors with us. Pit bulls are very social dogs and thrive upon human contact. I have to force my own dogs to go outside and enjoy the sunshine. There are permanent smears on the door glass where they press their noses.

Her coat was a deep brown-black with an unusual sheen to it. I'd seen the color before at the supermarket. She was the exact color of a black Kalamata olive. Her underside was dreary brown like the olive's center. I named her Olive. She was one of the sweetest dogs I'd ever met. She seemed about two or so and her history stated that she'd come from a Hispanic family. The nephew had brought her home with him and then moved on leaving Olive behind. The aunt kept her outside where she played and babysat the family's toddlers, a modern day redux of the breed history.

Pit bulls are one of the most child and human friendly of all dog breeds. When the public began using the dogs for bull baiting and later on, dog fighting in the 1800's, the owners needed assurance they wouldn't be bitten when pulling the dog from the pit. All dogs showing human aggression were culled. Even with all of the horrible backyard breeding still rampant today, the need to bond with their human is a strong trait of the pit bull terrier. Olive was a very people and child friendly dog and remains so to this day. Olive is a classic tribute to the breed. The media exploits the tragic incidents involving mostly unaltered and untrained dogs. Many of the dogs involved in maulings have acted out in packs and with pack mentality. One doesn't hear about the hundreds of thousands of well-behaved dogs.

I had Olive a couple of months. During this time, I had the opportunity to house a couple of dogs at Pacific Animal Hospital and animal shelter. This hospital had a contract with CCACC to handle the medical for the city's animals. Their shelter was quite successful as it was located in a posh residential area. Olive was one of the first Round Up dogs to enjoy the lush benefits of this lush institution.

Olive wasn't what you'd call a looker. She was bypassed by most for the cuddly puppies at the adoption events we attended. I loved Olive, but even I knew she didn't have the superstar looks, which would improve her adoption potential. Whenever the stress of rescue and life weighed heavy on my shoulders, Olive would cheer me up. She was always in a good mood and always had a smile no matter what storm was brewing around her. She was oblivious to stress. To me, she had a beauty beyond description.

I got a call regarding Olive. A nice sounding woman had just lost her beloved boxer to cancer and was looking for a dog to save. Her son had found Olive's picture on the website and said, "Mom, I want her!"

I was kind of surprised, because there were so many cute dogs up for adoption at the time. I didn't want to get our hopes up. The son had been looking at all of the adoption websites and said, "that's her, Mom. This one is the dog I want."

That Saturday, I went in a bit early to walk Olive. It never hurts to introduce a dog for the first time a little tuckered out. A tired dog is a good dog and a good dog is a tired dog. Pitties are born hams and will get all worked up when they think someone's paying attention. We went for a little jaunt in the nearby upscale park filled with yorkies and the like. Olive didn't care. They were all just friends to her. She was happy playing with all of the other dogs in the sunshine, glad to be outside. Though she was a backyard dog who'd escaped the blue juice by a sheer stroke of luck, she couldn't have been happier had she been a Queen Elizabeth Pembroke Welsh Corgi.

We got back to the hospital and saw Olive's potential adopter sitting in the lobby amidst all of the local gentry and their pets awaiting appointments. She jumped up and ran over to us. "There's my girl! There's my Olive!"

It was truly a case of love at first sight. Olive was as smitten as her new mom to be. She turned and asked if she could take her dog for a walk. I knew it was meant to be. I've been through my share of failed meetings and letdowns, but when it's the right match, what a charge. You just know. What a great day this was for Olive and for me. What a great day for her new family.

I have posted a document on the website called the Step 1-2-3 Pit Bull Starter Kit. It shows the new adopter how to crate train a dog in no time flat. I have never met a dog that didn't respond to this system. The crate gives them confidence and centers them by simulating their den instinct. Most dogs sleep 18 out of 24 hours, at least the lazy ones I've met. By implementing a few training tips with the Kong and following the simple suggestions on the Step 1-2-3 doc, just about any person can have a secure and satisfied dog. When mom gets home from work, she is met by her happy dog, who's been chewing his Kong and napping all day, the radio playing soft music. To end the day with a nice dog walk is probably as good as it's ever going to get.

Olive and her new bff came back to the hospital on a cloud. Both of the girls looked very happy with one another. She loved Olive and was thrilled with how well Olive walked on the leash. She had to work the next week and asked if she could begin the foster to adopt process the following weekend. She was beginning her vacation and thought that would be the perfect time to bring a new dog home.

Scott and I loaded Olive up the next Friday night along with her starter kit and crate. Round Up tries to supply a crate, food, treats, toys and a free drop in training class for every dog in our program. This gets everyone off to a good running start and insures a happy, solid beginning.

Olive was a hit in her new home. Her adopter, like most people, was a little bit unsure about the pit bull thing. Her family was avidly against her adopting a pit bull. She was a dog savvy person, but had no experience with the breed other than what she'd seen on television. I let her know I was available 24/7 should she have any questions no matter how insignificant they might seem.

Olive's only problem was a little piddling in the house. This is common, especially among the females. They almost always have an accident or two. I have gotten more than a few calls over the years complaining they thought the dog was housebroken. I refer back to the Step 1-2-3 Starter Kit. Sometimes the dogs just need a refresher. Crating is not a bad thing, although some of the adopters have expressed doubts. They must be reassured and learn to stimulate the dog's natural inclination. In the wild, a dog will look for a den where he can crawl inside and sleep. To this day, Rebel greets me with a big yawn and sleepy eyes when I get home. I always have to bust him for sleeping on the job.

As Round Up became more successful at finding great homes for dogs on the CCACC euthanasia list, I was getting more and more calls from the shelter to take dogs. It was getting out of hand. I didn't have a city budget and huge facility with personnel to care for the animals like they did. In fact, this particular day, I got a call to pick up three dogs! Again, these three had been turned down by CCSPCA for 'no history' that meant they took no stray pit bull breeds.

Their names were Ollie, Oscar and Huckleberry. I had named Huckleberry and the shelter had named Ollie and Oscar. A kennel attendant was rounding up the dogs when I arrived to pull them. I noticed besides these three, there were no other dogs in the section of kennels in Room 114. This was the largest of three sections of kennel rooms used to house available dogs for adoption. These dogs were obviously not pit bulls, even though they'd been listed as such by Lydia Bench. I was getting used to her frequent mistakes. It would have been funny if a brindle spot didn't mean death row. To Bench, brindle coloring meant one thing....pit bull. Ollie and Oscar were obvious Whippet mixes while Huck had the leftover gene of a randy Greyhound.

The three dogs looked up at me from their kennels while the attendant on duty, Francisco, yelled at me to get them out of there. I asked, "what's the big hurry?"

He replied they were resurfacing the floor and needed to close off this roomful of kennels immediately. Per the system, the three had been offered to CCSPCA that morning and refused almost as quick. Fortunately, I had placed the holds or they would be headed to Room 132 for the sake of a shiny new floor. Brilliant.

One young lady was interested in Ollie, but here were not bites for Huck or Oscar. My first order of business was to change those names. Years before at the Video Bar, we held a festival called 'if you can't change your life, change your name'. Oscar and Ollie and I held a reprise of that good time that afternoon. Huckleberry's name was perfect. If Tom and Huckleberry had a dog, he'd have been just like Huckleberry. You couldn't tell what he was supposed to be, long and rangy, a goofy boy with a big grin. Huck was a misfit, but he was in fine company.

Ollie and Oscar looked something like young Barney Fifes gone way wrong. I named one Artemus Pyle and the other one, Dickie Betts. They looked like they'd grown up on Southern fried rock and had a meth lab in their resume. I was able to board them for about a minute at the fancy hospital since Olive had been adopted. Dickie went home with the young lady who'd shown an interest as a foster. She had never had a dog and was a tad nervous. Again, we were slammed on Craigslist for allowing people to adopt/foster pit bulls who didn't have pit bull experience. FYI, Big Top, Dickie wasn't then and still isn't a pit bull, but doing fine with the inexperienced home we placed him in. Jennifer, his mom, became a dog professional and works in a doggy daycare.

This sort of gossip doesn't do us or the dogs one bit of good. I held my own and continued fostering to adopt to people willing to attend class and abide by the guidelines of our program. The people without experience have ended up being the best adopters. I believe they are so determined to have the perfect dog that they follow the crating and other suggestions resolutely. The end result was perfectly behaved dogs in loving homes, their guardians proud and very rightly so. We had a little boot camp going. I asked the adopters to feed a high quality food in which I've upgraded to organic humane raw diet. I couldn't save all of the animals in the world, but have asked the families of these saved ones to not support pet foods made from inhumane and unhealthy sources.

When I consider all of the animals in research labs and rendering plants, I am ashamed. We can hope for a better day when people spay and neuter their pets. If more of us were conscious of animal overpopulation, there would not be so many homeless and unwanted pets. There would be no more corporate owned rendering plants where these poor euthanized souls end their days. I yearn for the day when ingredients like 'by-products' and 'bone-meal' are viewed as the travesty they are. I yearn for the day when we do not have to turn our heads to not see the horror that goes on.

Dickie Betts had landed himself in a great home. His new mom forsook the big city and left with Dickie for her home back in Wisconsin. They were the second family to leave Coastal County. The first, Chester Heidleberger, lives in the Czech Republic with his mom. At some point in each dog's rescue, it's time to let go and realize your work is done. To me, that is the hard part. Dickie wound up hobnobbing with the stars. His mom took Dickie to an Allman Brothers concert where he met his namesake, Dickey Betts. They posed for paparazzi outside the concert hall and next to the tour bus. Our Dickie looks like he doesn't know what to do with the real Dickey. It's my favorite picture.

Sluggo was another dog that wasn't a pit bull. Sluggo wound up on the euthanasia list just the same. He was three months old when Round Up was called to pick him up. He was adorable. He looked just like the stuffed animal, Pound Puppy. Sluggo was mainly American Bulldog, but he had those incredibly long Basset ears. He was all white with fawn tips and a couple of spots here and there. He had absolutely no muscle tone. He was a soft bag of bones. I made a mistake with Sluggo. A man, a policeman, applied to adopt him and passed our foster to adopt regulations. After the preliminaries and paperwork, I allowed him to foster Sluggo. I called to follow up and saw a completely different side of the man. He claimed that Sluggo was now his and he was keeping him.

I was unable to sleep. I asked two of my rescue friends to accompany me and we headed for the house where Sluggo was being kept. The police and animal control were notified and met us at the address. It was a very warm and sunny day. The ACO grabbed ad come-along out of the van and we all laughed. We told him he probably wouldn't need that particular piece of equipment, as Sluggo was only three months old. He reluctantly placed it back into his truck.

There was no answer at the door. We heard whining. The three of us rescue girls and officers took a look across the fence. There sat Sluggo, pure white in the blazing sun. His little eyes were sunburned. He was crying. One of the girls, D, had been his previous foster mom. He was very dependent on D. She almost started crying as well. The officers had to report back to work, but each pointed to the back of the house. The policeman said he wanted to explain to us clearly that those hills behind the house were fire trails which one could access the backyards of this subdivision. Point taken, after they left, we went to work.

D couldn't be stopped. She is a gorgeous statuesque blonde Irish girl and a former model. She hiked herself over the privacy fence and grabbed Sluggo. We got into the car and put the pedal to the metal. Do whatever you need to do to walk out with the dog. There was never a happier puppy than Sluggo was that day. As we drove home that gorgeous sun-drunk California day, I began to laugh. The two blondes in the front seat turned around and asked what was so funny. "Did you hear the one about the Jew, the Catholic and the redneck who stole the pit bull?" That was a good day. All dogs ought to have these three blondes at their back.

These two gals were the essence of rescue. We have all traveled on in search of our own destinies. B was a California artist who created the most incredible pictures of sad dogs in shelters. D was broken by this world. At the time I knew her, she had a beautiful home by a lush park. She shared her home with many animals in need. D was swindled out of her home by a crooked real estate developer. He put her and all of her animals out on the street. When D asked him what she was supposed to do with the dogs, he said, "I don't care. Call animal control."

This was the same ACC who routinely put all of the pit bulls and mixes to sleep. D didn't lose one dog. She found places to put her and the dogs up. She is still saving dogs today, persevering through hardship, her own story not too different from the stories of the dogs she saves.

She had a crazy brother who had a dog named Pig. Pig's full name was the Outlaw Josey Wales. This brother was just plain mean. He wore a full-length leather coat and was covered in ink. He was a charter member of a notorious motorcycle club and called D one night to tell her he was going to kill Pig and cut her up into little pieces. D, being one of the most fearless people I've ever met, broke into the chapter clubhouse and amid drunken passed out club members, stole Pig. Talk about walking out with the dog! She kept Pig safe by her side and very much loved until Pig's death many years later.

A lot of time has passed since we re-rescued Sluggo. Over the years, there have been some deaths and some happy times. Rare is the day in rescue when 24 hours passes by without heartache or a little ray of joy. That's just part of the deal. You have to do what you have to do to walk out with the dog. It won't always make you a lot of friends, but the relationships that do endure are priceless.

Chapter Eleven
More Dogs

Been Caught Stealing
by Jane's Addiction

The First Ones

Madeline was typical of the dogs I'd see on a daily basis at CCACC. She was only five months old, but for a pit bull, she was considered an adult. With any other dog breed I can think of, five months is regarded as a puppy in shelter life. Many pits do look like adults at five months. Madeline was adorable with a deep reddish brown auburn coat and white blaze and a spray of freckles across her nose that gave her the zestiness of a little French girl. She looks like a pittie version of Isabelle Huppert.

She marched with us at Gay Pride where she met her wonderful dad, Todd. It was another case of love at first sight. Todd was due to march in the parade, but made me promise on a stack of bibles I would not adopt Madeline to anyone else. He loved her and would do whatever he needed to do to become Maddy's new daddy.

There was a slight hitch. Todd was staying at his parents temporarily. They had Tibetan Terriers and weren't too hip on another dog in the house. He was in the process of moving and asked me to keep Maddy until he was settled. Before long, though, Mom and Dad met Maddy and they fell in love with her, too! Most pitties are very manipulative and will do what they need to do to make the situation work to their advantage. Maddy was not different and set her beret towards winning the hearts of even her most defiant objectors. This was many moons ago and not only is Maddy raw fed and homeopathically treated, so is her brother, Sluggo. Yes, Darren, Todd's partner adopted Sluggo who is now called Wiley. Maddy is nine, Wiley, seven and they have just added a new member to the family, Henry. Henry is a little deaf puppy who fits in very nicely in his new home. For anyone cautious about adopting a deaf pup, take a page from Henry's book. Adopt with another dog and they literally train themselves by watching the resident dog.

Sadie Jane was a leggy three-month old black pittie mix. She came in with her two siblings whom I named T. Boz, Left-Eye and Chili, but the custody lady changed to names a bit more palatable for public consumption. There were all put on the kill list. The shelter was full and I began scrambling for homes. Quick solutions take money and resources. Round Up was and is always a day late and a dollar short on both, but I still knew how to type. I posted an ad on Craigslist.

By that evening, I had a reply from a very nice man who lived up on the Russian River. He'd been thinking about getting a dog and agreed to come in and meet Sadie. I knew it would be a hard sell, as he had no pit bull experience. I told him if he'd work with me, I would adopt Sadie and foster to adopt to him. This plan became the standard operating procedure from that day on.

M met us at the shelter the next day. He fell in love with little Sadie. Who wouldn't? She had a habit of laying on her back in your arms with her skinny legs splayed all over the place. M played with her in the side yard for hours. By the time he had to leave for work, she had him wrapped around her front paw. He assured me he wanted to adopt Sadie and asked me to begin the process. Then something very strange and awful happened. That evening, a volunteer came in to walk the dogs. Sadie was unable to leave her kennel. She lay in the back and could not stand up. No matter how hard she tried, her back legs would not function.

The volunteer was emotionally distressed and afraid she had caused Sadie's lameness. After a bit of investigation, it was found that the last shelter employee to enter that section of kennels had been seen slamming the door on Sadie's legs, followed by a loud whelp from Sadie. His initials were scribbled on the kennel card attached to the cage. He was immediately given his walking papers. Stranger still, he'd been fostering a male pit puppy for the shelter. The puppy's record was expunged and deleted, unlawfully. A copy of that puppy's record remains with Deputy Jill Burns' signature right across the bottom. In effect, not only did this employee maim Sadie, but was allowed to keep another innocent puppy without any supervision or monitoring. Whatever happened to that dog is anyone's guess. The dog's record was hidden and he was given to a known animal abuser by Deputy Burns to save face of the shelter.

I called M and told him about Sadie. This grown man almost broke down. "She was fine when we were out in the side yard playing."

I told him we certainly didn't expect him to adopt a dog in need of thousands of dollars in surgery and rehabilitation. I asked him if he might consider adopting another dog. We had several younger pups at the shelter and if he found one to share his home with, it might buy Sadie a bit of time so we could figure something out. Robbing from Peter to pay Paul, so to speak.

He met me again at the shelter and found another love of his life, a little fat black and white boy he named Jackson. There are so many unwanted dogs, really good dogs, whose only fault is overpopulation. It was a go on Jackson and the foster/adoption process jumpstarted with Sadie's name scratched out and Jackson's penciled in. Sadie earned a couple of days' grace and we were able to save her.

She needed $6,000 for two TPLO (tibial plateau leveling osteotomy) operations, as both of her back legs had been broken. That's a lot of money to pay for an owned dog, but really hard for a rescue to come up with. In the meantime, a lovely couple, parents of a beautiful female pit, Nikita and a gorgeous Shar-Pei, Mao, offered to foster Sadie during her surgeries and recovery. This was huge. A very sweet little girl who'd won the heart of all her met her did not deserve the rotten hand she'd been dealt by the shelter and it's employee. We renamed her Sadie Jane.

How was I to come up with all of the money and quickly? I decided to have a fundraiser. My favorite all time movie is The Incredible Journey, referring to the original 1960 one starring Bodger, Tao and Luath. I love the ending so much when old Bodger, the bull terrier is thought to have died, but comes hobbling over the hill barking the unmistakable bulldog bark which sounds like their vocal chords have been cut. Only an evil serial killer wouldn't be moved to tears at this ending. When we watch this film, my cat, Buddy, gets on top of the tv and tries to swat the goings on inside.

Disney wouldn't allow us to use the movie for a straightforward fundraiser, so we got creative. We had tee shirts printed with 'Sadie Jane's Incredible Journey' and the Round Up logo. We charged $20 for the tee shirt that had to be worn into the theatre for admission. The result looked like an old 50's movie theatre photograph with the patrons wearing 3-D glasses. Instead, the theatre seats were filled with animal lovers wearing Sadie Jane tee shirts. The movie house even allowed our guest of honor, Sadie Jane, to attend the move. I get more out of any movie when watching with an animal. Just ask Buddy.

We raised a lot of money. Some of the people who couldn't attend the movie made outright donations to help Sadie Jane. There was the other Buddy, a big caramel cow-spotted Round Up pit bull whose dad, J, owns a popular barbershop. Buddy and J sold a lot of tee shirts to help Sadie Jane. Little Daisy Duke's mom, L, came. Daisy Duke was an 8 week boxer/pittie mix that had been found with her leg fractured in four places. Daisy Duke had been our first injured dog and who'd also needed surgery to repair her leg. The doctor put a bright yellow surgical wrap on her broken leg and this had inspired her adorable name. There were many people who helped raise money to save Sadie Jane. Todd and Darren threw out all the stops to help us raise the money to save Sadie Jane's legs.

Even though Sadie Jane's injury was caused by a rotten person and covered up by the shelter, the goodness of human nature prevailed. A gathering of gracious souls populated the theatre that day to watch the best movie ever made. I believe Sadie Jane's faith in human beings was restored that day. She never once showed any fear or aggression after her legs were broken. Sadie Jane was content to sit in your lap with her legs hanging down, relaxed and happy.

I learned to ask the community. There isn't always a magic cure for every problem, but people do want to help. All it takes is being willing to help. If more outreach were done, so many animals being euthanized due to surgical or other fixable problems could be saved. Most of the time at CCACC, the animals are destroyed without the public ever knowing they could have helped. Most people, even though busy and having problems of their own, will take a minute and fish out a dollar or two to help an animal in need. There is more good than bad in this world, I believe. With CCACC, though, someone does need to monitor the goings on. To this very day, animals are still slipping through the cracks in the CCACC system.

When the time came to schedule Sadie Jane's first surgery, she was under the care of the best TPLO surgeon in the area. The nurse took Sadie Jane to the back for current x-rays. When the doctor met with us, he said he had a bit of good news. It seemed Sadie Jane's situation was rather a toss up. Her legs had been broken at such a young age that they were growing back together and in good form. Had this happened to an older dog, the surgery would have been critical and necessary. The doctor told us we could go ahead with the surgery, but it was my call. Either way, with surgery or naturally, the legs might have a slight limp. He suggested we wait and see if she continued to heal on her own.

Over the next few months, we went to the large dog park nearby the foster couple's home. Each Saturday morning became a dog party, full of dog loving folks who brought their beloved pets. These Saturday mornings became an opportunity for Round Up dogs to join in the fun. Any Saturday, you'd see Tutti Frutti or Zorro playing among the family pets. Sadie Jane would be laying peacefully on the grass, watching the other dogs frolic in the sunshine, looking like the Andrew Wyeth painting, Christina's World. Everyone was so good to her. She had become a favorite at the park, all of the patrons paying their respects beneath the huge magnificent palm trees swaying in the ocean breeze.

The good fresh air of freedom and lots of love had helped Sadie Jane avoid the knife. Right about then, another pup that had also been in Room 112 needing saving and surgery. He'd torn his cruciate, a common malady of the pittie breeds. We were able to rescue him and pay for the surgery to repair his leg. A volunteer at the shelter fostered him, fell in love and formally adopted him. He went on to become Chester Heidleberg and now lives with her in her homeland, the Czech Republic.

Sadie Jane met her new dad at the park. He'd recently lost his longtime companion dog to old age and fell in love with Sadie Jane. He lives in a fabulous three story home right on the Pacific Ocean. Nothing like that salty sea air to heal the spirit and whatever else might ail you. Sadie and her dad watch the sunrise every day with the wind right on their faces. From a rocky beginning, Sadie Jane had an incredible journey to an idyllic life.

Jackson was enjoying his new life on the river. As luck would have it, though, several years later, Jackson tore both acl's and had to have surgery on both legs. I had tried to save Jackson's dad from dealing with the expense of surgery and rehab by taking Sadie Jane and giving him Jackson. He and Jackson had to endure not one, but two surgeries and Sadie Jane healed on her own. It just goes to show, you can't manage nature.

With the torn cruciate being such a common ailment among the pits, we set up a deal with a local vet who gives Round Up a special price on the surgery. It is not the TPLO surgery, but the old school cruciate surgery. This is the same surgery that Mookie, my own boy, had on his leg. Mookie wasn't a pit bull, but tore his aco one Christmas when he literally 'hit the wall' at the dog park.

The dog's main two options are TPLO or the old style cruciate surgery. I prefer the old cruciate surgery. It's not as trendy, a lot cheaper and a bit less invasive. However, over the years, I've come to prefer conservative management and homeopathy. There are huge strides being successfully made without having surgery at all. If you are going to have to crate your dog until the surgery heals anyway, why not go ahead and crate beforehand? With conservative management and homeopathy, you and your dog have nothing to lose and nothing but restoration to good health to gain.

Mookie had a frightening experience. He'd made it through his surgery and was recuperating like an old soldier in a VA hospital. He was on a very strong pain medication and anti-inflammatory. I was hesitant to use it due to the warning of liver failure in some dogs. Now that I know better, it's homeopathy all the way for the dogs, cats and the birds. I have even broken my toe a couple of times and treated myself homeopathically. I felt no pain and walked 10 miles the day after the break. Mookie somehow got into the pain meds and ate the entire bottle. Right next to the chewed up bottle of beef flavored tablets was an empty can of fish food. My sister, Martha, remarked that old Mookie had a hankering for surf and turf.

Mookie was as stoned as he could be. He was sitting on his dog bed a howling his Mookie yowl, mouth wide open and head lolling back and forth. I rushed him to the hospital where they immediately went to work pumping his poor old stomach. Mookie was saved, but it was a close call. Another reason to question the use of such a serious medication.

Waylon was an adorable soft brindle boy in a kennel with his sister. I named them Waylon and Jesse after the Jennings. He was very shy and about four months old. They were beautiful puppies with deep luscious coffee and chocolate tones throughout their velvety coats. Amazingly, the CCSPCA adopted Jesse. Occasionally, the CCSPCA would sashay through the adoptable side and save a token pit bull. They took Jesse and left Waylon sitting alone in the kennel. There were several other dogs that had passed temperament tests, but for some odd reason, the experts chose to break up the bonded siblings. After their team left, it was noted on Waylon's kennel card that he was hand shy. When Waylon's time was up later that afternoon, Round Up took him into our program. Ironically, we found a wonderful foster home for him and she worked for the CCSPCA.

We all worked together to train Waylon. He surprised us right away as he began to shed his shyness exhibited at the shelter. I am amazed at people, those recognized as expert in the world of dogs, not acknowledging how a dog behaves in a shelter situation. It is quite difficult to capture a true reading on a dog in a loud, clanging facility with new dogs coming and going at all hours and constant loud, terrified barking. It took Waylon a little while, but he became quite happy to go on walks outside. At first, he was frightened of cars, but the more we encouraged him and gave him treats, the better he began to respond. Repetition strengthens and confirms and positive behavior is rewarded.

Waylon met two wonderful men and their Golden Retriever, Jake, at a mobile adoption event. They lived in a lovely Victorian down the street from one of the city's popular dog parks. Here was this little shy street urchin about to hit the big time. The couple fell in love with Waylon and the feeling was mutual. They changed his name to Benny. I never thought old Number One would've wanted a scaredy cat to carry his name. Jesse had become the guinea pig for a new training procedure at CCSPCA and unfortunately, had become afraid to go outside. I understand the only way the trainers could get her in or out would be with another dog. I'm still unclear about how their training was supposed to work.

Benny's dad began to have hearing problems and was

diagnosed with progressive deafness. To lose one's senses is terrifying, but Benny came to his rescue. His new dad began teaching Benny sign language and Benny became a hearing dog. This time, the dog rescued the rescuer. Benny became a very large hearing dog. At last weigh in, Benny tipped the scale at over 120 pounds!

Tish was still looking for a forever home, but quite settled in with her young foster mom and foster sister, Coco, a chocolate lab. We took Tish out every day to different dog parks around town and other sites of interest. At Pacific Animal Hospital, we were part of a big festival where folks came from all around to donate and see the adoptable dogs and cats. A nice family had written me about Tish. I set up our meeting to take place that spring day at the festival.

The dad was a single parent, a stay at home writer in Marin County with three daughters. Tish was all over them like glue and they fell in love with her. It was all good, a sure case of instant karma. The middle daughter looked like Scout in To Kill a Mockingbird. She had short straight brown hair and kept her arms wrapped around Tish all day. In the evening when we were packing up to go, she grabbed my tee shirt. "Can I have my dog? Can't I please take my dog home?"

Who could refuse that request? That was well past 8 years ago. Tish was renamed Roxie and except for a torn cruciate, she has lived a life full of luxury and love with the Marin headlands as a backdrop. I just looked at a photo of Tish after her mange had cleared up. She looks like a little pit bull princess. She wears a pink halter and leash and resembles Rowdy Cowgirl in coloring. Tish weighed 32 pounds that day we took her from CCACC, but she's put on some real life love handles since then. She's no longer a teacup.

At CCACC, a high profile case was boarded in the custody animals' section for over a year and a half. The green volunteers, such a pack unto themselves and always full of advice, weeded their group over this dog and long legal battle which ensued around her. Though there was never hope this dog would see the light of day, it was known she was going to be put to sleep as soon as the controversial trial ended in which she was an exhibit. Most pit bull pundits were very arrogant about the case and this dog, which was caught in the middle. Everyone had an opinion. The dog was being kept alive only until a verdict was reached.

One world-class trainer, renowned in rehabbing vicious dogs, had offered to take her into his program. I had seen recorded evidence of this man's work. He'd taped some very seriously abused and dangerous dogs completely turned around into sweet family pets. One dog who'd previously had bottle caps sewn under his eyelids and dragged through gravel by automobiles was sitting in the yard gnawing on a bone amidst chickens and crawling babies. Phenomenal work, yet Doc scoffed at his offer and refused to entertain the thought of rehabilitation.

After the case rested, blame and guilt properly allotted, the day came with the dog was scheduled to die. Whenever all seems lost, I am usually blessed with a pocket of hope. That day, my hope showed up in the package of Dulcie. Dulcie was a huge black and white cow of a pit bull. She'd been found as a stray at a huge park with a dead dog that had been hit by a car. Dulcie could have gotten away, but she'd stayed with her friend, the dog who had died. The two, Dulcie and the black lab, had been sighted for about a week or so at the park running and playing with one another. When they loaded Dulcie onto the ACC van, the ACO officer told me she saw a tear in Dulcie's eye.

I was outside with Dulcie when they euthanized the notorious custody dog. One of the cameramen was photographing us while I held a Frisbee up for Dulcie. She cleared the ground and did a spot on imitation of Snoopy as the camera captured her likeness for the news. He lowered his equipment and asked me, "what is it do you think that makes them so mean?" Without looking away from Dulcie, I answered with the truth. "The media."

A wonderful woman who lived across the street from that old park adopted Dulcie. She was so moved by Dulcie and the love Dulcie had for her friend, the lab. The nice lady who saved Dulcie had two older dogs that accepted Dulcie into their loving family. This nice woman was a gardener by trade. Each morning, she and her three dogs walk the lovely trails of the park where Dulcie had run with her friend. Sometimes, the dark clouds do have a silver lining.

Tucker was not a pit bull. He was a big red looking dog. Perhaps his history included a shepherd or maybe some retriever. This was the time of year they held the blessing of the animals. People bring their pets from all around to have them blessed. The blessings were held at an old downtown Spanish cathedral. Local shelters brought dogs and cats for the priests to bless. It was a huge public affair and a big media turnout. Somehow, I wound up with Tucker. My good friend and sweet, secret Round Up volunteer, Cathy worked as a kennel tech at the shelter. She took a dog and I got Tucker. Cathy had to fly under the radar in regards to Round Up. They didn't like employees to 'volunteer'. She was a caring soul who made sure the cat would have a blanket or the dog, a toy. This was a practice Deputy Burns frowned upon as a waste of time.

Cathy took a pit bull named Katie, which left Tucker. Every other dog in the available section had been selected but Tucker. Tucker was what Warren Zevon called an 'excitable boy'. Tucker started barking the minute we got out of the van and began to head toward the church. It must have been the shepherd, because he sounded a lot like Mookie. Mookie and I had recently begun attending anti-vivisection protests at the local medical university. Even though Mookie had been punished for barking in the past, he'd recently found his calling as an animal rights activist. We'd arrive at the protest and Mookie would start up with his resounding and repetitive barking. Instead of being hit or yelled at, though, the young protestors would clap and cheer him on. "Moo-kie, Moo-kie, Moo-kie!"

Tucker didn't have the same reception in the austere cathedral setting. That day of the blessing was extra special, because Jane Goodall was there. I was lucky enough to get to meet her in person. I had longtime been an admirer and reader of her books on primates. She was petting her stuffed monkey when I gushed out, 'this is Tucker." As he barked and barked excitedly, I added, "he's vocal."

Jane replied, "so I notice."

Everyone congregated inside the church house and settled down, everyone except Tucker, that is. He had no religious training and went on a barking spree. He was what we Texans call right proud to be there. They had a couple of priests running interference, one who finally came over and asked Tucker and me to leave. That was ok with us. We were non-denominational anyway.

Tucker and I went outside while the service proceeded and the blessings administered. There were several hundred animals to be blessed, so we had quite a long wait. There was a giant flowing fountain and surrounding pool to the right in the courtyard. Now, that was for us! Tucker and I looked at each other, like 'yeah'! Tucker was a water dog. He flat tore that fountain up. There was water everywhere. He splashed and partied like there was no tomorrow. For the next couple of hours, Tucker and I had the time of our lives. It was beautiful. To me, that was the blessing of the day. God might have been in the house, but he stepped outside with Tucker and me that wonderful, happy afternoon.

Chapter Twelve
T. Rex

A Song For You
by Gram Parsons

T. Rex

About that time, I met Scooby Doo. The small hospital where I'd boarded Olive and Sticker, the little bitty brindle girl, called me. Sticker had been adopted to a high school teacher and skateboarder. She was living large and learning to one eighty. I hadn't been by the hospital for awhile, so I was more than a little surprised when I got the call that day.

They asked me to take a look at a dog in their boarding kennels. What looked back at me was a version of what Scooby Doo would have looked like in real life. His left eye was glazed over. They told me he'd been beaten so badly, he'd been blinded in that eye. I looked at him and said, "oh, boy." He stared back with his good eye. "Grrrrrr." He looked so helpless in that kennel, so completely alone.

That night, I couldn't sleep. I tossed and turned all night with the vision of that poor puppy in my thoughts. I called the vet the next day to get more details. A longtime client of the vet had discovered this dog being abused by the owner. The old man, John, was on disability and HIV positive, but gave the abuser $40 out of his pocket to save the puppy from a horrible situation. He already had senior cats and dogs, but brought the puppy home anyway. When the old warlord landlord found out, he demanded John get rid of the pit bull. John boarded Scooby Doo at the vet office and paid the hospital out of his meager budget to vaccinate and neuter the little pup as well.

I called the man and we spoke for a while. I asked him should I take on Scooby, would he be willing to help me care for the dog. I wanted our trainers to look at Scooby and assess him. If for any reason they found him to be dangerous, I wouldn't be able to help. I am like the rest of the population who doesn't want to get involved. We all want a happy Hollywood ending, but sometimes, these only happen in the movies.

I made friends with Scooby. That wasn't too hard. He seemed to sense I was there to help him. Once he got out of the hospital kennel, we went for a walk. He was immediately great on the leash. That was a plus. Usually, when the dogs see me, all bets are off. They start jumping and I start yelling 'off' and they have no idea what I'm hollering about. Not jumping is an easy one, which just takes a little patience and standing like a tree stump. If you need patience, get yourself a jumpy dog. When the dog jumps and starts acting like a maniac, stand still and erect. You feel like a total goon, but after awhile, it really works. The dog gets bored and sits. Good boy, here's a cookie.

Scooby wasn't a jumper, though. His only issue was his trust in humans had nearly been destroyed. Both of the trainers I worked with met Scooby and did in-depth temperament tests with him. Each assessed that Scooby was a workable, though indeed damaged dog. Both trainers assured me if I were willing to put in the work, we could overcome his issues. Little did I know what course the path of my life would take after meeting him that first morning.

He was boarded at the facility I had recently started using to board dogs. It was an ideal situation and in Andy's own home. The dogs played all day and went to the dog park in groups throughout the day. There was nap-time and we supplied the kind of food we wanted the dogs to be fed. It was almost as good as being in a real home and better than many actual homes.

Scooby's real name was T-Rex. The old man had named him Rex and I couldn't pronounce that without laughing. I suggested we add a 'T' like the old 70's band, not the dinosaur. I agreed to take T-Rex on against my better judgment, but not against what my heart told me. I lay awake unable to sleep with the memory of little T-Rex growling pitifully at me from his kennel. I knew my job was to help T-Rex.

At first, T-Rex was skittish of most people, but he quickly began to respond to positive training. He was thriving in day care and at the boarding facility. Soon, Andy was sending me hilarious photos of T-Rex and Roy. Roy, another Round Up dog in boarding with Andy, was adopted soon after, but while

in boarding, those two became best chums. One of my favorite
photos was a particular day at naptime. All of the pit bulls were
asleep on Andy's bed, but T-Rex was sitting bolt upright as if to
guard the rest of the dogs while they slept. No sleeping on the
job for T-Rex. It was sad to watch T-Rex when all of the other
dogs went home at the end of the day.

He lived there for five years. During that time, T-Rex
went to the dog park every day. One day, a large dog at the
park began to pick on one of the smaller dogs in T-Rex's group.
The situation intensified at the big dog bullied the small one.
T-Rex came to the rescue. He stood between the little dog
and the bully as if to say, 'hey, bud, if you want to mess with
shorty here, you're gonna have to go through me'. After careful
consideration, the big dog finally gave up and wandered off.
This was the special kind of dog T-Rex was.

I suppose there was some Dane in T-Rex as he was
stately and golden. He could also be silly, both acting and
looking. We went everywhere together. We would visit an
old park that had been converted from a deserted army base.
We would explore for hours and hours to find a secret nook
populated by a single wild white rose. We would watch a
skittish pigeon yodeling his coo at us for disturbing his solitude.
We were the city's hideaways, its misfits. We would watch the
regulars swim the icy bay year round. We'd go out to the tip of
a small peninsula near the yacht basin where we'd listen to the
natural organ of wind at high tide. We'd watch an old wrecked
ship for hours. Some days, the sky was as plate grey as the
ocean. We loved it. We were twin souls, T-Rex and I.

One day, we were walking down the high-end street
toward Pacific Animal Hospital, T-Rex squeaking the red
plastic bone in his mouth. As we walked, he'd chew it to make a
funny hee-haw noise. Busy people looked up from the sidewalk
at the disturbance only to see this funny boy with his noisy
bone. It was nice to see a smile replace an irritated look. One
day at Castle Lake, T-Rex saw his first swan. He just didn't

know what to do with that critter. He play-bowed and barked at the swan, but could not get any reaction. The swan just looked blankly at this silly creature. The swan finally glided on by while completely oblivious to T-Rex's antics. Quite a crowd had gathered to witness the commotion, laughing and applauding.

We were always invited to local animal events. On one occasion, we attended a popular dog get together with T-Rex and Tutti Frutti. She was a bigheaded brindle girl who'd been put on the CCACC euthanasia list for pulling on the leash. The volunteers didn't like to walk her, so they wrote on her kennel card and she was moved back to the stray section. She might have been a handful, but she is a good-natured handful. She certainly didn't need to be killed for leash pulling. Tutti Frutti was a rambunctious girl just looking for a good time. T-Rex entered the doggy costume party as Vegas Elvis. Tutti was supposed to be a pink poodle, but looked more like a deranged saloon girl. T-Rex won first prize that day.

T-Rex got some good news. It came in a bittersweet way. I was going to adopt T-Rex. He'd been boarding with Andy for three years. I brought him home with me and kept him separate from Girl, Junior and Rebel. We'd lost our Mookie recently. He'd passed away in his sleep after suffering for years with mega-esophagus, a rare disease causing the dog to regurgitate his food. We had tried everything. All animals had been switched to a raw organic diet. Mookie ate little meals throughout his day from an elevated feeding station. He had responded well to acupuncture. We boarded Mookie and Rebel with Andy for a much needed vacation. I received a call from Andy that Mookie had passed away in his sleep. I no longer take vacations.

T-Rex had been in a couple of foster to adopt situations. The first had been with a young man with deep-seated personal and emotional issues. That one didn't last. The next foster home had been with a young lady who'd worked for our veterinarian. She had a dominant and aggressive female Akita, but T-Rex got along with her dog quite well. He was respectful of the 'office-manager' type dogs. I underwrote his continued training with Billy Best and she would bring her Akita along as well. T-Rex had been in training since he was a four-month puppy. He was great at obedience work.

After T-Rex had been with the young woman for almost a year, I received a call from her late one night. She had moved in with her boyfriend's mother. The mother would take the aggressive Akita, but not a pit bull. It was back to Andy's for T. Scott and I had a long talk and decided to take T-Rex and try and make it work. We incorporated much of the training we had done with Junior and Rebel with T-Rex. We took long seaside walks with T-Rex and Junior in hopes of bonding them. I knew it would be a stretch. Both were young, male and medium to large red males. We brought in Girl, then Rebel and the next thing you know, we were the best looking dog pack on the coast. We enjoyed many beautiful walks along the beach and the mountains behind our lovely coastal digs. The terrain was incredibly lovely and wild. There were so many places to explore. Those walks remain some of my happiest memories. This is how I'd imagined rescue work would be. We spent many days exploring the wild parkland right outside our home in a tiny seaside village.

T-Rex loved nature. It was funny to watch him gently smell a wildflower in bloom. He would lift his head up and feel the wind blow soft on his floppy ears. He seemed to be wondering what kind of flower he was sniffing. He loved birds and would sit and watch them take flight for long periods of time. Our house and lawn were the habitat of a regal red-shouldered hawk. He'd been there for decades. My neighbor across the road had been watching him train those young hawks for years from her front porch. They would sweep majestically through the branches of the sequoia and redwood in our backyard. The trees I'd named Mother and Father were each over seventy feet tall. I would sit in the back with T-Rex and we

189

would watch the raptors. For a short time, everything was in its place and I was at peace with the universe.

One evening, out of the blue, T-Rex growled at Scott. I do not know why. He growled again. It was as if he had suddenly lost his trust in Scott. I suspected that it was connected to the abuse he'd suffered as a pup. For someone to bash a dog's head so hard as to blind him could possibly have caused neural injury. I was afraid. I couldn't take the chance that T-Rex showed human aggression. I called the trainer who knew T-Rex well. He loved T-Rex, but suggested we euthanize. I was devastated, but felt I owed Andy the truth. He loved T-Rex, too.

We made the appointment quickly. It was set for the next afternoon. I had been awake all night crying. I felt helpless and alone. The idea of putting down an otherwise healthy dog was something I had a very hard time with. I did not understand. This wasn't why I was in rescue work. Surely there had to be another answer. How was I going to hold T-Rex while they took his life? I had let T-Rex down. I felt I had betrayed him.

I had put other dogs down for aggression. There is nothing quite as awful. I am remembering Maybelle. Maybelle had been Lydia Bench's favorite dog at CCACC. Maybelle would be allowed to sit with Bench at her desk during work hours. Maybelle was a staffie bull mix, ruddy red in color with short, bowed trademark legs. She'd been used as a breeder and had the teats dragging the ground to show for it. Many dogs like Maybelle are used as moneymakers, churning out unneeded babies. These dogs all too often end up on the streets. When her time at CCACC ran out, I got the call. We took Maybelle into our foster to adopt program immediately, assured by Bench that this was an extraordinary dog.

Maybelle did well in foster care. She was at D's house, in very good hands, the best hands. A woman contacted us about Maybelle. She liked Maybelle's look and had a male who resembled her. We conducted a dog on dog temperament test with her boy and she filled out the application. After a home check, Maybelle was placed along with crate, food and treats to begin the foster to adopt process. The foster-adopter is carefully instructed how to crate and care for the dogs in their care. When not under direct supervision, the new dog is always to be crated.

I got a call from the woman that night. The two dogs had gotten into a fight. I wanted to be sure what happened. According to the woman, Maybelle had become possessive when on the bed with her. She was not exactly sure what happened after that, but a scuffle ensued and the woman had a hard time prying the dogs apart. She was very upset. I didn't want to make the wrong decision. D agreed that Maybelle did have some aggressive tendencies and the decision was made to euthanize her.

I took her for a long walk the next day. She was not interested in walking. Looking back, I believe she knew it was the end. Even though I hate MacDonald's, I tried to take Maybelle there for a double cheeseburger. She didn't want any part of it. She knew something was going on. She became frantic and upset. I remember that day too well. I hope I never forget it. When I carried her into the vet office, it was clear to her. I felt like a loser. I had let Maybelle down.

Where was the renowned behaviorist, Lydia Bench, now? Maybelle, her favorite dog from the shelter was going to be euthanized and all she had in her life was me. Was I allowing my fears to override rational decision-making? Was I so afraid of retribution from the militant rescue and shelter community that I was putting Maybelle down to avoid public scandal? There was a strong contingency that ruled the Craigslist forums. I'd already been the brunt of their daily slams using that platform. The small groups like Round Up and Outer Space Rescue have always been blasted by certain pit bull groups. These groups are always quick to euthanize prior to investigation.

Rehabilitation was never an option to these people until the Michael Vick extravaganza. When the lights went up and the television cameras began to roll, out came the Norma Desmonds of rescue. These groups never pulled one dog from CCACC, yet would travel across the entire country to the state of Virginia to save Michael Vick's dogs. For people who'd publicly chastised those of us for saving local 'sketchy' puppies, suddenly, rehab had become chic.

What was the answer? I couldn't take Maybelle home with me. We lived in that tiny cottage and had four dogs, four cats and a bird. It was an accident waiting to happen. I couldn't take her back to her foster home. With her aggression, she would debilitate in a boarding kennel. There were not enough places for gentle dogs to go and certainly no place for Maybelle to go. This was the cold, hard reality. I made the decision to put Maybelle down. It was an awful, black day, dismal and cold outside. The sun was a forgotten memory. I remembered the day Girl had gotten a hold of Ray. There is nothing more desperate than letting down an animal that depends on you for their life.

Angus McPherson wasn't even a pit bull. He was a big huge spotted black and white dog, a dead ringer for one of F. Horak's laboratory dogs. He had a pointed nose and some sight hound features. A woman had fallen in love with him at the pound and wanted to help. She already had a dog and couldn't adopt, but was willing to foster him until we could place him in a permanent home. The volunteers form CCACC had called me about Angus. I adopted him under our rescue with a blessing from Lydia Bench and Lt. Dane. Angus was a favorite among the staff and volunteers. Perhaps it was his unusual look. We did a one on one with the lady and her dog and the two seemed compatible. After his paperwork was completed, he received the mandatory vaccinations and was released to Round Up Rescue. I brought Angus to the loft where he'd be fostered along with the crate, food, treats and toys. I gave her the same list of instructions and criteria every foster person receives.

That night, I received a frantic call from the foster mom. She was afraid. After having tried to place Angus into his crate, he had snapped at her. He was roaming freely around her house and exhibiting strange behavior. She was unsure what to do. I asked her if she thought she could get Angus into her car. She was able to get him outside, but he became aggressive when they reached the car. At this point, I told her to wait and I would call the shelter. The situation had escalated to the point where I felt she was at risk.

There were only three people on duty at CCACC, the counter person, a kennel tech and an ACO officer. It was nearing 8 o'clock and the shelter was soon closing. The counter person dispatched an alert to the on duty ACO officer. He had been sprayed by a skunk and refused to pick Angus up. I called the ACO myself and begged him to pick up the dog. I even offered to pay him! I was sincerely afraid for the foster mom's wellbeing. Finally, the kennel attendant agreed to remain late at the shelter. Luckily, the foster lived only one half mile away. In light of the Whipple incident, this sort of situation should never have been allowed to occur.

After a three-day hold period, Angus was euthanized at the shelter. Much later, I would see that same sort of behavior surface among other dogs who'd been over-vaccinated. Aggressive behavior is a regular symptom of over-vaccination. It would be several years before I would discover the realities and dangers of mandatory vaccinations. I would look back at what had happened with Angus, Maybelle and T-Rex and question whether or not I could have tried to help them. I do not know the answer. I do know I will work as hard as I can to find the solution.

At the time, I only knew there was no place for these dogs to go. I made a promise to Angus that day. I would never allow another animal to be euthanized at the shelter. I hoped I would never again have to euthanize an otherwise healthy pet. I do feel as though I let the dogs down. I think about them often. I hope wherever they are, they know I am very sorry. I have learned things I didn't know at the time. I know about flower essences and Chinese Traditional Medicine. I know about a raw, organic diet and purified water. I know about Waiora Cellular Defense, a supplement that pulls vaccinated toxins, metals and other toxicity from the body. I can share my experiences with people who have pets exhibiting aggressive behavior and who feel overwhelmed as I did. I can help other animals with the knowledge I've gained over the years. I may not have been able to save Maybelle and Angus, but in their memory, maybe some other animals can be saved. Hopefully, the day will come soon when we will not be forced by law to inject these poor creatures with deadly, harmful vaccines.

Chapter Thirteen
A Girl Like Slappy

Ohio
by Neil Young

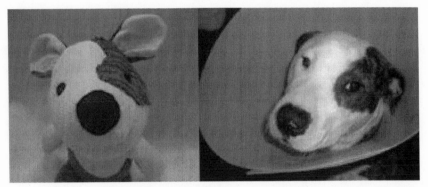

Slappy

When Slappy became available at CCACC, the place was fraught with chaos. A test of wills mingled with heavy discontent permeated throughout the shelter. Always a noisy den of clanging, banging and barking, the tension in the air was especially thick. Although Round Up Rescue had figured a way to close the gap and save many of these dogs, we had earned our share of enemies. The clique of women who volunteered with custody dogs had always shown antagonism, never missing a beat to make members of our group feel unwelcome at the shelter.

Two of our board members had become a part of the custody group. One of them had even disclosed that she felt most pit bulls should be euthanized. As in the meeting when Doc suggested we destroy all pit bulls but the spotlight dog, I felt sick to my stomach when I heard these words. This was a woman I had respected since my early picture taking days. I had trusted her to sit on our board. When she resigned from her post, I was happy. Sometimes the good lord takes care of us when we step aside.

By the time Slappy arrived on the scene, the battle lines had been drawn. There had been some ugly speculation in the hallways, emails and public internet forums. A girl who worked in a pricy downtown doggy daycare owned by a co-founder of Big Top Pit Bull Team volunteered to foster a Round Up pup. The pup had been found by the daycare manager upon opening one Monday morning in her crate, no food or water, and covered in her own urine and feces. This was unacceptable for any dog, especially a puppy. We took the dog back, but this unleashed a torrent of accusations and inflammatory gossip about our rescue.

My main focus was to find good homes for good dogs. When Slappy showed up with her big white happy face and lovely black, grey and white brindle body, I set my attention toward finding her a perfect home. Slappy had a lovely smile. It went on forever. When she smiled, everything lit up. You couldn't help but smile along. She was an extra special dog. There wasn't room for negative thoughts around Slappy. She just radiated happiness, even in this sad and complicated place. I took her photo and posted her on my site as well as the shelter site. A young couple emailed me almost immediately after Slappy went online.

I was held up elsewhere and couldn't show Slappy myself. I asked Cathy, who'd adopted Katie from the blessing of the animals, to show them. She was working as a kennel tech that afternoon at the shelter. I hung up the phone elated. Slappy had a shot at a new life. The couple had filled out our online application and was perfect for her. The young lady had grown up with pit bulls and loved the breed. There was hope.

That night, the young woman who had been scheduled to meet with Slappy called. She said they had loved Slappy and wanted to proceed with the foster to adopt. She mentioned there was something else that had happened. Was it customary for a dog to be sprayed with a hose during an introduction? The lady who'd showed Slappy to them in the side yard had apparently sprayed the dog with the outdoor fire hose.

I was surprised to hear this. Certainly, Cathy hadn't sprayed the dog. Cathy was gentle to a fault. In fact, we'd exchanged several conversations about the dangers of the firehose. Slappy's potential new mom explained that Cathy wasn't the person who'd introduced Slappy, but a volunteer in a green apron. The volunteer had appeared surly when she told the couple to wait outside in the yard. After a long wait, the volunteer led Slappy out on a plastic slip lead. This alone was against CCACC protocol. Pit bulls were to wear a flat or Martingale collar attached to a standard lead for all outings. Slappy had been spayed the day before and was not supposed to go outside under any circumstances. All newly spayed and neutered animals were to be introduced in the get acquainted room, CCACC rules.

Even fresh out of surgery, pit bulls love to perform and

Slappy wasn't any different. She knew this was her big chance. All it took was a little bit of encouragement and she was off and running. She had an instant connection with the young couple. The adopter's mom was a longtime rescuer and champion of the breed. To this day, she hikes her rescued pitties through the mountains every morning. Slappy started to wiggle and dance, jumping up and happy to meet her new family. She was a typical ham, standing on her hind legs and aping it up. She was such a clown.

With no warning whatsoever, the volunteer grabbed the fire hose and turned it on Slappy full blast. She opened up the spray nozzle full throttle and shot the powerful stream right at Slappy's face and body. When I heard this account, I was speechless. To open a hose of that strength on an animal, especially one fresh from surgery, was flat out cruelty. Slappy's behavior was in no way aggressive, just typical show-offiness. The girl went on to say that despite the incident, they had fallen in love with Slappy and wanted to take the next step toward adoption.

The next morning, I got a frantic call from Carol, the vet tech who'd named Girl, from the shelter. Carol was hysterical. "I'm at Pacific Animal Hospital with Slappy. I don't know if she's going to make it." Carol was crying. We called Carol the vet tech who cared. It wasn't unusual to see Carol walking through the halls with a baby kitten attached to her shoulder.

Carol told me an alert had gone out over the PA system calling her name to the kennels that morning. When she got to the dog kennel, she found Slappy sprawled on the cement floor drenched in blood. Her intestines were spread over the floor like a scene out of Alien. She was pitifully licking herself and about to go into shock. Carol scooped her up and got her into the vet office. She hoisted Slappy onto the steel surgical table and manually pressed her own body against Slappy to try and keep her insides together and attempt to stop the blood. She insisted the on duty ACO officer pull the van around to rush Slappy to the emergency hospital.

If Carol had not been on duty that day, Slappy would have died. The standard operating procedure was euthanasia for any traumatic medical issues. Carol's insistence for emergency room transport saved Slappy's life. Before they left the building, Carol had the wherewithal to take photographs of Slappy's injury.

Five feet of Slappy's intestines were removed that day in emergency procedure to save her life. It was touch and go, but Slappy is a survivor and a champion. She has that quality which medical science can't tag. Slappy has a powerful will to live. I called the couple and told them the awful story of what had happened. They were appalled. The girl began to cry. I knew how policemen felt when they have to keep a sober attitude when relating bad news. I tried to be still and strong for them and for Slappy. We had a serious situation to deal with, but the important matter was to save Slappy. We would all need to remain cool, positive and clear-headed to help her pull through. She took down the hospital information so she and her boyfriend could visit Slappy.

I got an immediate email from Doc. It was Sunday and Doc never worked on Sundays unless it involved a weekend retreat on his river getaway. One infamous story involved management at CCACC. Everyone was lounging in the hot tub when suddenly, Deputy Burns complained of the heat and took off all of her clothes except her brassiere and high-rise drawers. Poor Jane Everly was more shocked at the thatch of grey hair escaping Burns' underarms than her old-fashioned granny underpants. Doc wanted to know what my plans for Slappy were. He referred to her A-number rather than by name. I remember that. I knew his true purpose was to avoid the shelter being saddled with her medical bills. If Round Up were to adopt, we would automatically incur her hospital statement.

I made the suggestion that we wait until Slappy was

restored to good health before talking about adoption and the like. I stayed very professional and polite in my communication, minding my p's and q's like momma taught me to. I then received another email from Deputy Burns requesting a meeting first thing the next morning in her office. It was strange hearing from her as she took her weekends near as serious as Doc took his. I had a feeling they were burning up the phone lines between them. I replied at once and asked why the hurry. She replied that we needed to finalize some things. Keeping it real, I asked which matters she wished to address. Finally, she replied about the dog Slappy, referenced using the identification number mandated through their Chameleon software. I thanked her and asked if the shelter planned an investigation. She replied that the shelter indeed planned on investigating the incident. I ended the exchange by requesting she contact me once the investigation was completed.

Meanwhile, Slappy started her long road back to good health. She'd been through a lot. The couple went to see her every day and decided to foster her directly upon her release so Slappy wouldn't ever have to return to CCACC. Even though she'd come so very close to dying, that sad Saturday wound up being a very lucky day for Miss Slappy. What a beautiful beginning for this sweet girl who had endured so much.

I am always amazed when the animal shows no retaliatory aggression after such a clear case of animal abuse. She had to have experienced intense pain, but Slappy didn't have a mean bone in her body. She was interested only in enjoying life. We must endure and overcome the hurdles life hurls at us. That is a lesson Slappy taught me.

I wasn't surprised when I heard about the rash of meetings Monday morning at CCACC. I received another email from Burns again requesting a meeting with me in her office. I was justifiably hesitant. At this stage, I felt it prudent to keep all dealings with her documented. I agreed to the meeting, but asked if my rescue attorney might attend as well.

Burns swiftly shot off an answer absolutely refusing the request. In fact, she became incensed at the suggestion of a bipartisan witness in attendance. We went back and forth, literally regurgitating the same request and questions over and over. Had it not been such an unfortunate issue, the exchange would have been rather humorous.

Finally, I received an email from Burns stating that the shelter had completed its investigation of the matter and it had been decreed that Slappy had 'dehissed' her stitches. They felt that Slappy was a 'chewer' and had bitten open her own sutures and pulled her insides out with her own teeth. Burns referred to the adoption introduction as Slappy "becoming out of control" and had to be "misted" with the water hose. Talk about adding insult to injury!

The next email I received came from Doc. He was quite angry regarding my caution to meet privately with Burns. He went on to say that I was banned from doing business with CCACC and to never return. I was not "needed or wanted there". If the circumstances hadn't been so awful, I would have laughed out loud. I was from Texas, but his letter sounded like it was straight out of the wild, wild west. Under the Hayden Act, no rescue can be banned from any city or county shelter. To ban a taxpayer personally from a city office is as ludicrous as prohibiting a library patron from checking out a book.

I concerned myself with the most important matter, getting Slappy well. Since I was banned, we arranged for her to be adopted long distance. She was allowed to go home with her new parents directly from the hospital. She would never have to set her paws back at CCACC again. Still not completely out of the woods, she came with a laundry list of medical instructions. She must eat little meals throughout the day for the rest of her life. All of this was due to one person's irritation with her and Round Up Rescue. The volunteer who sprayed Slappy that day in anger was the same person who'd recently resigned from our board and felt that all pit bulls should be euthanized. That person still walks dogs at CCACC in her green apron.

The shelter was wrong on several accounts. Slappy is still very happy and the apple of her mom and dad's eyes. Since the first day she came home and had to be crated most of the time, Slappy never once chewed or tried to nibble at any of the many stitches in her lifesaving surgery. She never even exhibited puppy chewing and was allowed to free roam due to her good behavior. Her favorite pastime was to pile up on the bed and snooze. For a dog supposed to have chewed out her own spay stitches, this was certainly a breakthrough turnaround in behavior.

I contacted PETA about Slappy. I had been a longtime advocate of PETA and admire most of the work they've done to stop animal brutality. I sent them an account of the incident along with the photographs and medical report. Included were testimonials from Carol and the adopters who witnessed the incident. After several months of communication, PETA concluded they must ally with the shelter on "this one". They went on to state how friendly Doc, the director of CCACC, was to their organization and they didn't wish to rock the boat. They did, however, wish Slappy well. The letter ended with the final comment that at least Slappy didn't die.

I was saddened to realize the group I'd revered most of my adult life was based on myth. The simple concept of the animal or the politics had reared its head once again. For me, the choice, as always, was very simple. Their group does some good work, but my path is with all of the animals, not just some of the animals. Since Slappy, bad press has followed PETA regarding pit bulls and their founder, Ingrid Newkirk, who's publicly decried the breed. A former dogcatcher, Newkirk still carries a grudge for being bitten by a pit bull. That day, I really couldn't see any difference between Sue Sternberg, Ingrid Newkirk and Deputy Jill Burns.

Carol was let go from the shelter soon after the Slappy incident. A homogenized reason was given for her dismissal, something relating to budgetary confines. Those of us who'd been party to Doc's and Burns' performance in the past knew the real reason behind Carol's sudden departure. There was simply no room in the budget for a vet tech that actually cared about the animals. By insisting Slappy be rushed to a real emergency hospital, Carol had signed her own termination papers.

A few years ago, Slappy's mom sent me a very emotional letter. Slappy had fatty liver disease the vet told them to humanely euthanize. She and her now husband, Slappy's dad, had each tattooed Slappy on their arms before they made the appointment to have her put down. Slappy's mom was devastated. I asked her if she could hold on a minute and would she be willing to try an experiment. I had been having some good success with feeding a raw diet and homeopathic treatment with the dogs and cats in my own home. She was all ears. Any ideas were most welcome. She wholeheartedly agreed to visit a homeopathic vet for a second opinion. Slappy was put on a transitional diet to ease her system towards a raw diet. For now, Slappy would dine mostly on cooked chicken. She was given a homeopathic work up and the practitioner suggested a classical remedy to try. Along with the diet and remedy, Slappy survived.....again!!!

Fairy tales do sometimes come true. Slappy's mom is attending law school to pursue a career in animal rights. She is dedicated to helping all animals, but especially the very misunderstood pit bull breeds. Slappy has become a big sister to several pit bulls over the years that her parents have rescued as well as a real big sister to the couple's new baby.

Like the commercial says, life comes at you fast. Sometimes it can be a blessing. You don't have time to think or get mad or get even. There are some people in the world of animals and rescue that I'd rather not be around, but there are also great people like Slappy's parents. I have been very lucky to know this good people and I'm very grateful to have been blessed to know a girl like Slappy.

Chapter Fourteen
Junior

Sunny Came Home
by Shawn Colvin

Junior

We were still living in the little oceanside town when Junior was killed. The mayor of San Francisco, Gavin Newsome, had joined forces with Senator Jackie Speier to author a bill, SB861. SB861 is a document thrown rashly together in a state of panic after a young boy, Nicholas Fabish, had been mauled to death by the family's pit bull mixes. The family had been trying to breed the two dogs and sell the puppies, a common and unfortunate practice called backyard breeding. The female had been pregnant at the time of the incident. Left home alone with a chair jammed against the door to his room, Nicholas Fabish was killed by his own dogs. No one knows what actually took place that day, but everything about the story was wrong on all counts.

The city, still reeling over the Diane Whipple death, flew into frenzy after the young boy's death. The story was all over television, radio and the news. Newspaper reporters were assigned to the neighborhood to gather all the sordid details. As the facts began to surface, neighbors were quoted as saying they'd seen some strange goings on around the Fabish home in San Francisco's Sunset district. The young boy had been witnessed abusing and hitting the dogs with his hands and sticks. It was noted as well in several accounts that the boy was sent home due to issues at his school. The dogs had been in custody at least once in the city's animal control and had been relinquished to the family intact.

The boy's death should never have happened and could easily have been prevented. There were many things wrong with this sad picture. Even though all Round Up dogs are thoroughly temperament tested and trained with the new adopter, we insist upon crating when unsupervised. So many incidents can be avoided with simple training and an ounce of prevention. We ask that the whole family attend class together. No only is the playing field leveled and the group uses the same words of command, but the dog and family unit is strengthened.

Under extreme circumstances, unaltered dogs come into the rescue. For example, we often would get a call from the shelter regarding a dog with kennel cough. The dog cannot be spayed or neutered when ill and must go into foster care until the operation can be performed. In those cases, we sign an agreement with the foster parent stating the dog will be fixed as soon as the dog regains his health.

SB861 became mandate through the help of pit bull rescue Bad Rap's Donna Reynolds and phone tips from Denver's City Attorney, Kory Nelson. Nelson was behind the Denver, Colorado extermination of over 300 family pets who resembled pit bulls. One Denver family contacted us with their story about their beloved family member. He'd been trained to always walk on leash, even in the family's own fenced yard. One night, a knock sounded on the door. It was animal control with an order to confiscate their pet. He was taken into custody and euthanized by a stranger down at the city dog pound. This dog and many others were taken from their loving homes and killed by strangers. Their only crime was looking like a pit bull.

The events during this terrible time caused me to remember the Carolina Parakeet, our country's native parrot. When the parakeet became a nuisance in the 1800's, farmers shot them in mass quantity. They are now extinct. SB861 is the gentleman's approach to getting a shotgun and killing dogs. Period. Again, we render extinct the first native breed in the United States, the American Pit Bull Terrier.

Junior, Girl and I met the newsmen on a cold grey evening at an ocean park. The wind practically knocked us down, but we attempted to remain upright and composed for the interview. They asked me the usual questions about education and training being the real answer and not useless bans which have been proved ineffective over and again. I based my opinion on dog and master having a solid relationship through training. With a trained dog who minds his person, there will be no accidents. All of the attacks I've ever heard about occurred without supervision.

I tried to talk a little about fixing one's dog and attending obedience classes. At the moment I was attempting to get one more plug in about training, Junior took off running and jerked me along with him right out of the frame. It was like a cartoon and it wound up on tv! Despite the circumstances, it really was funny. Talk about a jump cut. Here I was going on about controlling your pet and couldn't even hang on to my own dog.

Girl and Junior were best friends, completely devoted to one another. They would play together for hours on end. Scott would throw a piece of driftwood into the ocean and off they'd go. Girl, being the athlete, would always reach the floating piece of wood first. Junior, the typical pesky kid brother, would lock onto Girl's piece of wood, neither giving up. This is not recommended dog play, but it was Girl and Junior's game. They would stand for hours, nose to nose, attached to the wood like a double two-headed dog statue. It was like time-lapse photography. People would gather together and watch them with the magnificent Pacific Ocean in the background. One group would move on down the beach and another would gather to take the last group's place. This is the memory of Junior I hold in my heart.

It was early in the morning when I heard yelling. I didn't even recognize Scott's face. He was hysterical. I ran to the front door and there he stood, crying and holding Junior in his arms. "He's dead. Junior's dead! They killed him. They killed my dog!"

I couldn't understand what had happened. Scott was so distraught. It was very early, before 7 a.m. and barely daylight in the hazy fog. I had never seen Scott in this state. I took Junior from him and tried to make sense of what had happened.

I have walked through several animals' deaths and almost have a natural ability to walk through the necessary steps calmly for some reason. I told Scott to go inside and I would handle what needed to be done. I would take care of Junior now. It's my nature to move through a frenzied situation by handling the physical aspects. There would be time for sadness later. For now, I had to see to Junior.

Our hospital was right down the highway. If I could only get Junior to the hospital, we could begin the preparation for cremation. As I drove down the highway, Junior already stiff and cold beside me, I noticed how quiet it was. I didn't pass one other car either way as I drove. The ocean was as dark as the sky. It was September, a cold, sad Saturday.

Mom was sweeping the kennels when I got to the hospital. She was a wonderful woman who always had time to give that special attention to the dogs and cats at the hospital and in boarding. She always had a cookie or a cuddle for the animals being boarded. She began to cry when I carried Junior inside. I remember we had to put his body inside a plastic garbage bag before he was placed inside the freezer. Putting Junior there was horrible. There is nothing so final as the life force leaving the body. It was truly the end.

As I drove home, I only passed one other car. It was almost 8 o'clock and the day was just getting started. It was going to be a long day. When I arrived back home, Scott was still torn up. He blamed himself. He'd taken Junior running early in the morning. They'd gone too far down the beach and had gotten tired. He called a taxi, but the cab driver refused to allow a dog in the car. He asked a guy at the convenience store to give Junior and him a ride home. The man agreed, but made Scott tie Junior in the back of his truck. They took off down the highway. Junior's kennel card flashed in my mind's eye when I heard this part of the story. The writing on Junior's card all those years ago read, "chews through leash. Must use chain leash with this one."

I remembered when we used to go on those long all day mobile adoptions, Junior and me. We would sit outside the pet store and he would go do the perfect sit for each person who passed by. I remembered how his canines stuck down below his lip like Scred's. I remember when I was training him and saw his crooked little bottom teeth that crossed. I remember joking with his trainer that Junior would need braces someday. I remember wondering if I would be the only person to ever notice those crooked little teeth and I remember thinking he must really be my dog.

There is a tony eyeglass store where I used to fill my prescriptions. I really liked their beautiful frames. This store also had a great insurance policy that allowed duplication the first year should your glasses become damaged, no questions asked. You just needed to bring back all of the parts. As you enter the boutique geared toward the fashion-conscious sight impaired, there sits a glass covered display case. A mangled and gnarled set of black high fashion eyewear sits inside with a note reading, "chewed up by customer's dog." Junior chewed those very eyeglasses up the first night he'd been with me. That is the memory that breaks my heart.

The wonderful thing about animals is the saddest thing as well. They bring us such intense joy, but leave such a devastating hole. When Scott got out of the truck and ran to get Junior, Junior was still alive. Junior had loved Scott so much and couldn't stand being apart from him in the back of the truck. He was used to riding shotgun with his dad. Junior should never have been in the back of the truck. No dog should ever ride in the back of any truck. Period. Scott picked Junior up out of the road and began running back to our house. Not one person pulled over to help. When I heard this, my mind was made up. I was going back home to Texas. I was not going to live where the law dictated what kind of dog I could have. Say what you want about Texas, with all its bad and all its good. When you're walking down the road with your hurt dog, people stop to help. It doesn't matter who you are or what kind of dog you have. It was time to come home.

Chapter Fifteen
Box of Rain

Learning to Fly
By Tom Petty

Girl

I am sitting in my own version of paradise, surrounded by the dogs left in my family. Tex is a six year-old deaf white pit bull that hitched a ride out of town from Half Moon Bay. Rebel is still going strong. Etta James is singing on the radio and my girl, Rowdy Cowgirl has her lovely head in my lap. Cubby has joined us from his second home gone badly in California. I sign a lifetime agreement with each adopter providing a promise to re-home should the adoption not work out for any reason. Cubby was not happy, but now he is happy, end of story.

I would never have imagined the direction my path would lead all those years ago when Angel Divine wandered up to our little house. I never dreamed I would spend 24 hours a day, 7 days a week rescuing pit bulls. The hard parts are hard to remember and it's easy to forget the miracles. Jenna was a re-homed girl like Cubby, twice. She landed in the home and hearts of the sweetest family with two little girls. The family had never owned a dog and were at first, a little hesitant about adopting a pit bull. They became staunch anti-SB861 protesters and made a video with their two daughters and Jenna. Dad kept the camera running and took Jenna out for a shred on the skateboard.

I think about Trinity, the little girl who was almost killed due to mis-information from CCSPCA. She was re-adopted by a wonderful couple in a lush Victorian. Trinity was renamed Trixie and helped her mom reinvent herself as a dog duds fashionista designer. I received a photograph and letter yesterday that Trixie has passed away. Her years were spent being treated and spoiled and loved.

We lost Frenchie this year. She lost her battle with lymphoma and broke her dad's heart. Frenchie was an incredibly beautiful boxer/pittie mix whose picture is tattooed across her mom's back. I was pulling so many dogs from CCACC when I got Frenchie, until she met her new mom and dad that I didn't know she could roll over and shake hands She is remembered on the memorial page and always in our hearts.

We lost Zorro a.k.a. Jakie's dad, a retired policeman to cancer. He is with the aged Maltese, Granny, in heaven. Jakie and his mom received a message from them with an animal communication transcript. When Granny had been rescued, she didn't have a tooth in her head. Jakie and Granny's dad had lost all of his teeth as a result of the cancer treatment. According to Granny's transcript, she and dad are together in heaven and they both have new sets of teeth. Everybody in heaven has teeth.

Rocco is still with his family and sister, Vega. Mia is still with her mom and they are both rescuing pit bulls. Buddy still works at the barbershop. Dickie Betts is living kosher and has a baby brother. Oliver is big brother to a real baby, too. He has quit chasing the movie stars since the day he knocked down Sean Penn for a face-licking. We are always looking for a volunteer who will help upload photos so we can keep up with all of the happiest endings.

There is a grey cloud over the valley. I am not so worried about what the cloud is bringing, but content to watch it approach. Whatever it brings, I can withstand it. If I keep running my whole life, I won't get to know the place where I am. Things are not perfect back here in Texas. I still secretly pull dogs from CCACC shelter. I show other people how to get the animals out that the shelter says are too ill or behaviorally unsound. I even rescued a white parakeet from CCACC who was there for a month with scaly face mites and weighing only 25 grams. Her name is Alamo and the wonderful rescue group, Mickaboo, flew her to me with a volunteer visiting family in Texas.

I had already been feeding a raw diet and a member of the SF Raw Feeders co-op located in the bay area. I fell into raw feeding quite by chance. Alibaba, the old Siamese, taught us about raw and homeopathy. I decided one day if I couldn't save all of the animals, I could focus some energy on nutrition and diet. I began to feed raw by supplementing with the expensive kibble I couldn't for some reason quit feeding to the dogs and the canned paste for cats. Even though Alibaba's homeopathic vet warned me that these bought foods were still processed and the animals required and needed a whole diet just as we people need to thrive. Dogs and cats need a raw, organic meat diet to maintain a robust immune system.

The bay area raw feeding group was founded by a vegan. She is a testament to feeding raw the correct way. I am still a member of this co-op even though I'm far, far away. I learn something new about diet and animal health every day from this group and the local raw feeding co-op I joined here in Texas. I began an online chat group for raw feeders as well as another holistic chat group just for cats and those of us who choose to treat our cats homeopathically and through diet. I encourage every animal person to feed his dogs and cats a raw diet. It's cheaper and healthier, easier and no matter if you subscribe to Darwin or God Almighty, the sustenance your animal was created to eat. It's never too late to start, just ask Rebel.

Anyone can start a local co-op and seek out humane sources. More and more animal people are seeking a more healthy way to raise their beloved pets. I would never be able to afford to feed all of these rescue animals a processed food diet when taking into account the benefits enjoyed by a raw fed diet. In over 8 years, I haven't given a flea or heartworm monthly preventative to any of the animals in my home, either rescue or permanent. We live in a Mecca for heartworm and fleas. Our daily food cost per dog is around twenty cents per day. Factoring out the cost of those unneeded and toxic medications along with yearly teeth cleaning, which raw fed animals do not need, the cost of feeding raw is too good an offer to pass up. The benefit of seeing your animal stop mid meal with a chicken leg or back hanging out of his mouth to look up and thank you with those big eyes makes my heart burst with happiness every night.

The first thing I hear from people is 'what about the bones'? My answer is what did animals eat before Gravy Train came to town? I remember when I was a girl growing up in southeast Texas, the family dog ate scraps from the kitchen table. During the day, dogs ran the country roads scavenging for a bird or rabbit. Of course, this would be unacceptable in today's world. The point is, these animals were rarely sick. Nobody had to go to the vet every five minutes for this pill and that shot. I'm not an expert, but I've lived with animals that never go to the vet and enjoy pretty good health. Having been on both sides, I must credit the raw diet and homeopathic/holistic treatment as the reason. A great starter site for the novice is to Google Raw Fed Dogs for dogs and Raw Fed Cats for your feline friends.

Seems like every day, I get a reminder card from the vet. "Where is Rebel? Rebel is due for his bordatella, his heartworm treatment, his flea treatment, his rabies shot, his dhlpp booster, his teeth cleaning…" If Rebel were following that curriculum, he'd be too worn out to enjoy being a dog. I file those reminders in the round file cabinet where they belong.

Rebel is almost 16 now. He suffers from lipoma fatty tumors. I have tried for years to get rid of these nasty looking lumps. The same vets who send me those belated treatment notices are the same ones who'll say, "oh, all old dogs get these. They're harmless. Just keep an eye on them." That advice never sat right with me so I decided to do a little research. New information has surfaced which links these tumors to vaccination. I'd wanted to be a good mom to Rebel. I wanted Rebel to live forever, so I did everything I'd been told to do for him. Rebel had been vaccinated every year for years.

Based upon research, I have discovered that these so-called harmless lumps are believed to be linked to vaccinations. In wanted Rebel to be safe and healthy, I had compromised his wellbeing instead. In the past, I'd documented the cats' records where and when they'd been inoculated. I had heard of vaccine associated feline sarcoma way back when and told not to worry, because 99 percent of the cat population doesn't develop the tumors. What about those poor cats and their people that fall into the one percentile, though? What if it were me and my cat?

I quit giving vaccinations to my cats. Due to the processed food they ate, Roy developed chronic renal failure. Against veterinary advice, I transitioned Roy to a raw diet at fourteen years of age. It took a while but he came to love organic free-range chicken necks along with livers and gizzards. He and the rest of the bunch would tolerate the requisite muscle meat making up 80 percent of their diet, but that took a little extra trickery on my part. With homeopathy, Roy lived to be twenty years old. That's six years of living with CRF. The chronic renal failure didn't kill Roy. He died when his old heart finally gave out due to the hypertension associated with his CRF. I haven't heard of another cat diagnosed with CRF as a senior living as long as Roy lived with the disease. I believe Roy enjoyed a long life due to his diet and homeopathic treatment. I believe he lived as long as he did, because I listened to my heart and not to allopathic advice.

The last three cats that have moved here were all kibble fed cats. Each one was gobbling up his raw dinner inside of a day. One of the boys, Fernando, suffered some trauma. It was touch and go, but the vet ultimately decided to wait and see if Fern could recover on his own without surgery. I gave Fernando Arnica and other homeopathic remedies specific to his symptoms and he recovered completely in under a week. The vet mentioned when he looked at the initial x-rays, he could tell Fern wasn't a cat food cat. You might say raw food saved Fern's life. When people ask me about the bones in the raw food, I tell them about Fern. Those bones make for strong bones.

Another discovery I made on the past three cat adoptions was in regard to allergy symptoms and cats. I have the worst allergies and asthma of anyone I've ever met. Several years ago I had a sinus operation to clear out my passages from problems associated with my allergies. As each of these past three cats came into our fold, my head would swell up and I'd begin sneezing and tearing something terrible. The asthma would kick in along with awful bouts of insomnia. As each cat was transitioned onto a raw diet, my allergy symptoms would disappear. By the adoption of the third cat, I realized that we aren't allergic to the animal, but to what they are eating. When the cats and dogs are eating raw, I'm not allergic and exhibit no symptoms. When I get the calls and emails to re-home someone's cat or dog due to allergies, I ask the family to try a raw diet. While you're waiting to re-home the pet anyway, you might have a healthy and happy discovery as I did and keep your beloved pet. Now if I could only figure out how to cure myself of cedar fever.

I have not had to take any of the cats or dogs to the vet for teeth cleaning since I began to feed raw. All of the cartilage and gristle is nature's dental floss. My old homeopathic vet used to ask, "have you ever seen a wolf with a toothbrush?" The benefits of a raw diet are evident the first minute you put the food dish in front of your dog. I'll admit, it takes a little longer with some cats, but usually the dog looks up at you like, "now, you know what I'm talking about." Feeding time at night is my favorite part of my day. The feeling I get from knowing the animals are getting exactly what they need to thrive and survive is huge. It's as good as it gets.

It's been said that life happens in threes. Just as the last three cats came, three dogs appeared in my life. These three dogs couldn't have been more different, but they each had a profound impact on my rescue work. The first dog is called Raspberry. Raspberry is a lovely red Staffordshire Bull Terrier mixed with a drop of Boxer. She has a black muzzle tipping up into an under bite. Her white blaze is dotted with pigment, spraying big freckles across her chest.

Raspberry was found by a young man who works at
the place where I buy my tea. Like much of the population,
he didn't know what to do with her and certainly didn't want
to turn her over to the overwhelmed local dog pound. With
all of the breeding going on, there just are not enough homes
for these dogs. All over, shelters are overwhelmed and must be
honest with these people whose lives have been interrupted by
a stray dog. The prognosis for most of these unwanted pets is
death. My good friend Kathleen who tirelessly networks online
for unwanted shelter dogs that have run out of time says, "we're
living in a virtual bloodbath!"

He called and told me what a wonderful dog Raspberry
was. She was super kid and people friendly. He allowed her to
free roam with his small dog while he and his girlfriend were at
work during the day. They visited the local dog park frequently,
Raspberry running alongside him while he rode his bicycle.
With his assurance of her temperament, we courtesy posted
her on the websites. Occasionally, we'd get an inquiry about
her, but the Staffie Bulls draw a strange crowd. Most of the
candidates asking about Raspberry hadn't yet completed a class
in grammar and their email handles contained phrases like 'got
game'.

When the tea guy and his girlfriend were due to leave
for vacation, Raspberry was out of options. The foster room
was vacant since Joe, who'd been with me for over a year had
been adopted. Joe had been abandoned in the backyard of a
house right out of Texas Chainsaw Massacre. The girl who
owned Joe had left him with the sister. The sister ran out on
the husband, a rodeo rider complete with a lasso and a black
toenail. The toenail is in Joe's before picture.

Joe had been the worst case of abuse I'd ever seen. The
vet office called me very alarmed. This hospital usually runs
every possible test imaginable, but were afraid to even put
Joe up on the exam table. His gums were so white, the doctor
was concerned that Joe might go into shock and die. He was

221

infested with whipworm and had a severe case of heartworm. He was covered in fleas, emaciated and very depressed. He was alone in that nasty backyard next to a filthy Igloo doghouse.

Joe was with me for over a year. I took my time with Joe. Not only did I want to make sure he was well physically, but I wanted to make sure he was emotionally well. Since I was sure Joe didn't need me anymore and was adopted to a wonderful young woman and her Chihuahua, John Henry, I offered to foster Raspberry. I am always hesitant to take on a new dog or cat, because they usually stay with me for at least a year. Brownie Rose and Bullfrog, the semi-feral puppies were with me a year and a half before Joe came. Bullfrog came back three years later under the lifetime contract and just went home last night to a Basenji farm. Bullfrog takes a little bit of my heart wherever he goes. If I didn't have so many, I'd keep him myself.

Raspberry arrived the night the couple left for Florida, a bundle of joyful wiggles. She was a super dog, very friendly and playful. She loved games. I also noticed something else. She was in heat! I made an appointment at the free clinic for pit bulls to have her fixed. They took us quickly and I dropped her off the next morning. When I dropped her off, she was all waggy and happy and everybody was a friend. This was an adventure! When I picked Raspberry up that afternoon, I picked up a different dog. She was fine with me, but seemed traumatized. As I signed the paperwork for her release, I saw where the printed breed information Staffordshire Bull Terrier/Boxer mix had been rudely scratched out. The paper was very near torn. The words 'pit bull' were scrawled in ballpoint underneath. "Oh, boy," I though, "here we go again." I asked the young lady checking us out about the breed information being crossed out and mentioned that pit bull itself isn't a recognized dog breed.

Scott and I were playing with Raspberry and she went for his face that night. I was concerned. I had put dogs down for showing less aggression. I knew a little about rabies vaccinosis, but I was about to get a crash course on the subject.

I have been lucky enough to benefit from some great e-groups online. Many of these forums discuss nutrition and treatment issues that the average pet owner is not remotely aware of. Over vaccination has become a hot topic with many concerned parents as well as pet owners participating. I was up pretty late that night Googling and searching. Thank God for the internet. I joined a couple of groups knowledgeable about vaccination. Some of the stories were shocking. I read about animals that suffered from aggression, like Raspberry, and had been perfectly well-behaved before inoculation. I read about animals that had exhibited excessive licking and itching, extreme cases of fur loss and sores, epilepsy and seizure and loss of limbs. One person's heartbreaking story about her dog ended in her pet's death. She tried everything to undo the awful symptoms which vaccination had caused her dog, but lost the fight. Her story is linked to my site so others can make conscious choices with their own pets.

The rabies vaccine contains mercury, formaldehyde and aluminum among other nasty and toxic items like lead and anti-freeze. The rabies vaccination reportedly causes neurological damage and literally eats the lining of the brain. Little wonder Raspberry went ballistic. Her body was burning from the inside out. She could hardly stand to be touched. I knew enough to consult a homeopath and already had her on a raw fed organic diet with plenty of fresh purified water. Of course, she would not be given any kind of flea deterrent or heartworm preventative guaranteed to complicate the problem and further distress the immune system. I contacted a classical homeopath who immediately began treating Raspberry for rabies vaccinosis.

Right after Raspberry's reaction, I received word about two California dogs, Nell and Howie. Both had received vaccinations and both had immediately reacted. Howie is a little mix of Beagle, Basset, Corgi and Pit, quite the adorable chap. He was found at a schoolyard. He was loving and huggy. All of his photos form the shelter were pictures of people hugging him. He was given a dhlpp vaccine upon release from the shelter. The foster to adopt gave him another dhlpp vaccine, a rabies shot and neutered. He was immediately administered with toxic heartworm medication, pain meds for the neuter and had a microchip japed beneath his skin. On top of all this, she applied more toxins in a monthly dose of flea preventative. Howie was completely overwhelmed and immediately began to exhibit fear-related issues.

Nell was given her dhlpp and fostered by a woman in a beautiful antique-filled home. Nell, who'd always been perfectly behaved, reacted to her reflection in the mirror. Unfortunately, the woman's home had tons of mirrors throughout. I later found that fear of shiny objects is another symptom of vaccinosis. Nell was removed from the woman's home and is currently being boarded.

The ideal is to feed the animal organic raw meat and purified water. Most homeopaths and holistic vets are now insisting on a raw diet before treating homeopathically. The main difference between allopathic and homeopathic medicine lies between treating the symptom and treating the disease, respectively. In allopathic medicine, one treats a cold by killing the symptom with antibiotics. In homeopathy, the cold would be seen as a symptom of a greater disease. A homeopathic remedy is administered according to which symptoms fit the correct remedy. One patient might feel better lying down with fewer symptoms in the morning rather than at night. These issues are very important to the homeopath in treating his patient. Ultimately, one remedy might be correct for one patient and completely wrong for another patient. For this reason, it's highly recommended that a person work with a classical homeopath specifically for each of his pets.

The initial price tag usually scares most people off, though quite comparable to a first visit at an allopathic veterinary clinic. When one takes into account that most homeopathic consults can be taken care of online, the perspective becomes quite different. I have benefitted immediately from being able to call or email my homeopath during an emergency. My little deaf white pit bull, Tex, had a violent case of heatstroke one summer afternoon. After his remedy and the homemade electrolytes of honey, water and sea salt were administered, Tex was restored to his healthy self within half an hour. The attack had been so severe, Tex had urinated on himself and begun to convulse.

It's amazing stuff, this homeopathy. I have personally known it to save animals from giardia, demodectic mange and even a torn cruciate ligament. I'm not saying to never visit an allopathic vet, but today when I visit a conventional veterinarian, I am able to make rational, informed and researched decisions.

There has been relatively little research performed regarding rabies vaccinosis. Based upon my own limited experience, I am curious as to how many dogs in shelters waiting to be euthanized due to behavioral and medical issues are where they are due to over vaccination. If this is indeed the truth, we could save many animals. People could treat the problems at home and their pets might never see the insides of a shelter or face euthanasia. If we are required by law to over-vaccinate our pets, the very least we can do is mandate they be treated humanely and holistically. It's time for a wake up call!

Chapter Sixteen
Word To Your Mother

Good Day
by Paul Westerberg

Sasha

One out of every five U.S. citizens will find a pit bull this year. Judging by all of the calls and emails I receive every day, it sure seems like one out of every five people is finding one. I get tons of letters and calls from all over the U.S. and beyond. I recently spoke to a lady in Nova Scotia whose entire community united to help a stray pit bull. All of the pleas sound alike. "The nicest dog wandered into my yard. I'd like to keep her, but I already have three dogs. She is very good with my son and the dogs. She is so skinny. Her tail just wags, though. I can see she wants to be friends. Can your organization take her?"

First, I tell everyone to be careful. If you have access to a dog trainer, have them assess the dog. I have uploaded a section on my site for all of these good people to refer to. Crating and leash walking are at the top of the list. If the animal shows any kind of aggression at any point, contact animal control. However, in over twelve years, I've never had an experience with anyone finding a dog they couldn't handle. Most of the dogs I've been contacted about have just been hungry for food and attention. Most of these dogs just want a little loving.

Even though I'm back in Texas, I've never given up on the dogs in Coastal County. That is where I began Round Up Rescue and I feel a sense of loyalty to the dogs and animals from Coastal County. Since I am especially aware of the flaws in their system, I am able to tell the average person how to retrieve the dogs that have been turned over to that shelter. I have monitored the numbers at that shelter over the years. I visit the Pet Harbor website as anyone can do. When I type in the zip code and follow the prompts for lost dog, I am able to see just exactly how many dogs are currently in the stray section. Each animal is supposed to be photographed on intake for the $9,800 software program paid for by that county's citizens. If you don't see a photograph for that animal, the county is being robbed and that animal is being robbed of his chance for life.

After the stray period is over, the animals are supposed

to be put up for adoption. Countless upon countless dogs and cats fail this test. Both of the last puppies we secretly pulled from this shelter failed their temperament tests for pulling on the leash. Both dogs are doing great in their new homes and leash walking on a daily basis, no complaints.

Over the years, I have received other calls regarding a found dog. Often, the finder called CCACC and began to suffer misgivings. Time after time, dog after dog, each one of these finders had placed a hold on the dog so they could be called when the animal found a home. They'd always read in the newspaper about this wonderful low-kill shelter and seen the director interviewed with incredible live release numbers. Each time I received a call at the last minute from the person upset that the dog they'd found and shared a car ride with failed his temperament test and was going to be euthanized. "That dog was not aggressive. He licked my hand and let me pick him up and put him into the car. He rested his head on my lap. He was so good with my dogs." On and on, I hear the same thing from every person who calls.

I am reminded of my first and best lesson I learned. Trust your own instincts. With many of these people, I can tell them which rescue to call. We, as rescues, can have our trainer take a look at the dog and pull the dog under the Hayden Act if the dog is of sound temperament. Every one I've been involved with passed our temperament test. Every dog we've helped with is in a great home, eating raw food and has graduated from the Billy Best obedience classes. For those people who pulled over and saved the dog and called us when the shelter let you and that dog down, thank you. You know who you are and better yet, the dog you saved knows who you are and what you did for him.

When I hear of legislation such as SB861, I am justifiably terrified. I have seen firsthand what harm misguided panic and fear can do. The worst case happened to a friend and her family. She had a little rescue dog named Peanut.

Peanut was a mess. He attended our aggressive dog training classes, which I recommend for any dog who is experiencing space issues or dog on dog behavior problems. I have seen dogs completely turned around in this class. Sometimes you have a pushy little so and so who needs some manners. That was Peanut's description. Peanut had a huge case of what we used to call 'showing his ass'.

Peanut's mom and her lovely six-year old son attended class every single Saturday with Peanut. I have never seen anyone more dedicated to training and working with their dog than what I observed with Peanut's family. If Peanut was awful in every other respect, he had one brilliant and gleaming redeeming quality. He loved that boy. To watch the boy and Peanut was a joyous thing. Under the instruction of our trainer, many of our own rescue dogs were trained to properly behave with children with this little boy's help. He probably has no idea how many dogs he's taught to be proper good citizens.

CCACC got involved. The high paid dog behaviorist Lydia Bench insinuated herself into that family. Lydia Bench, the same behaviorist who was so very wrong about Maybelle, Angus McPherson and others too numerous to name, had notified child protective services. CCACC threatened her to relinquish Peanut and she refused, God bless her. The little boy was removed from his mother and placed in foster care. This is an upstanding member of her community, a registered nurse who spends all her spare time as a loving parent and volunteering.

The little boy was sexually molested while in foster care. Ultimately, he was returned to his home, but his childhood ruined. He was robbed of his innocence by people who were messing where they shouldn't have been. This is what can and did happen when unfair legislation is passed and creates an air of panic. This is what happens when government agencies and their employees have unclear authority and incompetent people allowed to enforce the law. Somebody needs to control animal control.

Even though I had been banned, I continued to hear about the terrible goings on at this shelter. I started a small group based on a saying by Margaret Mead. "Never doubt that a small group of thoughtful, committed citizens can change the world; indeed, it's the only thing that ever has." That quote had such a huge impact on me. I felt like the crow turned to black in mythology, a harbinger of doom and revenge. I was good and mad, angry at what we were allowing as a society to be inflicted on our animals. I was just one person. What could I do to change things?

I made posters with my little group's name, CAW... Citizen's Animal Watch and the silhouette of a beautiful, black crow, beak open. I told the story of a little six-month pit bull mix that had been picked up as a stray and taken to the shelter. She was forgotten about in the stray section. For thirty days, the pup was never taken outside and went completely crazy in the dark. She was then euthanized.

I put the posters up all over town. The story of the little pit bull was in the same groovy coffee houses, animal hospitals, surf shops and pet stores where I put up posters of Round Up dogs for adoption fliers. Wherever I could find a community board, I put up a poster about the little dog. I felt something like Dalton Trumbo during the Hollywood blacklist. Even though no one but the directors of CCACC could change the awful things going on at the shelter, at least I could spread the word with my fliers. "Caw, caw, caw," quoth the raven.

We can all vote. Breed specific legislation is attacking the free world like a nasty virus. PBRC or Pit Bull Rescue Central's website presents an informed and intelligent look at breed specific legislation and how it has failed time and time again. Not all of us can pick up and move when the government tells us what kind of dog we can share our homes with. Very few states have laws prohibiting municipalities from passing breed specific legislation. I am happy to live in one of those states. We are safe, for now. What would I do if someone came knocking at my door to confiscate Girl or little deaf Tex for looking like pit bulls? These laws and their enforcers are not too distant a throw from 'Invasion of the Body Snatchers'.

One sunny day, I happened to be in San Francisco with my good friend, Gary. We were strolling at the Palace of Fine Arts. How serene and graceful white swans were gliding across the lake. I was walking the two Akitas, Lola and Bella. There was a crowd gathering and a table being set up with cookies and refreshments. The city's mayor, Gavin Newsome, was gearing up with his little cue cards to give a speech. Gary went down to help himself to a cookie while I proceeded to walk the Akitas. I can't say what it was, but something overcame me. I looked at the Akitas as though to ask, "should I do it?" They gave me their full-hearted encouragement and I began to chant loudly. "Gavin Newsome, mayor of San Francisco. Leave our dogs alone!" I shouted for all to hear the wrongdoing of SB861. I shouted in memory of the pit bulls confiscated and killed in Denver, Colorado. I shouted for all of the thousands of dogs over 35 pounds exterminated in Germany. I should for all of the people who were being told they could not have a pit bull for a pet. I shouted for Junior.

A pudgy aide began to run toward the Akitas and me. He kept putting his finger over his mouth and going, "shhhhhhhhhh, shhhhhhhhhhhhhh," I must admit, the scene was comical as I continued to chant my mantra. "Gavin Newsome, mayor of San Francisco. Leave our dogs alone." The mayor fondled his index cards and refused to acknowledge me, pretending not to hear. I saw Gary trying to disappear into the crowd with his cookie. Looking back, I am not sorry. I am glad I took that opportunity to voice my opinion, so to speak. Bella died soon after that day. I will always remember him egging me on that day. I had clearly crossed over the line to become a certified animal rights nut that day. My only regret is that I didn't cross over much sooner.

I got sick of seeing awful cartoon caricature pit bulls on television every night, so I started a pit bull Frisbee team. It didn't take much training. We selected appropriate music for the events in which we performed, Guns and Roses' "Welcome to the Jungle" and Charlie Daniels' "Devil Went Down to Georgia". To see the crowd scream at those pit bulls flying through the air for their Frisbees and running back to their handlers was awesome to behold. Most of those people had never seen a pit bull other than the evening news doing something awful. How novel to watch them hamming it up with a Frisbee.

How about adopting a pit bull or a pit bull mix and being seen with that dog? Every time you go out in public with your perfect pit bull, you are making a statement. You are honoring all of those dogs that don't have a chance by walking your pit bull smiling loud and proud down the street in your neighborhood. You are making the world a better place. If uncomfortable about adopting from a shelter, adopt from a rescue organization. Most rescue groups depend on foster homes. This way, the adopter knows that dog is good with other dogs, people, kids, cats, birds, whatever. They know if the dog is hyper or a couch potato. If you aren't ready to make a commitment, foster. If you can't foster, go down to your shelter or find a rescue group and walk a dog. One citizen can make a difference. Save one dog. Pull that one dog from death row and foster until you can find him a forever home. This is how I have saved hundreds and hundreds of dogs, one dog at a time.

Some days I feel sad. There is only so much one person can do. I get all of the mail from people giving up their dogs and cats, from fellow animal lovers with petitions to sign about animals who've been tortured or hurt, about foolhardy legislation and so on. Sometimes when I'm feeling blue, I look at Girl with her big smile. I remember those months I would play with her and have to take her back to her kennel afterward. I remembered all those year ago when I would promise her

night after night I would get her a home. Well, I did. I got
her that home. On days like this, I get up and walk over to the
refrigerator and get out a cup of yogurt. I see that big old grin
light open her face as she laps up that first sloppy bite. When
Girl looks up at me wanting another bite, life feels pretty good.
Life is real good.

CINDY MARABITO

Chapter Seventeen
A Day in the Life

Fall on Me
by R.E.M.

Raspberry

I had pulled a blind 10 year old pit bull and he was pretty much out of time at the foster home. Their resident female cattle dog just didn't get him. She was over his blindness and it was causing trouble. He had nowhere else to go He was found walking down Pico Boulevard in Los Angeles. In a movie, it would have been funny. My guess is he was wandering amidst the management offices and big time talent agencies looking for that big deal with Animal Planet. He wound up at the local shelter. Jack was redlined when I heard about him. The staff and volunteers had fallen in love with him and I saw him the day they were supposed to euthanize him.

I should have learned by now to hit the delete button, but something compelled me to contact the group networking Jack. I found a foster family right outside Santa Cruz. Our transport group, Streets of Bakersfield, brought Jack all the way to his new foster home. He was there for four months. I thought Jack would never find a home, but a miracle happened. A sweet dog walker saw his posting and called us. She and her boyfriend have one of these 'office manager' girls I like to call them. However, she took to Jack who is now Carmine. He is home! He gets around by following the sound of his sister's dog collar. Now, his song is "Jingle of a Dog's Collar" by the Butthole Surfers as well as Pearl Jam's "Santa Cruz".

I get an email about Kashi, a five-month pup we pulled who was put on the euthanasia list because his ears had been butchered. I could tell by his muscle tone he was more American Bulldog than pit bull. He's a pretty perfect dog. His foster sister is also a cattle girl, but she really likes her foster brother, Kashi. I get this email letting me know that Big Top Pit Bull Team has released a statement that pit bulls can't be read until age two when they hit puberty. What? The guy who sent the email cited his own PhD toting behaviorist as saying no dog can be assessed until age 2! Does this mean she doesn't train dogs under two?

These kinds of blanket statements are terrifying,

especially when coming from a renowned group often quoted for their sage advice regarding pit bulls and yet another behaviorist moonlighting as a breeder. The poor man really cannot be blamed, but here is yet another potential adopter operating on bad information. The very people who are supposed to be helping, a rescue and a so-called behaviorist, are in fact hurting. The man ended up purchasing a dog after researching ad nauseam. The puppy turned out to be impossible to live with. The young man tried everything suggested by these pundits before eventually returning the Vizsla to the breeder. Kashi was adopted by his foster parents and is living large and happy with sister Darcy. There is much to be said for flower essences and emotion code work, note to breeders and firebrand rescue organizations.

Again, I'm amazed at the willingness of otherwise intelligent people to take what is heard about pit bulls as gospel. Hell, I used to and I'm fairly well read. Now that I've been in the game a few years, I've born witness to how the media actually slings these stories together. Unfortunately, an incident will occur and media goes into overdrive. It's my understanding in Coastal County that scanners are set to only alert pit bull incidents. After a bit of monitoring on my part, I began to notice stories neglected to mention dog breeds unless a pit bull was involved. In every situation I've been party to, the reporter had no dog knowledge and was on deadline, meaning had to have the story finished within an hour or so. My question is how reliable is information slammed together in an hour? A greater authority might be someone who's spent every waking hour with the breed for a chunk of time.

All too often, some hotshot reporter needs to throw something together by quitting time, so they call the shelter and get ahold of someone like Doc or the new volunteer coordinator. If it wasn't so tragic, his remarks could be comic. Imagine the idiocy of a comment like, "pit bulls are notoriously unpredictable." What kind of shelter director issues such a statement? Or, "threat of a death sentence was what kept pets in their homes." Some of the lunacy Doc has issued to the media rivals George W.

On Easter Sunday, I had better things to do, though. I had to take Raspberry for her daily walk. I was thinking about the fearful statements from the man about Kashi. I was sad. I had checked the PhD behaviorist's website for information and was surprised to see that most of her specialty work with dogs required over-vaccination. Here I was walking a poor dog down the middle of the road in a gated community, because her dog aggression was so bad. This was a direct symptom of vaccination.

These ideas repelled everything I had learned first hand in my own work. I might not have a PhD handy in dog behavior and my pit bull mixes don't rival the poster supermodel pit bulls of Big Top Pit Bull Team's rescues, but most of my guys have been pulled at a year or under. All of Round Up's dogs are crated and otherwise trained and leading exemplary lives in their families and communities. All of them.

Raspberry had to be crated much of the time. She was doing better and I could see a degree of progress. She was no longer human aggressive, but still over-reacted around other dogs and wildlife. We had attended three dog obedience classes. Two of the classes, we'd completed, but the third had kicked Raspberry and I out before finishing. This was our area's most well respected training center, but at least they refunded a portion of the cost and our Kong training document came from this trainer. That document alone was worth some of the $400 some odd dollars we shelled out to attend and go through the one on one required assessments.

The year I spent with Raspberry practically broke me. It was just Raspberry and me. I couldn't find anyone to help us. I had no experience with rabies vaccinosis and except for the long term treatment homeopathically, there was no help for us. There was nowhere for Raspberry to go. She spent 24 hours per day in the music room. I kept music on for her, but I had other duties and a job as well. I couldn't spend every spare minute babysitting Raspberry. Except for our walk each morning, she was by herself in that room.

Scott had refused to allow Raspberry to be aggressive with him. He is like Steve Irwin, the Crocodile Hunter, just fearless. Even when Raspberry was baring her teeth and lunging at Scott, he would go down into the music room with a handful of biscuits. He'd throw a biscuit at her and she'd eat the cookie and then bark at him. He'd do this until he ran out of cookies and then call me to rescue him!

We were having a really hard time with our business and finances. We had and IRS audit that lasted a year and a half. I even allowed the agent to come into our home for 8 months. Even though she was a born again Christian, she wasn't an animal person. The dogs had to be outside or crated all day during her visits. I wasn't surprised near the end of our ordeal to find that she'd run over her own family cat.

With all these pressures, I hadn't the patience necessary to handle Raspberry's situation correctly. I'm high strung anyway and one needs to be calm when working with dogs. Much to Raspberry's credit, she hung on like a champ. She is a super dog and very special. There were days on our walks I am ashamed to admit I just lost it with her. We'd be walking and she'd see another dog. She'd go ballistic and I'd break. A couple of times, I just kicked her in the butt. I am deeply ashamed of losing my temper with Raspberry. I questioned my staying in rescue. Even the homeopath told me to quit rescuing. I felt like a loser. Raspberry never gave up on me, even when I gave up on myself. I'd end the walks on those days by kneeling down and telling Raspberry how sorry I was. She'd lick my face and let me know it was ok with her. She forgave me.

I am talking about this, because I know there are people who have lost their temper with their dogs. When the world's problems become our own and the stress of life becomes too much, we break. When we lose our temper with our dogs, because they don't behave as we want them to behave, we feel badly. I want to share my experiences with Raspberry, because there is a solution.

I woke up one Sunday to Scott yelling out in the road. He was hollering and hollering to hurry up. I managed to drag myself out of bed that morning and downstairs to the front door. What do I see but Scott, Cubby and Raspberry leashed and walking down middle of the road. Scott was barefooted which added a trailer park panache to the photo.

Not all of the days were filled with hope and progress. That whole year, the only exercise Raspberry got was walking down the main street in the gated community with leash laws. The town has a history of being a retired military settlement. Gone were the days when I'd hike the greenbelt with Girl. Those hikes had become my salvation, traipsing seven miles of primitive creeks and hills, oak and ash juniper where we could lose ourselves. I couldn't take Raspberry due to that dog owner who might not obey the leash law. Were something to happen, the leashed dog would be the one blamed, not the untrained off leash dog. Girl is so trained that when another dog charges us, she immediately retreats behind my legs and allows mom to handle the offender.

What about Raspberry's future? I worried that Raspberry would never find a home. I worried that she'd always be stuck with me living a substandard life. I could leave out the part about losing my temper, but I owe the truth to Raspberry, to other rescuers, to other people who've become overwhelmed and to all the dogs we've lost our temper with. There are times when all the training and behaviorists just don't seem to help. These are times when you just feel so alone and helpless.

I began to listen to my senses as I'd never listened before. Raspberry taught me that. On those days as we walked, I would look into her eyes and see what the writers talked about, that unconditional love. Raspberry forgave me. Instead of looking at the world as dark and hopeless, I began to see it as an adventure I could share with Raspberry. This is what Raspberry was teaching to me. I began to look forward to our walks. I knew even though she might go leash crazy, I could redirect and turn the other way. It took a bit of doing, but we began to enjoy our new system.

They built a new outdoor mall with a three mile decomposed granite hike and bike trail. Raspberry and I thought we'd died and gone to mall heaven! We began walking the trail with a new leash on life. It was pretty and you could see another dog coming in time to turn around or segue over to another part of the trail.

I had another realization. Even though we'd been to three group dog classes, I had reached an end point with Raspberry. I was no longer helping her. In fact, I had regressed with her. When we'd see another dog, I'd tense the lead and she'd overreact. I knew I needed to help Raspberry, but I didn't know what to do other than attend classes. By providence, something happened which laid the answer at our feet. I had re-homed a found puppy and become friends with the foster mom. She told me about a wonderful man who was like the dog whisperer and ran a local doggy daycare where the dogs all ran around off leash. She suggested I contact Mr. D about Raspberry.

I called him almost as soon as we hung up the phone. He wasn't concerned about Raspberry's aggression or rabies vaccinosis. As a matter of fact, he couldn't have cared less. He told me to bring her over the following Saturday afternoon. I sent a request in to the animal communicators group of which I was a member. This was the same group who'd helped me discover Raspberry's treatment at the hospital where she'd received her rabies shot and spay surgery.

Two wonderful ladies performed some session work with Raspberry. I had asked them to let her know she was going away to a doggy daycare with a man who understood dogs. I didn't want her to be afraid. We went about our week, Raspberry and I. We continued our walks at the mall and explored Kong recipes to keep her occupied and busy during her hours in the music room.

I got an email from Linda, one of the two ladies. Linda does emotion code work and wanted to know if I'd noticed a difference this week in Raspberry's attitude. I answered yes, indeed I had! Scott had mentioned the night before how happy Raspberry was. Linda told me that she and the other lady, Jayne, had been helping Raspberry all week through reiki and emotion code work. It had come to her attention that Raspberry was experiencing some aggression due to the mercury still in her system from the rabies shot. There was a product called Waiora Cellular Defense that safely removes metals and toxins from the body. Linda suggested I dose Raspberry for three weeks with Waiora and that should help the problem.

The next day, Raspberry and I met Mr. D. I was scared. I knew Raspberry was frightened, too. For the past year, it'd been just Raspberry and me. Soon and very soon, all that we knew was going to change. We pulled up into Mr. D's long driveway. The sound of barking dogs filled our ears. Raspberry and I looked at each other. "This is it, girl. You can do this." I smiled at her, but I was as nervous as she was. Mr. D met us as the car with his own leash. Mr. D is brilliant with dogs. He is the head of the pack and the dogs all know it. He has quite a set up. Aside from the main house is a large, fenced area with toys strewn about and a big swimming pool for the dogs.

Adjoining is another fenced area where he took Raspberry to sniff the twenty-five some odd dogs lined up to meet her. It was like a commercial. There were dogs of every size, shape, breed and age. Mr. D's own dogs wore bright orange collars. Raspberry was kind of stiff, but I could tell she wanted to meet the others. There was no aggression!

First, Mr. D let in his own dog, Buddy. Buddy is a big

gorgeous red boy who reminded me of Mookie. Buddy's job seems to be to break in the new guy. He came through the gate and size Raspberry up. He sniffed her while she politely allowed him to inspect her tail and tummy. He then allowed her to return the favor. This was her first chance to interact with another dog in over a year and she did just swell. You could tell she wanted to romp and cut loose, but she also knew a lot depended on this introduction. I watched her restrain herself and behave like a good girl.

Mr. D let in another one of his own crew and then another and another. Before I knew it, she was surrounded by all twenty-five plus dogs. It was the dangdest thing I'd ever seen and my eyes filled with tears. There was Raspberry in her element. She'd made it. Thanks to Mr. D, thanks to the two ladies who believed in her, thanks to Scott and thanks to God, she'd pulled herself through the horrible vaccinosis.

Mr. D let her romp with the others and it was something to behold. This is what I was meant to do. I couldn't save them all, but I could help that one. Raspberry came running over to the fence where I was. She was grinning. "Look at me," she was saying. "We did it. We made it!' There was no room for blaming myself for the times I'd lost my temper. There was only time to rejoice and celebrate. Raspberry was happy. Raspberry was healed.

As if I didn't have enough to be grateful for, the unbelievable happened. One day, I was talking to Mr. D on the phone. He said, "when the day comes to give back Raspberry, it's going to be a sad day for me." I'm like, "what do you mean?" Mr. D said he'd really gotten attached to her and they had become soul mates. We talked for a minute and he asked me about how to go about adopting. I answered him pretty quick and told him however he wanted to go about it!

The next time I went to Mr. D's, Raspberry ran to meet me at the fence. She was radiant. Around her fat little neck was a brand new bright orange collar. She was a very proud new member of her daddy's pack. Dangling from the collar was a rhinestone-encrusted sherbet colored dog tag reading, "Raspberry". Dreams don't come any truer than this.

Mr. D told me the story about Tommy. Tommy came from the foster mom who'd told me about the daycare in the first place. Tommy had always been something of a loner. Tommy would run around with the rest of the pack, but didn't have any real buddies. Not until he met Raspberry. Raspberry and Tommy are bff's, inseparable. Tommy lets Raspberry do things to him he'd never allow any other dog to do. They play and play for hours. When it's time for the afternoon nap, all tuckered out, Tommy lays on his back with Raspberry straddling him. She nuzzles and nibbles Tommy's neck while his tongue hangs out. Mr. D said that even if he hadn't adopted Raspberry for himself, he'd have adopted her just for Tommy.

Raspberry has taught me a lot about rescue, about dogs and about life. When I start to become overwhelmed at the 2,000 plus emails and messages I receive every day, I think about her. I remember her success and her happiness. Whatever life chooses to place in my path, whether a cat or a dog, a sentence to finish, a dish to wash, I stop and count my blessings. I think about Raspberry who would surely have been put to sleep had she not come into my life when she did. I think about all of the others who're benefitting from her story.

Chapter Eighteen
A Day in the Life
Part 2

Talk About the Passion
by R.E.M.

Pali's Dogs

Not all of the emails and phone calls I get each day have to do with animals in need, but most of them do concern animals in some respect. We are living in a terrible time. The shelters are full of unwanted animals and getting fuller by the minute. More than ever before, it seems we are hearing about someone's old dog or cat sitting in there confused and afraid. They can hear the other animals being euthanized as they wait on their own turn. And you ask why people hoard.

I have been lucky enough to find a network of others who care about animals like I do. God bless the internet. Talk about the information highway. Thanks to Pet Harbor supported by some of the better shelters and this tireless group of people, we are able to get the word out and save many of these forgotten and unwanted ones. Even our own president and his family wasted the most valuable commodity a rescuer has, time. By promising to adopt a shelter animal, he got the necessary votes to become elected while hundreds of rescues wrote letters and pitched their dogs and wasted time needed to save lives. Shame on our president for accepting a purchased dog as a gift when had an opportunity to make a difference. When I see the sad faces day after day, I wonder if the president knows or even cares that some 8 million animals are being killed in our shelters each year.

The lack of funding is constant. I have dogs in boarding with no way to pay. When I'm overdrawn, I'll go sit in front of the Starbuck's or grocery store with my rescue jar and table. When I get a little bit of extra energy, I'll try one of these groups with a foundation program to help dogs. I had to raise money for Davika's surgery recently. She needed the three tumors that sprouted up immediately after her shelter rabies shot removed. I called one of these groups of many who've sprung up in the past few years mindful how corporate the nature of rescue has become.

"Hello."

"Yes, Miss Marabito?"

"That's me."

"You called our group for help to raise money?"

"Thank you for calling me back."

"Well, you probably already have tried, but our first suggestion would be the large pet store chains."

I reply. "Yes, I have tried." The largest one of these chains recently told me they were too broke to help with a donation of $1,000.

The lady had another suggestion. "You might try some local resources, such as putting a collection box at a nearby vet hospital."

"The problem is Davika is in California and I'm in Texas."

"Then you should consider limiting your rescue efforts to local animals."

Here we go. "I began the rescue in California and am still networked heavily in the state. This dog was on the euthanasia list in Martinez. I couldn't just turn away when I am able to help.

"Miss Marabito, you've selected a difficult path. It's going to be very hard for you to raise money for animals from so far away."

"Rescue is difficult no matter where one is located."

"Perhaps you should consider working in your own area and turning over these others to rescue groups in California."

"That would be great had there been an abundance of such groups when these guys are looking at us from death row. At the time Davika was about to be put down, I was the only rescue who stepped up."

"You might consider a bake sale."

Time to hang up. If I have to depend on cakes and brownies to save pit bulls and others like Davika, we're all up the creek without a paddle. I might as well figure out a cure for cancer. All in all, Davika looks like she did beat the cancer. We did raise the money necessary to remove the three tumors. She also received a dental and had several extractions. While the doc was in there, he found even more trouble, an embedded and infected foxtail for years causing her much pain and suffering in the back of her jaw. There has been no return of the cancer. Along with the homeopathy, Davika, now known as Chika Chika and her brother Boom Boom, have been traveling. Their only agenda is daily hiking and we have the photo album to prove it. With a grade-five heart murmur, surgery was a huge concern, but I knew something for certain. When I happened to see Davika's photo by accident that day in the med ward at Martinez while she was awaiting euthanasia, I saw a girl that wanted to live. Against all odds, Davika showed me once again how powerful a thing the body could be when it wants to live. And she's not even a pit bull!

When I pulled Davika, I pulled an old Aussie, Daily who is now Romeo. He was 10 years old and put in the night deposit box by his family. Sadly, Romeo's story is the same as so many. I know people are broke, but I can show them how to feed their pets so cheaply. At the same time, I took Marla. She looked so pathetic with he paws on the bars of her kennel. Plus, I needed to pull a pit bull that week, right? Marla became Taffy, but now she is adopted to my good Pacifica friends and the staunchest pit bull advocates around. Stranger than fiction, Romeo's adopter is a longtime friend of Sasha's family.

I receive an email from Jack, now Carmine's, foster to adopt parents. They are moving to the east coast and wanted to update the rescue. For an old blind guy, Carmine sure gets around. Since I met him, he has traveled from Los Angeles to Santa Cruz to Oakland and now to Connecticut! What a life! What a miracle!

I have Pearlie boarding in a sanctuary. She was one of the three blue girls who were pulled last fall. The other two wound up in great homes, but Pearlie wasn't so lucky. She wound up in a dicey situation. Nice home, nice people, but like the man says, when you get behind closed doors. You don't want to think of the mistakes or bad things that happen to the dogs we love, but Pearlie showed up at the sanctuary with scarring across the muzzle. That didn't come from any gentle leader.

Yesterday, I got a call from one of the foster parents. The Sonoma shelter had a Round Up dog and wanted $500 plus dollars to return her. This was a first. Seems the foster dad went into the house for a minute and the Jasmine managed to get through a broken slat in the front yard fencing. He contacted the shelter immediately, but no difference. They had rules. With all of the incurred charges and fines, no one could afford to bail Jasmine out. I called the shelter and tried to be nice, but that didn't last too long. Before I got off the phone, the supervisor called me a hoarder. "I'll have you know I'm a high class hoarder," I told her.

The phone rings and it's a real adopter. The man actually sounds cohesive and qualified, a rarity for Texans. I can say that, being one. We start talking about Festus who I had to remove from the foster to adopt. The foster to adopter failed to follow some of the simple suggestions like attending the free training classes and missing the complimentary neuter appointment. I have two dogs that interest this fellow, Festus and Bullfrog. Bullfrog came with his sister, Brownie Rose three years ago. They were abandoned in the country and had been 'denning' themselves just like the paperwork reads in the head of a dry creek bed. Bullfrog came back under our lifetime guarantee.

The man wanted a nice family dog. Both Bullfrog and Festus were Animals First dogs. They just didn't have enough pitty to pass the cut. They were an amazing mix of Vizsla, Chesapeake Bay and lab. I called them Texas Brown Dogs. Bullfrog had turned out beautifully streamlined. He is a calm and easygoing fellow. I was determined to place him in the great home he deserved this time. The man went on to say he needed an outdoor dog. I asked him, "what's an outdoor dog?"

"Well, we have our daughter's longhair dachshund inside and we need a dog for the outside."

This was an intelligent sounding fellow who worked for the school system. I asked him why he wanted a dog for the outdoors and he answered he wanted a large dog to stay outside. I tried to educate him about what dogs really want. For some reason, people in Texas think dogs all want to be outside. In all my years, I've only got one outsider and that's Rebel. Ever since 9/11, Rebel's been on watch. When they shut down the Golden Gate Bridge and posted the National Guard, Rebel and I said we could have saved the country a lot of time and money. Word to the wise, don't leave your jet stream where Rebel can see it if you're interested in peace and quiet. Either way, every dog I've ever known wants to be where the people are. If you are outdoors, then they enjoy being outside.

This man wasn't having any of it. I'm trying to think of a way to say his name without getting into trouble. It contains part of the notorious dogfighter zero and football hero along with a French article. That cinched the closure of any deal on my part. The only other call I had that day had been from a Waco clown, no, a real clown, driving through town and wanted to adopt Daisy, the Brittany spaniel. Bad day for adoptions, but a good day for clowning around.

About once a week, Scott tells me to get out of rescue. That's a joke. Anyone who's in the game will tell you, it's like the mafia. You can't just quit. There is no getting out. "Just when I thought I was out, they pull me back in." If somebody asked me how to describe myself, I'd have to say part Big Love Lois, part Bunny Rabbit and part Wendy and Lucy. I have a very simple life. I don't require much. I don't need to have pedicures and attend fancy luncheons, not to say there's anything wrong with that lifestyle.

This morning, I got up and I was glad to get up. How many 56-year old women love to get up? This morning was a special day. Yesterday, the litter of orphan kittens went into general population with my old guys. Since Roy passed away, it's been kind of lonely. We have Martha Kate and her chronic eye condition that just about drives me insane. With all my Granny Clampett tonics and potions, I can't seem to lick it! She came to us out of the Petsmart. There's my Street Cat boys, Fernando and Germ, short for Germany a.k.a. Jeremy Meowrice. My friend, Byrd, says Germ looks like an old Mauriceville cat. He does! Buddy is 19 and Candy is 18 or so. She won't tell us. Now they're about to crap all over themselves with those five kittens in there.

The kittens came from Mr. D. Mr. D, who to me is about as close to God on earth as you can get, called me one day and said he had something happen to him that had never happened before. A momma cat had left four kittens right outside his doggy daycare. I offered to post the news on all my sites and help him get them a foster home. Being kitten season, they wound up here plus one. Black Patsy Cline, the militant runt was yet to be caught. After the mom had safely delivered the kittens to Mr. D's, she'd been hit by a car and killed. Please slow down, everybody. The day after I picked them up, Mr. D heard a commotion and the dogs were all lined up barking at the spot where the kittens had been. There was a big, old rat snake with his mouth full of a Norway rodent right smack dab where those kittens had been.

These kittens were about four weeks old when they came and took up residence in the music room. I crated them and started them on raw and kitten replacement milk. I must say, they were in extraordinarily good health. The mother had lovingly nursed them. They were social and adapted to me easily. There were two Bengal looking-brown tabbies with white markings like Germ and Fern. I named the boy Slim Harpo and the girl Prima Donna. I call her Darcy Doucette. She's the middle girl, easy and fun, loves to eat and gets fatter every day. The tortoiseshell girl is Gypsy Kristine after Bella and Lola's beautiful mother, but we call her Turquoise. Her markings caused me to nickname her Lil' Possum along with her other nickname, Butch Hancock. I named the blue and white boy Douglas after his savior. The runt of the litter came last, Black Patsy Cline, the littlest Black Panther you ever saw.

If life ever gets you down, save yourself a litter of kittens. Nothing on God's green earth is more precious than kittens. To cherish means adore, hold dear, dote on, be devoted to, revere, esteem, admire, think the world of, set great store by, hold in high esteem, care for, tend to, look after, protect, preserve, keep safe, treasure, prize, value highly, hold dear, foster, nurture. To see those precious kittens visit the enclosure and safely play on the cat furniture, discover the trill of a songbird and learn to manage among some grouchy elder statesmen is exactly what I had needed and hadn't known.

The kittens taught me a great lesson about rescuing. The whole time I've been in rescue, I've been planning, manipulating, placing this one there and worrying about that one. I didn't know how to let things happen as they are supposed to happen. As the tea bag says, 'know that you can move through every change of tide'. I can pretty much say I can take what they throw at me.

Epilogue I
The Story of Pip

Everybody's Talkin'
by Fred Neil

Pip

Pip was in a shelter outside Bakersfield for over a
year. To the shelter's credit, they kept her alive. Bakersfield,
California is an example of a modern day Auschwitz. Something
like 500 unwanted dogs come into the Kern County Shelter
every week. Due to the tireless round the clock internet work
of men and women in my peer group, a small portion of these
animals are being saved. However, most of the time, it's a
slaughterhouse. For a country as wealthy as the United States
and such a bounteous and lush state as California is, these
statistics are a horror story. When I began the rescue, Gray
Davis was our governor. Times were great. Now, the governor
is famed bodybuilder Arnold Schwarzenegger. He's made huge
strides during his tenure to lessen the stray period so we can
slaughter more animals more quickly. Danke schoen, good
buddy!

Pip is just that, a pip! She is a quirky anomaly. The
definition of pip on the internet is a disease of poultry, a minor
nonspecific ailment, shoot: a kill by firing a missile, a small hard
seed found in some fruits, spot: a mark on a die or on a playing
card, worst: defeat thoroughly, blip: a radar echo displayed so as
to show the position of a reflecting surface. Pip is the dog that
defines dog. She hates sex and loves toys. She will spend hours
throwing an old stuffed Christmas tree that's been chewed
on by a ton of foster dogs up and down, up and down, up and
down all day and night. She is gentle and soft-mouthed. Labs
are supposed to be soft mouthed to retrieve game, but the other
day, this fat lab named Bruno just about took my arm off. Pip
must have been a ballerina in another life. When she pees, she
actually plies!

I was pulling dogs out of this tiny shelter when one of
the volunteers contacted me about Pip. Pip had been there
a year and her time was up. I pulled a lot of dogs from this
shelter, but like most of us, they became careless in their rush
to save the dogs. They forgot to mention Pip had never been
inside a house before. I adopted her to a family in the headlands

with an antique filled house. Upon her release that day, she was vaccinated. By the time she reached her new home, she reacted violently to the hundreds of reflections throughout the mirror filled home. The family called animal care and control and had Pip removed.

Through some quick thinking, we got Pip out of that high kill shelter and on a transport all the way back down to the little shelter outside Bakersfield. This time, they weren't so glad to see Pip and fired back at me for the next four days. As usual, I was broke and had no tricks up my sleeve. I had one friend in Bakersfield and I called her. My good friend, Gabby, was partnered with a girl who ran a rescue franchise. I'd never heard of rescues branching out before. I didn't realize we were making that much money. This outlet was part of a bigger operation back east.

What they concentrated on were these puppy litters at the high kill shelters they'd pull for free and sell for big bucks. My friend, Gabby, is a good person who went into this venture to save animals. She had dogs like the rest of us who had to be shuffled about while they waited to find that perfect home. Her dog was Shelly. Shelly was a five year-old mastiff mix that Gabby had championed since a puppy. When mere babes, Shelly and her sister wound up at a high kill shelter. The sister was adopted and Shelly was lucky enough to find Gabby.

Over the next four years, Gabby was able to move Shelly around to the various groups and organizations where she volunteered. This dog managed to stay alive in one of the highest kill areas for animals in the United States for four years. This is amazing stuff. When I met Gabby and Blake, the chic young woman behind the actual organization, Shelly was boarded at the facility. Gabby suggested I speak to Blake about rescuing Pip.

I called her and was happy to find that she would visit the small shelter Pip had come from and where Pip had been returned. I told the young lady I would help as I could with

$50 per week should she take Pip on. Over the next couple of months, I got a clearer idea of how this outfit truly functioned, as did Gabby. Gabby was beginning to have doubts about her involvement with the group. I was scrambling to raise money for this one to have an operation and to meet that one's boarding costs when I fell behind in the fifty-dollar payments to the tune of $150. I'd been hearing from Gabby about the human error snafus at the old vet office cum kennel. You don't get the best help for hourly wage and someone was always leaving a gate unlatched and the inevitable was bound to happen. And happen it did, almost daily. The day it happened with Pip, someone left her cage unlocked and she tried to nail a Golden Retriever who'd been staring her down as she walked by each day to go play. Finally, Pip had enough and jumped the Golden. Pip's a Dobie/Malinois with a dash of Dutch Shepherd and a piss-poor fighter. She lost this one and badly. The Golden tore Pip up pretty good.

When Blake called me that evening, her squeaky voice escalating even higher while going on about that awful Pip dog, I asked her to keep Pip contained while I tried to come up with something. I'm pretty good at throwing things together, but I'm no magician. I called Gabby to find out what actually occurred at the kennel with Pip. Gabby had interviewed the crew and her other associate at the facility for details surrounding Pip-gate. Indeed, the Golden had been allowed to challenge Pip day after day until today when the door to Pip's kennel was not secured.

Before I was allowed to come up with plan B, Blake took Pip to the high kill Kern County Shelter in Bakersfield. This shelter intakes some incredibly high number like nine thousand dogs a year. Blake turned Pip in as a stray dog. I know, because I have the paperwork. I also have the paperwork with her name and her rescue's name as the adopter from the smaller shelter Pip originated from. To turn a dog like Pip into a high kill shelter as a stray is the same as placing a loaded gun to her pointed head and pulling the trigger. The Golden was retained at the rescue center and later adopted for a large donation.

I was scared and I did what I always do when I get frightened for the animals. I wrote a letter to my animal communication friends I posted Pip's photo and asked for their help. During the next 24 hours, some amazing things took place. First, Pip knew she was going to die. She told the first communicator that. She just hoped that the people in her life learned something about dogs. I took that to mean me. I hoped I could learn what Pip wanted me to learn.

Pip told the communicator that she was a big, strong and smart girl. She told her AC that she needed someone who got her, Pip's words. She liked and needed training. She thrived on it. For a dog who'd never even been in a house and who'd survived in a shelter most of her life, this was sage. I was writing back and forth through the next day with the group, the next day being a Saturday. Another AC piped in. This was an amazing day. Right as she piped in, my friend, Gabby, went down to the county shelter to try and see Pip. The #2 AC sent a message from Pip to the group. Pip said that someone there at the shelter 'got her'. Now, I never expected the right soul to show up at the very last house on the block. This was like finding Jesus in Pelican Bay lockdown.

Right as I was reading this message, I was speaking with Gabby on the phone. Gabby's voice rose excitedly and she told me she had to go, that she'd call me later and hung up. I was dumbfounded, but I'd learned to trust the greater power. I had just learned it and it's an art I haven't quite perfected just yet. I'm still working on the just breathing part. But, I tried it. I tried it for Pip's sake. Her transcript where she had said she was just waiting to die was hard to take. I could at least try to breathe for her. That's what I could do.

Gabby called me back after about an hour. She had a plan. There just happened to be a person at the shelter who was willing to board Pip at her kennel down in Palmdale. This woman really knew dogs and had been in rescue for a good number of years. For $300 a month, we could buy Pip some time and a stay of execution. During the next couple of hours, we sent the necessary paperwork to adopt Pip and hitch her a ride to the desert. I wanted to make sure all our t's were crossed and i's dotted so Pip wouldn't get yet another vaccination. The one thing there never seems to be a shortage on is vaccinations!

During the next year, I got to know Tess pretty well. Tess is the woman who 'got' Pip....in more ways than one. Pip was boarded for one year down in Palmdale. That's where we truly learned that Pip loves toys, namely a big orange snake. I didn't see it at the time, but was this an omen? Orange is THE color in my town and sometimes I've wondered why the state animal hadn't been a rattler instead of the Mockingbird. Tess would work with Pip over the next year, but Pip was still in a kennel. Pip is a dog that needs to be owned and worked.

Right after Gabby saved Pip at the last minute, something terrible happened. We all have husbands and partners who aren't as gung ho as we are in the rescue world. One rescue lady recently sent out a group email with a corny poem about how wonderful her husband was. At the end of the piece lay the realization that the woman speaking had her husband mistaken for the bottle of wine. Gabby's husband had forced her to go away for a few days. For a normal person, a getaway is a blessing, but for a rescue gal, it's pure torture. It takes so much to train somebody to feed this one and that one, chop this up for the birds and give that cat his remedy. It's so stressful to prepare, that it's just easier to stay home.

While Gabby was away, Blake had Shelly euthanized. Shelly, who'd managed to keep herself alive in one of the highest kill regions in the state for four years, wound up dead at the rescue facility! Shelly had been taken on a walk with a small dog, a Boston. Shelly did not like snappy little dogs and the Boston Terrier was a snappy little dog. The kennel attendant, in a hurry, had grabbed Shelly and the Boston to take them for their daily 10 minute walk. Shelly was wearing a faulty collar that broke apart. She grabbed the Boston with her teeth and the dog suffered a puncture wound.

When Blake found out about the incident, she immediately drove to her facility and picked Shelly up. She was angry. I know, because she called and left a message for me. She needed to teach Gabby a lesson. She took Shelly, a dog legally owned by another rescue, Gabby's group, and had a vet euthanize her. When I heard what she'd done, all of the pain and rage over Pip rose in me. I sat down at my computer and posted Pip's story along with Shelly's story. Poor Gabby. She loved Shelly and for Shelly to die without the company of those who loved her and tried to keep her alive was just plain wrong. Shelly died alone in some vet's office, dropped off by a pissed off girl who has no right to call herself a rescuer. Unfortunately, there are many like her who take advantage of these overpopulated shelters and pull purebreds and sell to the highest donator.

Rather than harbor negative feelings, I tried to put my energy toward an area where it could do some good. I couldn't bring Pip to Texas while I had Raspberry. I had my full-time foster dog. Pip was kenneled for two and a half years. She made herself a lot of friends during that time. She traveled up and down California and earned herself quite a reputation as a companion and passenger. She was lovely in the car. Everyone she met decided a different breed for her. With one, she was a shepherd, another was sure she was blue heeler. The tiny shelter and police station where she originated had her listed as a Dane and Blake just called her a pit. I love pit bulls and spend all my time trying to figure something out for them, but Pip ain't no pit. The discovery I made from her description was sadly that this woman hated pit bulls. Mr. D has a funny thing to say about breeds. He told me the other day that nowadays, just about everything has pit in it. That made me laugh. I'm incorporating it into my sales pitch for why to adopt from a shelter.

Mr. D really saved the day when he adopted Raspberry. I was finally able to bring Pip to Texas. She is not a dog park dog, hates sex and loves toys. She really likes to chill out in the music room and toss her toy. I realized more than any of the other dogs every, Pip is me. No matter how hard we try, we can't seem to make it through the day without getting into a fight. Pip likes to chew her rawhide ever so often and we go on a morning walk each day and enjoy nature together. She'll watch a bird for an hour if you let her. Today, she was as mesmerized as I was by a huge fluttering butterfly. I know a joy you can't put a price on when I walk with Pip. She is such a Pip.

Epilogue II
Arthur

Forever Young
by Bob Dylan

Arthur

We rescues might not always get along, but the good ones rally when an animal is in jeopardy. That's what is happening today with Arthur. I pulled Arthur and his sister, Molly about a year before this writing. They were even kenneled together at a high kill shelter. Most rescues and shelters have a tenuous relationship. Granted, there is a need for shelter 'A' numbers and rules, but we should all be on the same page in regards to saving lives.

A particular rescue who I'd enjoyed a longtime relationship would often pull dogs for me and transfer ownership to my rescue. Most of us are working class individuals without the benefit and luxury of staff, payroll and basic help. Most of the rescues that I know and work with are one-man operations, the downside being extreme exhaustion and stress and the occasional overlooked detail.

Arthur's third foster to adopt home sprang up when a couple applied for Jack, the blind 10 year old by way of Los Angeles. Jack was recently placed in a marvelous home with lots of love and photos, his eye drops refilled for another year and enjoying his new life with dog walker mom, dad and sister, Fiona. Being an entrepreneur, I was getting Arthur back from the second foster to adopt home after the foster mom was diagnosed with muscular dystrophy. I pitched Arthur.

The application looked great. The couple worked for a big hospital and had a dog and a cat. It looked like a potential home sweet home happily ever after type of deal, the rescuer's dream. Long story short, it was a perfect home. The couple brought their dog and met Arthur at the mobile adoption and we spoke at length on the phone about our program, about Arthur's raw diet, about treating with homeopathy, about Arthur's crate and Kong training, on which we'd worked so very hard. When Arthur entered this home, he was about as near perfect as one could hope for.

I began emailing the next day and didn't receive a reply until several days later. The woman apologized for the delay in responding, but Arthur was doing wonderfully and getting along perfectly with their dog and cat. They even sent a picture. I sent several more emails over the next month without reply. I fall prey to the same potholes in the road as other animal lovers do. I love these dogs and want to believe that everyone else loves them, too. That's where I leave myself open to error. I believe that's what has happened in the case of Arthur. I wanted to believe this was a perfect home.

I finally get a reply email about a month later. Everything sounded perfect. In fact, it was almost a repetition of their first email. Then two months passed with me growing more and more concerned. Life is busy in the rescue community, like today as I'm still sitting here at the computer in my boxer shorts and my wife beater just a typing away. Take a deep breath and plug on ahead. Like the man Mr. Flaubert says, "Be orderly in your normal life so you can be violent and original in your work."

Again, I answer over and over to nothing. No replies at all. I call several times and begin leaving messages at the woman's job. I find it disconcerting that her three references all work for the same company. I begin to research. Funny word, research. In fact, that's what the woman does for a living. She works in a medical research facility. The couple's home is owned by that facility. My poor mind begins to dramatize and drive me over the brink. I am chilled to the core of my being. I feel frightened as I've never felt before. I remember all of those Saturdays and Sundays I would protest with Rebel and Mookie against the illicit horror of skinning and anally electrocuting beautiful creatures for their fur. When I see a person wearing one of those puffy homey jackets with the German Shepherd collar, I'm reminded of the HSUS underground tape of the German Shepherd being skinned alive. I remember that PETA film of the little white fox looking into the secret camera, pleading for help when there was no help for her.

I am terrified. I cannot get access to Arthur. I have no

proof that he is alive and well. No one has seen the dog in three months. The volunteer who fostered Arthur tries to call. The number's mailbox is full and both of us are unable to leave a message. We set up a time for her and her partner to visit the home where Arthur is being fostered. The house is dark and the shades are drawn.

The next day I ask a fellow animal rights activist and one of the adopters to visit the home during the daylight hours. The plan is to see Arthur, take him for a walk and make a wellness appointment at our vet. We want to be absolutely sure Arthur is not being used in medical research experimentation. Mainly, I just want Arthur back safe and sound. The couple violated the agreement and I do not want to go forward with an adoption.

The two men knock on the door of the facility owned duplex. They are on VA property and accompanied by a member of the facility police department. The house is as dark as it was the night before, shades drawn. There was the sound of one dog barking indoors. A security staff member approaches the rescue representatives and the policeman. The security guard informs them by the security person that they are trespassing and are ordered off the property. At that moment, here comes the foster husband. He is carrying his laptop computer and saying something to the effect of how he's been communicating all along with me. My representative was struck that the gentleman went to the trouble to boot up his laptop and bring it outside. Why not just bring Arthur outside? Again, why can't we see the dog?

Before the dirt's allowed to settle, I receive a terse and angry email from the foster wife. Rather than any mention of Arthur, the email opens with her statements about living on federal grounds and being protected. I can't help but think about the Nancy Grace show and when some husband is asked about his missing wife. It's always rather suspicious when the husband immediately demands an attorney. If only I would have received communication of any sort during the past three

273

months and had been able to set up an appointment to visit Arthur, this ugliness could all have been avoided.

I do not answer the email. I know I'm a hothead, but I also know to let someone else speak for me. CCACC gave me a prime education in that respect. My good friend and rescue attorney, Grace, offers to call the woman. She is not in any respect acting as our attorney, but just trying to diffuse the situation. I wait. I will do a lot of waiting in the next few days.

The foster wife began by trying to out-lawyer the lawyer. Over the next forty-five minutes, Grace listened and tried to center the conversation as the woman went from angry to tearful pleading. In fact, when Grace called me after the phone call, she asked me to re-consider allowing the adoption. My friend said she truly believed Arthur was in a good home. When Grace began to recount the conversation, my stomach caved in. I realized Grace had been snowed.

The woman sent a joint email that evening to both Grace and myself. The letter was nasty and vitriolic. She hit below the belt. Rather than try and find a solution to this situation, she went digging instead to see what kind of dirt she could dig up on Grace. I've known Grace for twelve years. She is a lovely, soft-spoken person whom I met walking dogs at CCACC after she'd studied hard all day at law school. Rather than entering one of the areas with deep pockets, she dedicated herself to saving animals. I've never met an individual more hardworking and caring. For this woman to speak to her in such a manner was unacceptable. If I had any misgivings before, I certainly did now. I did not want Arthur in that sort of environment. I just wanted the dog back.

The next two days were a nightmare. The first night, a helpful facility policeman attempted to knock on the door of the residence. Again, the house was dark and silent. He offered to return the next day. Like me, he mentioned he was suspicious of foul play. I waited all day the following day for him to return to the facility residence. He visited the home that afternoon to find it closed, dark and still quiet. We spoke repeatedly over the telephone during the day. That night at 10:20 central standard time, I received a call from the officer stating that he'd just visited Arthur and Arthur was just fine, a very happy and waggy dog! He told me not to worry and that he would send the photograph I requested. At least, if my rescue was unable to see Arthur, this kindly policeman from the facility was able to hold and pet Arthur.

I checked my emails throughout the night. I wasn't sleeping much this week, anyway. I checked first thing in the morning and several times throughout the a.m. hours. Nothing. I finally called the poor man again to see if he had the right email address for me. "Oh, yes," he answered, "Miss Marabito. I'm still working on it." Finally, at 3 p.m. central time I received the photo. There was a very blurry square inch impression of a white dog. The dog was curled up next to some sort of weird structure. Whatever it was, was indistinguishable and I was unable to identify just what it was. It didn't look like furniture or resemble the only two photos I'd received two days after Arthur entered the foster residence. This photograph was terrifying to me. I've seen the photos of dogs in labs. Whoever the dog was in the blurry pixilated photograph, he did not look like a happy, waggy dog. I've seen enough dogs to know what one looks like.

I received the email from the officer's Hotmail account yesterday as I sit and write today and try to organize and make sense of the events. I try to remain level headed. I know I screwed up by not checking the foster's application more thoroughly. Had I called the three references she listed as knowing for five years, I would have received the same voicemail I listen to every time I call the foster's work phone. They all work in the same research lab. I would have discovered that for the application to be truthful, the three women and co-workers at the research lab would all have to have attended the same ivy league university as this woman who graduated only three years ago. The red flags were starting to outnumber the positives. It's hard for me to remain calm, but I must for Arthur's sake.

I plod forth through the red tape and the details. God is in the details. If I remain strong and even, I will be able to do some good, I will be able to get Arthur back. Without remaining centered, it's easy to fall prey to panic. My job is to email, write, call, post, do what I can do to have Arthur returned to our rescue. I call the local animal control, yet another big swanky outfit with lots of departments, lots of outreach, lots of behaviorists and lots of money. Here we go again.

I started out by jumping through the right hoops. The very first phone call I'd made had been to the animal control. They don't call it animal control, but instead a long drawn out name with lots of animal friendly euphemisms in the title. Bottom line, it's another high dollar dog pound, just like CCACC. Just like the CCSPCA, lots of donors and lots of puff pieces in the media, lots of fat wallets on the payroll. The director pulled down over 300K in 2008. That's a lot of dogs. I'd had dealings with him in the past. My old buddy, Colleen, had hired on as their animal control supervisor and had caused static around my rescue cell tower. I try to remain focused and just walk out with the dog, but the average Joe has absolutely no idea how much time and effort some of these individuals invest in making sure they remain in absolute control. To me, the soft-spoken corporate guys like this one were the scariest of all.

I am thinking of Vivienne today. Vivienne came from this very facility. Human aggression was what their dog behaviorists labeled her with. She came to us by way of one of their own, an animal control officer who'd had a bellyful. It isn't difficult to get sick of watching dogs die. This officer contacted the homestyle facility where I'd boarded T-Rex, Tutti-Frutti and so many others. The officer outright adopted the little dog and she was brought to Andy's. I posted this little one on the websites and before too long, I had a reply. Friends of the couple who'd adopted Frenchie asked if they could meet Vivienne. Amazingly, Frenchie's new parents and this young couple were all from Texas, right down the highway from my hometown. Both couples had moved west and each couple had a dog walking business.

That was many years ago. Vivienne went on to become certified as a canine good citizen. She lives with a Chihuahua sister, a pug and a red nose. She did do something very scary a few years ago. For Halloween, Vivienne dressed as the MGM lion. We had to keep reminding her to stand up, though. It's hard to look fierce when you're lying down.

I called this facility to ask for help. They are huge, so there were extra hoops to jump through. I ate a good breakfast, took a deep breath and got to dialing. After about 10 minutes of automated instructions, I punched the last zero and waited. I finally got someone, a nice girl at the counter. Some people really try hard for the animals and this was one of those people. She gave me the inspector's line and I left a short message in regards to our fears concerning Arthur. I waited for a reply call, but none came for several hours.

I didn't mind. I called the inspector again and was able to ask the lady to dispatch my call to her line in the field. When I explained my concerns about Arthur, I was met by the same rhetoric that would become a sickening echo in my ears for the next week. I was beginning to wonder if the humane societies and the police departments, the attorneys and the media were all reading from the same teleprompter. I heard the same format many times over and over and over, morning, noon and night. I began to feel like the sick dogs and cats force-fed that pre-digested pulp they sell at the vet office. I was having a hard time keeping mine down, too.

The inspector corrected me first off when I referred to her as officer. "In-SPECK-tor!," she corrected. I apologized and altered my salutation. I tried to explain our situation, explaining that Arthur hasn't been seen in over three months and we were concerned for his welfare. "That's a civil matter. You need to call a lawyer. We don't get involved in civil cases." Again, I was getting attitude for caring about an animal. I kept my calm and asked her if she could just check on the dog. We just want to make sure he is alive and cared for. I was prepared to do what I had to do to walk out with the dog.

She promised me she would go in and do the check. I asked the inspector if she would call me and let me know as soon as she saw the dog. I had her word that she'd return my call and let her know that I'd keep my phone on me. I let her know I respected her schedule and didn't want to add more to a busy overload. I waited. I called other agencies while I waited. I emailed everyone in my rescue database. I posted on Craigslist. I also spoke with a nice sounding officer from the facility police, so helpful.

I didn't hear back from the inspector by five p.m., so I called their shelter and held while the automated menu accessed. I typed in all the ones and zeros, etcetera, and got the inspector's line again. I left a message at the risk of being a pest. Why should it be a nuisance to ask the local animal protection society to protect an animal? Something was wrong with this picture.

When I didn't receive a return call, I called the counter again. After the regimen of automated menus, ones, zeros and recorded messages, I finally reached a live person. This time, the live person was not as unstressed as the earlier counter person. This one sounded like she'd had a long day. I understood. So had I. "Look," she said. "Inspector_____ is very busy. She can't check on every dog." I answered her with calmness. I let her know I wasn't expecting special treatment, but our dog was thought to be in harm's way. After 10 minutes of pleading, she finally told me the inspector left at 3:30. Boy, what I'd do for hours like that. Most days, I'm still hacking away at the computer by mid-afternoon. Today was one of those days.

The next day, there was a catastrophic explosion and the inspector was caught up with the rest of the community saving animals in distress. I am all for helping the animals and understood better than anyone why she did not ever return my phone calls. I swallowed hard and decided to call the director of the facility. It took all day, but he actually returned my call that evening.

He authored a blog, hearkening back to his poetry writing schooldays, which tackled subjects like diet preferences and claims that fish have no souls. His seven-year deal includes a million-dollar house he and his family kick back in each night in this lush, upscale neck of the woods. All in all, I can't help but think of how many dogs I could save with that wad of green as I scrounge every week to put together Pearlie Girl's $100 boarding. Pearlie's a dog that wouldn't last a millisecond in this place. The whole deal is just plain wasteful. Sorry. Blog that.

I guess I'd laugh, too, and that's just what this guy did. I tried to breathe and not sound too crazy. I tried to just stick to the facts, ma'am. I am violently passionate. I know that. I try to hold it back around this man with his exotic office pets, aquarium lizards who belong in preserves or their natural habitat. I explained the story surrounding Arthur and asked him please for a wellness check. This is when he began to laugh his empty Johnny Carson laugh. This was not funny to me. I asked him to reconsider, as I was fearful for Arthur's wellbeing. More laughter. He then went on to explain how the law works and began to spew a few numbers to make his point. I guess he picked up a math minor along with his writing sheepskin. One thing about these shelter guys, they could sure crunch some numbers.

I realized I'd lost long before the call was finished. In fact, I knew it was over before I even picked up the phone to answer his call. He finally interrupted his chuckling to wrap it up with his opinion that I didn't have one leg to stand on. I felt no anger or animosity. The fight wasn't there. I answered him with calm. "No sir, you're right. I have three legs." He laughed again, but this time, he didn't sound as convinced.

I had bigger fish to fry. I thought about Mookie right now. He's gone, but I remember him every day. If I'd ever known truth, it was when I'd looked into Mookie's face. I recalled all those months we fought the government to keep Mookie's record honest and clean. Remembering Mookie gave me the strength I needed to help Arthur. All the dogs I've loved and known have released in me a power I didn't know I had. All those many walks I'd taken with Raspberry, not knowing what the outcome was to be. All those nights staying up late pounding away at my computer trying to find a foster for Hope, a girl from Bakersfield. T-Rex, who I'd let down. Maybelle. Angus. They are with me here in spirit as I write this.

Over the next seven days, I write and call every single police station, animal control, sheriff and what have you that will pick up a phone and has animal anything in the moniker. I call the facility's media arm, I call the lady's boss who runs the pain lab. I call the director and also leave a message for the assistant director. Nothing. I call Washington. I'm screamed at and hung up on by the hotline and get a frosty response from the top dog's office. I remain objective and rational, two words I'm losing from my vocabulary after this awful mess is over and we have Arthur back safe and sound. When Arthur's recovered, I'm dedicating myself to petting kittens, coo cooing the birds, walking the dogs. These are the activities I signed up for. I got into rescue to help animals, not argue with bloated overpaid posers who throw boring gala events in the name of animals, but refuse to help when an animal is truly in distress and there's no tv camera running. I didn't apply for the job to hold for an hour waiting to speak to some Nazi throwback demanding I click my heels and call her inspector. When I click my heels, I want to be holding a fuzzy little dog and all the bad people to go away.

My neck hurts so badly from typing and craning to hold my cell phone while I fill water dishes, feed the birds, clean litter boxes, not to mention my household chores. I do not care. I have found an attorney who'll take the case. He is awesome. He's all about the animals, but works for a great big law firm. To take the case, we need to raise $5,000 dollars and place in a trust for Arthur. I get that. It's business. We all love animals, but courts cost money.

The sad thing about this entire affair is the reaction I get from friends and family. I see their glazed eyes and understand when they overlook what the woman does for a living and that the couple violated the terms of the foster application. They don't understand the horror of not being able to see Arthur for over three months. They just think I'm being rigid. I really do understand their concerns, but to operate a rescue and one that saves pit bulls, I cannot afford to make a mistake. Some of these people would love to see Round Up Rescue screw up, but that is not why I'm such a stickler for maintaining the guidelines of our program. There is a good reason we are known as the home of the world's friendliest pit bulls. Part of our mission is to share our program with any dog owner out there who is feeling stressed. We have about a 50% success rate with calls from people on the verge of relinquishing their pet.

There are a few simple directions, carefully explained to every potential adopter who writes me about a dog or cat. There's a good reason I have 20,918 messages in my sent box, last count. These directions involve crate training, Kong training, diet and nutrition, medical treatment and obedience training. These standards are not only for the protection and welfare of the dog, but in consideration of the foster family as well. We have been successfully fostering animals to homes under these terms for 12 plus years. This is the first experience in our history we've had the foster lie on the application, lie to the police, lie to the feds, lie to animal authorities and lie to the dog pound and still be protected. In fact, we are the ones being attacked and treated as if we are bothering people. What about Arthur's welfare? Can't one representative knock on the door and see that Arthur is safe?

I had trusted the property police department who guarded the facility, who were employed by the same government who signed the foster applicants' paychecks. One officer in particular had extended a degree of kindness. He intimated he was suspicious of the couple and would stop by to try and see Arthur. This went on for the better part of last week. I began to become suspicious. Throughout the week, I held on the phone, left messages, sent emails and still, no one had seen Arthur or would try to perform a wellness check. What is wrong with this system? Just last week, someone here in my neighborhood reported to the sheriff's department that I had cats trapped in a large cage. The poor lady sheriff knocked on the door and apologized, but said they had to follow up on all calls. I had to laugh and motion her to come in. I told her she was just going to have to view this one for herself. The look on her face was absolutely priceless when I escorted her into our cat room and the adjoining deck enclosure. The large cage the complainer was referring to was an outdoor deck, 12' high and contained with 1x1 PVC coated galvanized. I had ordered the stock from a man in the Pacific Northwest. I had built the first indoor/outdoor habitat when we lived in California and brought the leftover materials back with me to Texas. Appropriately, I now had a Texas-size cat enclosure. The sheriff called dispatch, laughing, and told them she was on her way back to the station and this is one they just weren't going to believe.

This experience was just one example of how the animals are protected in my neighborhood as opposed to the last county I lived in when I was a California taxpayer. This is prime for remembering why I'd relocated back to Texas after Junior was killed. If I wasn't sure five years ago, I was certainly aware of the difference now. Last night I was cuddling the kittens and my old cat crew as we listened to a radio broadcast of All Things Considered. The story was about Istanbul, Turkey and the stray dog problem. In Turkey, they have an overwhelming problem with dog population, as does the rest of the universe. However, when a dog is picked up in this community, he's taken to the shelter, microchipped, spayed or neutered and his medical needs addressed. The difference between Istanbul and Arthur's county, is the Turkish dog is returned to the streets. The Turkish dog is protected. Depending on the affluence of the community, Istanbul dogs are cared for by the local shopkeepers. The dog focused in the broadcast was sheltered in a custom doghouse the merchants built for him. Another local restaurant fills the dog's food bowl with delicacies from his café. By Moslem custom, dogs and animals are thought to be unclean and not allowed into the home. This country could sure take a page from the Koran on how to treat animals.

I get a call from the inspector finally. Seems like she's got a handle on the explosion and can finally address Arthur's situation in which she was asked to perform a wellness check and refused. Of course, there weren't any national news cameras and reporters wondering about Arthur. Only me. I was in the doctor's office when she called and left a message. She'd decided that the couple were official adopters and advised them to vaccinate 'their dog' and let me know she thought they were good people and Arthur was very happy with them. Lastly, she warned me that I was harassing them and to stop it immediately. All that from one phone call! I bet she could fix the economy in two days and settle that spat over the Gaza strip short of a week. She was being wasted as an inspector for the local dog pound.

I called and left her a calm message, just to clear up a couple of minor points. I let her know that we planned to hire an attorney who agrees with the law that Arthur is owned by our rescue, that this couple has misrepresented the facts to police, the feds and the local dog pound, all of whom believed their fabricated story. I let her know in my message that this call was a courtesy call, the last call I would be making to her particular office. If she had any questions, I then directed her to all of the postings and alerts made on Arthur's behalf and which could be accessed throughout the internet and listed all of the URL's for her convenience. Lastly, I mentioned I would be making one last call to her boss, not the poet laureate that ran the corporation, but the animal control director. I ended the message with a heads up for the inspector. It was not her job to make decisions that will be decided in a court of law.

I actually get a pretty nice guy on the phone when I ask for the animal control division. I don't know if he's really a nice person, but he does get the law. I gave him a short rundown regarding my experiences with his inspector and her message about Arthur. I then told him this was a courtesy call and my attempt follow the correct protocol by their rules. I mentioned that I'd followed curriculum for the past seven days and I'd done it all their way. "Now," I said, "we're going to do it the Cindy Marabito way." I suggested he have a sit down with the lady inspector and tell her that by advising the people who have officially stolen Arthur to vaccinate him and ignore the rescue who owns the dog is opening their huge organization to a huge liability. He got that point loud and clear. I ended the conversation with the information that we were raising the money to hire an attorney to get Arthur back and that I was hoping against all hope that Arthur has not been abused. I asked him to consider public response should Arthur fall under harm's way. The community had grown just that afternoon when 100 plus of my fellow Texas rescuers put out a plea on Arthur's behalf to their network. "Oh, boy," he says.

I'm not angry. People are just doing their jobs. The difference between them and me is to them, it's just a job, bigwigs pulling down six digits while animals die in secrecy. I cannot afford to become hurt or angry. I cannot stop to fight

with these people. It's early and I have just begun. I have $3500
to raise and letters to write, phone calls to make. There will be
a time to walk the dogs and a time to pet my cats. There will be
time later to sing to my birds. When I feel overwhelmed, I will
try to think about my hero, Tom Joad.

Wherever there is a sad dog
chained up in someone's yard,
Whenever some animal control
wrongly takes somebody's pet,
Where there is wrong doing
that needs righting,
Wherever there is innocence and
someone's trying to take it away,
Look in those eyes and there I'll be.
I promise.

Acknowledgments

Thank you to everyone listed below who've made not only writing this book possible, but who've helped make it possible for me to follow my passion, rescue work.

This song's for you:

Wrote A Song For Everyone
by Creedence Clearwater Revival

Thank you to everyone who made this book a reality. Brandon Kent for the art; Lonnie Layman for the cover design/layout and technical support; Scott for eternal support; Martha for being my sistah; Paul Daniel; Toby, Gary, Philip, Byrff, Rox, Dolores, Raymond and Canis; Sutton and Jessica; Patty for the great notes;

Thanks to Sean Smiley Rogers for the lake shot; Adena for Sasha's photo and for being a great mom; Thanks to Rachel for Slappy's photos: Thanks to Kira Abrams for the stained glass of Patch; and thank you to my Texaco homies down the road and all of you wonderful people whose support and kind donations have saved so many lives.

Mia and Emily; Jessica, Rocco, Vega family; Sara and Misha, Todd, Darren, Maddie, Wylie and Henry; Alan, Lauren, Oscar and Frenchie; Duane, Sam and Lenny; Russell, Marty and Angel Divine; Doug and Raspberry; Sam, girls and Tish-Roxie; Rachel, Mark and Slappy; Adena, Matt, Reed, Russell and Sasha-GarGirl; Martha and Frida; Ruby and Barry; Buckley and Denise; Christina and Griffie; Chester and Andrea; Grant and Stevie Ray; Eric, Dennise and Oso; Tutti Frutti-Eliza and Gaye; Andrew, Erika, Jenna and the girls; Jeff, Felice and Kirbee;

Hillary, Daniel and Ellie; Jennifer and Dickie Betts; Nikki and Mrs. Billie Holliday; Brian and Nelly Belly; Dave, family and Mocha; Tom and Spottie; Jim, Pam and Sadie; Brandon and Ellie Mae; Michelle, Courtney and Cody; Hayden and Ashley; Buddy and Joe; Dave and Sticker; LeaAnne, Bill and Huckleberry; Dawn and Marvel; D.J. Gustafson clan and Mercy; Theresa, Andrew, Jordan and Quincy; Jeff and Sadie Jane; Kristin, Frank and Hanna-Banana; Jessey and Bosley; Brandi and Gator; Dierdre and No-Good; Kali, Kelly and Gobi; Lauren, Francisco and Mr. Petey Miller; Lisa, Brad, Simone and Lola; Kirstin and Ollie Two-Lips; Felix, Emily and Lexi-Lulu; Trav and Lorna Doone; David and Chino a.k.a. Donny Ray Ford; Chris and Olive...Jeff and Max; Nikki and Daisy Duke; Jamila, Cory and C.J.; Jen and Clyde; Angela and Dulcie; Walter and Rudder; Duane, Maria and Santos; Jennifer, Phil, Zorro-Jakey, Granny and Shadow; Wil, Lila and Droog; Jerzey, Norm and Hank; Sheri, Marco, Sophia and Morgan;

Chino and David; Bernice and Christian; Janet and Shadow; Walter; Rebecca and Dotsy-Garbo; Bullfrog and Denise; Barbara and Murmur; Bella and Sue; Colin and Brownie-Rose/ Iggy; Helen and Joe; Thomas and Skippy; Kashi's family, Patty, Tom and Darcy; Susan and Bosco; Leslie and Gauguin (Festus); Marisa, Mike, Fiona and Carmine;

R.I.P. Angus McPherson; T-Rex; Little Piggles; Maybelle; Trixie; Frenchie; Elvis; Teddy Theodore and Elroy; Sony; Johnny Cash;

Resources:

Linda DesMarais.....Emotion Code
  http://www.thebodycodetohealth.info/

Clare Metcalf.....Homeopathy and Animal Communication
  http://www.freespiritanimalcare.co.uk

Jayne Athey......Reiki and Animal Communication
  http://www.briarwoodpups.blogspot.com

Allison Peta......Animal Communication
  mail to: animalsofspirit@hotmail.com

Elizabeth Ohmer Pellegrin...........Flower Essences
  http://nolareiki.blogspot.com/

Louise Larabie...........Flower Essences
  harmony46@gmail.com
  http://abfe-info.blogspot.com/

Pamela Picard @
  Exempt Sick & Senior Pets from Rabies Shots
  http://aimees-law.blogspot.com
  http://www.petwellness-update.com
  http://www.petitiononline.com/tdsh2007/petition.html

Kasie Maxwell.........Raw Feeding, Whole Pet Care
  http://www.sfraw.com
  http://www.raraavisherb.com

Bob Gutierrez...........A Better Way Dog Training
  http://home.earthlink.net/~sfdogboy/

Lynnet @
  Jeffrey's Natural Pet Foods
  North Beach and Dolores Park Locations
  http://www.jeffreysnaturalpetfood.com

Shireen and Suzie @
 Pawtrero Bathhouse and Feed
 Potrero Hill and South Beach Locations
 http://www.pawtrero.com

Mary Quinn @
 All Aboard Animal Search and Rescue
 http://allaboardanimalsearchandrescue.com

Leslie @
 Two Hands Four Paws
 http://www.twohandsfourpaws.com

Lisa Tipton @
 AngelDogs Foundation
 http://www.angeldogsfoundation.org/

Pit Bull Rescue Central
 http://pbrc.net

God Bless the Tireless:

The Kathleens:
Who pound the keyboards to all hours of the night...

Kathleen Helmer

Jennie Adams

Susan Tyler

Zelda

Girly Girl Army Chloe Jo

Alexandra Touch

Bill Eckert

Astrid Dahlman

Shelley Davis

Annie Wang

Tamiko Kobayashi

Pat Smyklo

Lorraine Sakli

Vendetta

Carol Parks

Susan Wallace

Laurie Mecca

Melissa Maroff

Lisa Hester

Holly Murray

Marianna Gilshteyn

Tia Triplett

Barbara Kohn
Alicia Esken
Judy Bishop
Dana Dulaney
Linda Baker
Kristine from Nevada
Bonnie Witten
Diana Wagner
M. Karyn
D. Allard
Mindy DeBaise
Whitney
Tracey Jacobs
J.C. O'Connell

Megan Blake
Lisa Robertt
Patti Lopez
Lisa Cossettini
Kathleen Hendron
Kim Collier
Tony and Lori Perry
Antoinette the Doxy Den
Mother
Deana Whitfield
Steve Spiro
Mayte Delgado
Elsie nsync
Debbie Milne

The Transporters:

Streets of Bakersfield
http://pets.groups.yahoo.com/group/bakersfield

Roads of Hope Rescue
Ed for http://www.pilotsnpaws.org

John McAuley
Ben Kellogg
Periel Stanfield
Patti Lavine
Wendi Kusamura
Judi Daunell
Donna Bagwell
Carrie Marvin
Jane Almon
Nancy Osgood
Barbara Harmening
Glenda Ballengee
Robbin Grabowski

Janet Blea
Marlena Markel
Kathy Vossler
Patty Boles
Bonnie Whitten
Periel
Lianne Werner
Ronessa Biddle
Stacey Wololey
Roads of Hope Rescue
Donna Martin
Hannah Boxer Transport
Brad Moseley

The Rescues:

Kari and Kai @
>Ace of Hearts Rescue
>http://www.aceofheartsdogs.com

Diane @
>Westside German Shepherd Rescue of Los Angeles
>http://www.sheprescue.org

Lindy @
>Southern California Dachshund Rescue
>http://www.delgadog.com

Kay @
>Noah's Friends Animal Sanctuary
>http://www.noahandfriends.org

Linda Beenau
>Wonder Dog Rescue
>http://www.wonderdogrescue.org

Pali @
>Rocket Dog Rescue
>http://www.rocketdogrescue.org

Sherri @
>Muttville Senior Dog Rescue
>http://www.muttville.org/

Paw Printz Pitbull Rescue
>http://www.pawprintz.org

Angela @
>Family Dog Rescue
>www.norcalfamilydogrescue.org

Lori and Paul @
>Good Newz Pittie Pups
>http://www.good-newz.org/

Laurie @
>Hopalong and Second Chance Animal Rescue
>http://www.hopalong.org/

Patti @
>   National Brittany Rescue and Adoption Network
>   http://www.nbran.org/

Wendy @
>   Rat Terrier ResQ
>   http://www.ratterrierresq.com/

Patty and Patricia @
>   H.A.L.T. Rescue
>   Helping Animals Live Tomorrow
>   http://www.haltrescue.vpweb.com/default.html

Angel @
>   Big Dog Rescue

Marilyn @
>   Pups Rescue
>   http://www.pupsrescue.petfinder.org

Vivian @
>   All Creatures Great and Small Rescue
>   http://www.allcreaturesgs.org/

Lynn @
>   TaraSun Animal Rescue and Retreat
>   http://irena.patestdesign.com/

Debbie @
>   Yorkies & Friends Rescue
>   http://www.yorkiesandfriendsrescue.com

Everybody @
>   Barks of Love Animal Rescue
>   http://www.barksoflove.org/

Kelly @
>   Dogs Deserve Better
>   http://www.dogsdeservebetter.com/

Colleen @
>   All Souls Rescue
>   http://www.allsoulsrescue.org/

Shawn @
>   German Shepherd Rescue of Orange County
>   http://www.gsroc.org/gsr.asp

Valley Dawgs Rescue
    http://ww.valleydogs.org/
Carrie @
    Sacramento Independent Animal Rescuers, Inc.
    http://www.siarescuers.com/
Cheryl @
    Sporting Hope Rescue
    Coastal German Shepherd Rescue
    http://www.coastalgsr.org/index.html
Kim, Heather, Lori, Robyn and all the gals @
 Pit Bull Rescue San Diego
    http://www.pbrsd.com/
Tia @
    Villalobos Rescue Center
    http:www.vrcpitbull.com/
Barks of Love Animal Rescue
    http://www.barksoflove.org/
Bail a Tail Rescue
    http://www.petfinder.com/shelters/CA1574.html
Death Row Dogs Rescue
    http://www.deathrowdogsrescue.com
Animal Advocates Alliance
    http://animaladvocatesalliance.org/
Karma Rescue
    http://www.karmarescue.org/
Angels in Fur Dog Rescue
    http://www.angelsinfurdogrescue.com/
Bound Angels
    http://www.boundangels.org
Kerri @
    Muttmatch LA
    http://www.muttmatchla.com/
A Dog's Life Rescue
    http://wwwadogsliferescue.org/
    Meoowz Rescue
    http://www.meoowzresq.com

The Rescue Train
http://www.therescuetrain.org/
Modjeska Ranch Rescue
http://modjeskaranchrescue.org
CA Shelter Friends
http://www.casf.rescuegroups.org/
Laura @ Pets Without Partners, Redding, CA
http://www.petswithoutpartners.org
Shana @ Greyhound Friends for Life
http://wwwlgreyhoundfriendsforlife.org
Pets Without Partners
http://www.petswithoutpartnersinc.org/
Joy and Craig @
    All Breed Animal Rescue
    http://rescuemeinc.org/
Helping Animals Live Tomorrow
http://www.haltrescue.vpweb.com/
It's the Pits Dog Rescue Specializing in the Bully Breeds
http://www.itsthepits.org
Blake @ ResQPet Dog Rescue
http://www.resqpet.com/
Animals First Foundation
http://animalsfirstfoundation.org/
Joy and Craig @
    Rescue Me Incorporated
    http://www.rescuemeinc.org
Cheryl @
    A Passion for Paws Akita Rescue
    http://www.apassionforpaws.org/
Los Angeles Animal Services
http://www.laanimalservices.com
H.E.L.P. (A Home for Every Living Pet)
http://www.petfinder.com/shelters/help.html
Kristine @
    Safe Haven Animal Rescue
    http://www.petfinder.com/shelters/NV119.html

Abby Animal Sanctuary Rescue
>   http://www.petfinder.com/shelters/CA1641.html

Gail and Lianne @
>   Northern California Sled Dog Rescue
>   http:www.norsled.org

Mid-America Bully Breed Rescue
>   http://www.mabbr.org

Texas Size:
>   Spindletop Refuge
>   http://www.spindletoppitbullrefuge.org

Toni Liquori
>   Katy's Promise Rottweiler Rescue
>   http://www.kprr.rescuegroups.org

Donna @
>   Street Cat Rescue
>   http://www.streetcatrescue.com

Cathie Clark
>   Blazing the TNR Trail Across Central Texas

Dale and Amy Poskey
>   Independent Earth Angels

Debbie @
>   Heart2Heart Animal Rescue

AAR - Abandoned Animal Rescue
>   http://www.aartomball.org/index.html

North Texas Bully Rescue
>   http://ntbr.weebly.com

Happy Endings Dog Rescue
>   http://happyendingsdogrescue.com

Friends for Life
>   http://www.nokill1.org

Made in the USA
Lexington, KY
18 December 2011